*Solving the Iraq Crisis*

NEW YORK  LONDON  TORONTO  SYDNEY  SINGAPORE

# GAME

## SCOTT RITTER

Simon & Schuster

SIMON & SCHUSTER
Rockefeller Center
1230 Avenue of the Americas
New York, NY 10020

10   9   8   7   6   5   4   3   2   1

Library of Congress Cataloging-in-Publication Data
is available.
ISBN 0-684-86485-1
ISBN 0-7432-4772-8 Pbk.

Maps on pages 14, 30, 138, and 160–61, and
tables on pages 58 and 123 by Jeffrey L. Ward.

# Acknowledgments

I<small>T HAS BEEN</small> over three years now since *Endgame* was published, and I am very proud of how this book has withstood the test of time. The fact that the tumultuous events of the present were so accurately predicted bears witness to the quality of the work that went into the publication of the hardcover edition. For that alone, I remain grateful to everyone associated with that effort, especially Robert Katz.

*Endgame* is, if anything, more timely and relevant today than it was when originally published. For that reason, I am grateful for the hard work of my agent, Sam Pinkus, for pushing for this paperback release, and to my editor, Bob Bender, for helping me with the updated material in this book.

The past three years have been difficult ones, and I couldn't have persevered without the solid backing of my dear friends, especially Bob and Amy Murphy, Mike and Becky Steiner, Mark Gibson, and Frank and Annie Mellet. Thanks, guys.

To Chris Cobb-Smith, Roger Hill, Didier Louis, Norbert Reinecke, Tim Trevan, and my old boss, Rolf Ekéus, I owe special gratitude for standing by a colleague when it wasn't the most politically correct thing to do. Your integrity and dedication to the truth make your friendship all the more important.

To Don Epstein, Lisa Bransdorf, and the entire staff at Greater Talent Network, thank you very much not only for helping me support my family, but for your warmth and humor for a client I know hasn't been the easiest to support. Thanks for keeping the faith.

I have been supported by a tremendous network of American citizens who reached out to me during this time and helped spread the message of peace and justice as an alternative to war and suffering. To Suny Miller and Charles Jenks of the Traprock Peace Center, thanks not only for bringing the message to the people of Massachusetts, but the entire country. To Barbara DiTommasso, Carolyn Micklas, and all the other members of the Albany peace and justice community, I am deeply appreciative for giving me a forum to speak on Iraq when no one else was listening. To Stuart Halford and the British antisanctions movement, the same holds true regarding getting the message of truth heard in England. And I give a special thanks to Jennifer Horan, not only for her friendship, but also intellectual integrity in making sure that I never allowed my rhetoric to outstrip the facts.

Of course, in the end it comes down to family. To my parents, Bill and Patricia Ritter, my sisters, Shirley, Suzanne, and Amy (together with their husbands and families), to Aunt Shirley and Uncle Tom, Cousin Jenny and Sam, and to my brother-in-law Archie Khatiashvili and his lovely family—thanks for being there and providing support. To my father-in-law, Bidzina Khatiashvili, I owe special thanks for helping support my household during my all-to-frequent trips away from home. And above all, to my lovely wife, Marina, and my wonderful daughters, Victoria and Patricia, thank you for everything. Nothing would be possible without your love and support.

*In loving memory of
Lamara Khatiashvili,
who passed away on
Christmas Day, 2001.*

# Contents

# Author's Note

The Arab language is a rich language that makes use of subtle phonetic sounds to express different meanings. Although the Arab script renders these subtleties, the Latin alphabet of the English language does not. There are several schools of transliteration of Arabic into English. I am not an Arab linguist and have opted usually to defer to Amatzia Baram when transliterating the complex family names set forth in this book. However, for certain names, such as Saddam Hussein (Husayn is Professor Baram's preference) I have decided to use the common spelling because of its familiarity. Consequently students of the Arab language will note an inconsistency in my rendering of Arab names.

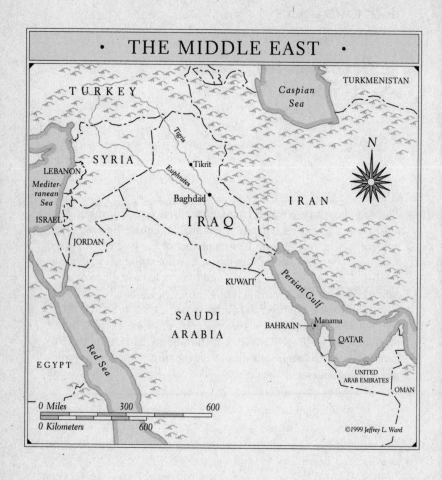

# · THE MIDDLE EAST ·

TURKEY

TURKMENISTAN

*Caspian Sea*

SYRIA

*Tigris*

•Tikrit

LEBANON

*Euphrates*

*Mediterranean Sea*

Baghdad•

IRAN

ISRAEL

IRAQ

N

JORDAN

KUWAIT

*Persian Gulf*

SAUDI ARABIA

BAHRAIN → •Manama

QATAR

EGYPT

*Red Sea*

UNITED ARAB EMIRATES

OMAN

0 Miles    300    600

0 Kilometers    600

©1999 Jeffrey L. Ward

# Prologue

# UNSCOM 255

AUGUST 2, 1998.     We were 10,000 feet over the Persian Gulf, headed out of the haze for blue skies and Baghdad. Even then we knew this was our last shot at beating Saddam Hussein at his own game. In the seven years since being pummeled by Desert Storm, he had proved himself to be the master of deceit—playing his sly, winning hand of concealing Iraq's weapons of mass destruction from the world, specifically from UNSCOM, the United Nations Special Commission inspection apparatus, of which I was chief inspector. But now we had an ace up our sleeve, a counterdeception all our own that would break the case wide open. It would all hinge on timing and the clock was running.

We'd lifted off from our base in Bahrain in UNSCOM's leased L-100. The white, lumbering aircraft was a civilian variant of the cavernous C-130 and there were only three of us in the flight cabin, sitting on a bench just behind the cockpit crew. I was briefing my boss, UNSCOM's executive chairman, Richard Butler, who was en route to Iraq with his deputy, Charles Duelfer, for routine talks with the Baghdad government. Officially, I was in Butler's party, which included an entourage of about twenty disarmament experts in the rear cabin, to provide technical assistance and advice during the course of his visit. But my real purpose, as chief inspector, was to command a series of surprise inspections—an operation we called UNSCOM 255—so called because it was UNSCOM's 255th inspection since its inception. We were set to begin as soon as Butler's visit ended on the 5th and he was out of Iraq. I had forty-two men on the ground in Bahrain and Baghdad ready to move in, awaiting Butler's green light.

The four inspection sites we were ready to pounce on were all exceptionally promising but one was a real gem, chosen on the basis of one of the hottest intelligence tips we'd ever scored: the precise location of a cache of ballistic missile guidance and control components, enough to equip a dozen missiles—the hardware and the heart of Iraq's chemical, biological, and nuclear delivery potential.

Under the 1991 Security Council resolution providing for Saddam's disarmament, Iraq was permitted to retain ballistic missiles with a range under 150 kilometers. Suspicion arose from the very start however that Iraq would seek to maintain a covert long-range missile capability. It had agreed to declare its inventory of long-range missiles and associated production capabilities. UNSCOM's job was to destroy this inventory. Within months of that declaration, it became clear to us at UNSCOM that our initial concerns were soundly backed by fact: Iraq had lied on every level. For example, aerial photographs revealed that Iraq had more mobile launchers than it had declared.

UNSCOM had engaged Saddam in a frustrating game of cat and mouse, trying to hunt down the evidence of Iraq's wrongdoing. Saddam had covered his tracks well, yet UNSCOM continued to isolate inconsistencies in the stories told by Iraqi officials, pressing so hard on their inherent contradictions that gradually aspects of the truth emerged. Many of these breakthroughs took place over the issue of ballistic missile guidance and control components. Iraq was gradually forced to admit to clandestine dealings with several German and British companies that had provided critical support. But it never revealed the entire truth, just tantalizing bits and pieces wrapped in a cheesy fabric of lies, old and new. Even now Saddam was hiding something and even more so, he was hiding how he hid it. We called this phenomenon "the concealment mechanism" and we were resolved to find out how it worked.

As we made our way north, skirting Kuwait and ascending the fertile valley between the Euphrates and Tigris rivers, the briefing was going well. Butler was fired up, and even Duelfer appeared upbeat. He was the pessimist among us. A longtime State Department official, he had risen through the ranks to become a national security expert.

We had been planning this inspection for some time, but things had been going downhill for UNSCOM for months. It had begun in April, with the U.S. pressuring Butler to radically restructure the controversial Concealment Investigations Unit, which I headed. We were controversial because the Iraqis vehemently opposed our operations—opposed them because we were good at what we did. And what we did was continually penetrate the mantle of lies by which Iraq retained prohibited weapons.

Our most recent and dramatic success had come in March, on the heels of U.N. Secretary General Kofi Annan's February agreement with Baghdad, reiterating UNSCOM's "unconditional and unrestricted access" to inspection targets. As a result, the Special Commission had been pressured into carrying out a quick test of that agreement. We had argued in vain for more time, but the United States had prepared a military option that required UNSCOM to make this test—and inevitably, it seemed, to generate a crisis—by the 7th of March. The pilgrimage of the Islamic faithful to Mecca, the Haj, would begin on the 15th, and the military strike, planned as one week of sustained air bombardment, had to be completed by that time. The U.S. had assembled a powerful armada in the region, and many in Washington were eager to use it.

We went ahead, of course, but insisted on fielding special support. For over a year I had been requesting, even demanding, that the inspection team be furnished with rapid assessment of all-source intelligence information.* For example, I requested the interception

* All-source intelligence is intelligence gained from looking at photographs, debriefing spies, and listening to intercepted communications and signals. The actual sources and methods of gathering a specific piece of information are closely guarded secrets, so when I refer to all-source intelligence, I mean that information relating to a specific event has been accumulated using one or more of the means mentioned, but how the information was collected is not transparent. All-source intelligence also refers to a systematic

of Iraqi communications by special teams of UNSCOM inspectors. This particular technique, considered the most sensitive of the work carried out by UNSCOM inspectors, provided us with unique insights into the Iraqi response, including how material was hidden from the inspectors. Such information would be transmitted to me and my team in Iraq, where we would be able to fuse it with the detailed observations we made. The result would give us the clearest picture yet of how the Iraqis responded to an UNSCOM inspection, and whether or not they were hiding material from a team during the course of an inspection. I had finally secured that capability and it had proved to be invaluable.

We went in that first week in March and by the time we left on the 9th the whole world was informed of how the Iraqis had met the test. We had attempted to gain access to a dozen facilities deemed sensitive by Baghdad. The Iraqis, in keeping to the letter of their understanding with the secretary general, had thrown open their doors at every one—and, yielding no apparent violations, had thus forestalled any excuse for a U.S. military strike. March passed peacefully.

What the world did not know, however, was that our new intelligence capabilities—specifically, communications intercepts—had racked up a major success. My team had been able to detect how the presidential security apparatus responsible for the protection of Saddam Hussein—the Special Security Organization—had evacuated material from sites in advance of our team's arrival, and how, when we got to a site where material was still stored, the SSO had created delays until it had been safely withdrawn. Here at last was the concealment mechanism in full-blown operation, and the man directing it, we knew, was Iraqi presidential secretary Abid Hamid Mahmoud—one of the most powerful men in Iraq, second only per-

--------

approach to studying a given problem using all available resources, not just limiting yourself to the study of data obtained from a single source of information. For UNSCOM purposes, all-source intelligence referred to our unique blend of information obtained from on-site inspections, imagery analysis of U-2 photographs, access to reports from spies operating inside Iraq as well as from defectors, and information gleaned from communications intercept operations run by UNSCOM.

haps to Saddam Hussein himself. Senior defectors had long talked about the immense secrets kept under Mahmoud's personal protection. But his close relationship to Saddam had kept us at bay. Now we had the goods on him. All we needed to do was catch him in the act.

But that was not to be.

Armed with the stunning results of our March inspection, I was trying to mount an inspection campaign aimed directly at where it made the most sense, at Abid Hamid Mahmoud himself. Butler, Duelfer, and I had agreed that the tests of the Kofi Annan agreement were nothing but political eye-candy; the real tests would come afterward, when Iraq would drop its guard and UNSCOM could send in a team armed with high-value intelligence.

But the enhanced intelligence system so painstakingly put together began to be dismantled piece by piece at the behest of my own country. Washington, even while claiming to be well disposed toward the idea behind this mission, was working behind my back to undermine critical support of two of the most important proponents of the kind of concealment inspections I was charged with undertaking, the United Kingdom and Israel.

The U.K. withdrew three specialists from my full-time investigations team in Baghdad, gutting that operation. The Israelis were next, informing me that support they had previously agreed to provide could no longer be given. The screws were then applied to my own boss. Butler was suddenly less than enthusiastic. He began to question the political viability of my work, citing French and Russian criticism of my methods.

I was up against a wall, my options being continually whittled away. I disbanded my unit. I proposed a revised organizational structure to accommodate the new reality, the current operational and political environment. Duelfer and I traveled to Paris, trying to engage the French. Together with Butler, we went to London, where we explained my new operational concepts. Both capitals promised support. But it was in London and ultimately in Washington where I got my new marching orders.

The criteria for launching confrontational inspections had changed, I was told. What had proved successful in the past—"shaking the tree," as we called it, by sending in inspection teams to stimulate and monitor Iraqi responses—was now viewed by the U.S. and the U.K. as too controversial. Now we could act only when the results would be guaranteed.

The Clinton national security team knew there was no quicker way to provoke Iraqi noncompliance with Security Council resolutions than through an UNSCOM effort to inspect Saddam's inner sanctums, regardless of the compelling nature of the evidence presented. Afraid to provoke such a response, especially without knowing what Iraq might be hiding, the Clinton team instead decided on an uninspired, no-endgame strategy of containment through economic sanctions of indefinite duration.

The inspection regime to achieve arms control was rapidly being reduced to a mere illusion of arms control. But my job wasn't containment, it was inspections.

Although disheartened by the new conditions being imposed on my operations, the one narrow door of "guaranteed results" had been left open and I got straight to work. I went about reassessing the data I had regarding Iraq's concealment practices, identifying critical areas, hoping to develop them into something that could be used in an inspection.

Then we had two important breakthroughs:

- One involved specific information about how Iraq was conducting covert procurement via Romania of prohibited ballistic missile guidance components;
- The other—the extremely perishable intelligence windfall mentioned above—was a site where Iraqi authorities were hiding ten crates containing guidance and control equipment that had been taken from dismantled Iraqi missiles.

The first item led me to develop an inspection target folder for Iraq's Economic Department of the Presidential Office, located inside the Republican Palace. An inspection target folder was a file where we would assemble all information pertaining to a given location in Iraq that we wanted to inspect—the background details, our all-source intelligence, high-resolution photography and detailed maps. This information would be used to plan the inspection, brief the UNSCOM executive chairman on the proposed inspection operations, and, if he approved the mission, to assist in the actual inspection itself. These folders were invaluable to the inspection effort. This meant that UNSCOM would have to undertake a new presidential site inspection. From our viewpoint this was an added bonus, since we knew that Kofi Annan, during discussions with Saddam's deputy prime minister, Tariq Aziz, in April, had promised that inspections of presidential sites would be finished by June 23. We now had a great opportunity several weeks in advance of that date not only to catch the Iraqis in the course of an illegal activity, but also to expose the underlying hypocrisy of the agreement.

But it was the site where that second piece of information led us that contained dynamite. From a description provided by our source, I had easily identified the building in question, which was located in Baghdad's downtown Aadamiyah section. The ten crates of missile parts were stashed in a basement of the Baghdad headquarters of Saddam's own Ba'ath party. If we could achieve surprise and surround the site before the Iraqis could evacuate the crates, we would obtain the ultimate catch-22 situation: let us inside as promised and we would find the prohibited material; bar our entry and violate the Kofi Annan compromise, and in the process invite a devastating air strike by the United States. UNSCOM would be prepared to camp out around this site until the situation had been resolved one way or the other.

Duelfer and I put together what we call a concept of operations, a plan that would enable us to carry out this inspection without tipping our hand to the Iraqis. At the same time, UNSCOM charted two other operations:

- unmasking an Iraqi remotely piloted vehicle (RPV) program that was suspected of being developed for the purpose of delivering biological agents;
- conducting an investigation of the Iraqi Defense Ministry's Chemical Corps aimed at uncovering evidence of a much larger chemical weapons program than Iraq had admitted to date.

By mid-June, the multiphase operation was in place. While the first two inspection teams were being pulled together, I flew to London, where I briefed British officials coordinating UNSCOM-related issues. Much to my surprise, there seemed to be genuine support for these operations. Buoyed by this visit, I returned to the U.S. to work with my counterparts in Washington, who likewise seemed favorably inclined toward the inspection. Butler was enthusiastic.

The countdown to a perhaps decisive four-day blitz of confrontation began, with the first inspection—Ba'ath party headquarters—due to take place on July 20. On short notice I was able to reconstitute my intelligence support. The first two inspection teams were dispatched to Bahrain. I was set to arrive there on the 18th. I would be joined by my deputy chief inspector as well as several operations staff. All of us were veteran inspectors, requiring no additional training. Instead, the clock was stopped.

The U.S. and U.K., Butler told me, were uncertain about going ahead. He needed to consult with them, he said, and on the 15th— my thirty-seventh birthday—I found myself pacing the floor of my office on the thirtieth floor of the United Nations Secretariat Building in New York, waiting for the results of these talks.

Butler came back. It was all bad news. The inspection was canceled. My carefully assembled team dispersed.

Clinton administration officials, torn between pressure from the Republicans to go forward and a reluctance to respond to any Iraqi confrontation (and there was sure to be one) with military force, had tried to convince Butler to postpone the inspection until "a more opportune time." Butler was convinced. To me, he called it a case of "bad timing." I viewed it as something else—an appalling lack of leadership, not only in Washington and London, but also on Butler's part. He was allowing a golden opportunity to slip through his fingers. I said as much in a long, critical memorandum that I wrote to him the next day.

The onus of leadership fell on him, I said, and if he would seize the initiative, Washington and London would have to follow. That may have been somewhat naive, but I firmly believed, I wrote, that UNSCOM was fighting for its very existence as a meaningful disarmament body, and inspections aimed at uncovering concealment remained imperative. It was a fight worth fighting, I said, recommending that we go ahead with the planned inspections regardless of the naysayers, though not without continuing to seek support. "In reengaging on concealment," I concluded, "the Special Commission will be waving a red flag in front of the Iraqi bull. It is essential that this red flag be backed by a sword, or else the commission will not be able to withstand the Iraqi charge. In short, the Special Commission's push on concealment must be 100 percent."

It was as hard-hitting a memorandum as I could make it. Butler accused me of overstating the lack of resolve in both Washington and London. But my argument over the need to get a concealment-based inspection on track did resonate with him. He authorized me to put together an updated inspection plan to take place following his August visit to Baghdad.

I didn't have much time. July was half through, and I needed to get a new forty-odd-person team assembled, trained, and deployed prior to Butler's arrival in Iraq on August 2. We would use the same basic inspection concept that had been prepared for July; the intelligence on both sites, I was assured by sources, was still valid but not for much longer. I would make use of some twenty-five inspectors resident in Baghdad with the monitoring groups, and I added twelve experts, selected on the basis of what the team needed for the planned inspection. I had a five-person command element fly to Bahrain with the twelve experts to train them. They were to stay in Bahrain after the training to carry out last-minute preparations and receive intelligence updates until they flew into Iraq on the same plane that would take Butler out on August 5. Somehow it all came together. The inspections would begin on the morning of the 6th.

I'd learned to read Butler's body language and he was getting a little nervous as we flew deeper and deeper into Iraqi territory. The reality of what we were about to do had begun to hit him. Duelfer teased him about how the Iraqis could solve everything if they just shot us out of the sky. Butler was not amused. He kept asking probing questions, reassuring himself that these inspection targets were of a legitimate disarmament character. "What makes us go to that site?" he asked. How do I explain it to the Iraqis? . . . How do I explain this site to the Security Council? . . . What do we expect to find at this one? . . . What happens if the Iraqis stop us from entering?"

Over Baghdad, he signed off on the required authorizations. UNSCOM 255 was on.

We landed and were greeted by senior Iraqi officials from the Foreign Ministry. We loaded up in their Mercedes sedans and were driven to the Al Rashid Hotel. A mob of journalists was waiting for us when we arrived. The ones with the better noses for news wanted to know what I—UNSCOM's concealment man—was doing in Butler's party. I whisked by mutely.

The tension was mounting hour by hour, of course, so I was pleasantly distracted when I ran into a colleague I hadn't seen in a while at UNSCOM's field headquarters in the former Canal Hotel. It was Jason Driscoll, commander of a small team of U.S. Navy divers that operated out of Bahrain. He'd worked for UNSCOM in the past to help scour the bottom of Iraqi rivers and lakes in an effort to find weapons components dumped by the Iraqis to conceal their existence. Driscoll had been in the news a few days back, the subject of Iraqi allegations that he was an American spy caught red-handed photographing Iraqi troop movements. The incident was quickly revealed to have been a misunderstanding and the matter dropped, but at the moment he was taking a ribbing from his men, who were calling him "Bond, James Bond." They were just back from a diving mission, unloading their equipment. Driscoll and I went off to the cafeteria for a Diet Coke break.

He and his men had been dredging the Saqlawiyah Canal, which links the Euphrates and the Tigris and feeds an irrigation system for the farmlands along the waterway. They had been looking for the same kind of missile guidance and control components that I was about to swoop down on, so after we had a chuckle over the spy business, I leaned in when he began to speak of the dive.

"Scott, you wouldn't believe what we saw out there," he said as his eyes suddenly took on a haunted look. At a loss, I speculated about unexploded ordnance, the bane of underwater work in a riverine environment. I stared back at him, the sensation growing that it was something far worse. I listened intently as he related his story. The team had been diving east of an area where components had earlier been found. It was the height of the flood season, when the flow of canal water moves faster than usual and underwater visibility—in conditions normally known as "Braille diving"—increases to about two feet. The divers were investigating likely spots where the Iraqis might have dumped the missile components, where roads or trails lead directly to the bank of the canal. It was in one of these locations where the team made a grisly discovery.

"It was a plastic bag," said Driscoll, "and it contained an object with some weight and mass, so we opened it to see if the Iraqis had placed some of the components inside before throwing it into the river . . ." He paused. "It was a baby, a newborn . . . and there were more bags around us. We probed around and found bodies of men, their arms and legs bound . . . body parts, torsos of women . . . we didn't count how many, but it was clear this was a dumping ground for people being disposed of in a Mafia-like fashion."

That day, forty-eight hours before our initial surprise inspection, Saddam's deputy prime minister, Tariq Aziz, a man I had heard more than once refer sarcastically to UNSCOM's search for components as looking for "dead bodies," met with Butler and threw his newest wrench into the works. He informed Butler that Iraq had decided to stop cooperating with UNSCOM. There would be no more UNSCOM inspections. Neither would there be any talks; they were suspended.

A few hours later, Butler, Duelfer, and I were formulating a strategy in response to Tariq Aziz's move. We were locked inside a secure conference room at the UNSCOM monitoring center in Baghdad. It was an electronically swept facility with double-door access and an encrypted telephone link to U.N. headquarters in New York, but we still didn't trust it completely. We had the air conditioner running as loud as we could and repeatedly used the large white marking board instead of talking.

I argued that at the moment Iraq's position was merely verbal. We had to test this latest refusal as a means of forcing a definition of exactly what no cooperation really meant. Was it the total rejection by Iraq of the guarantees it gave to the secretary general back in February? Those commitments had been endorsed in the Security Council, which had promised "severe consequences" if Iraq were to be found in noncompliance. It was clear to all of us that such a test of intent would be the planned inspections.

We knew that by moving forward with this inspection we were entering a highly charged political arena. However, Iraq had thrown down the gauntlet. The consequences of this challenge had to be very stark or else the Security Council and the secretary general would seek a politically motivated compromise. All three of us were in agreement that such a compromise would only harm the commission and strengthen Iraq.

Butler ordered me to remain in Baghdad and assemble my team for the scheduled start of UNSCOM 255. He needed to return immediately to Bahrain and go on to New York to coordinate closely with the Security Council on this matter. He was resolute in his belief that this was the right course of action. He threw up his fists in a boxer's pose, and said, "I'm ready for a fight, Scott . . . Let's take it to them." I could only agree.

Five days later I was back on board the L-100, flying out of Iraq for the last time. After consulting by phone from the U.S. Embassy in Bahrain with Secretary of State Madeleine Albright, who strongly opposed the inspection going forward, Butler had sent me instructions to postpone until August 10, giving him enough time to return to New York, present his report to the Security Council, and carry out additional consultations. On the 8th, he called me from New York to tell me to leave Baghdad. The inspections had been canceled. There was, he said, no support for them at this time. I was upset, to say the least, but there and then, high over the Persian Gulf, at last I knew for certain what lay on my horizon. I began to form the words . . .

"Iraq has lied to the Special Commission and the world since day one concerning the true scope and nature of its proscribed programs and weapons systems," I wrote Butler in my letter of resignation later that month. "This lie has been perpetuated over the years through systematic acts of concealment." I was high above the East River now, in the thirtieth-floor U.N. office I would shortly vacate, as I wrote reminding Butler of what I believed was our very reason for being. It had been Butler who had created dedicated investigations of Iraq's weapons concealment activities, which I had had the privilege to lead, and we had uncovered indisputable proof of a system-

atic concealment mechanism, run by Saddam Hussein and his security forces.

> This investigation [I went on] has led the commission to the
> doorstep of Iraq's hidden retained capability, and yet the com-
> mission has been frustrated by Iraq's continued refusal to abide
> by its obligations . . . [and] the Security Council's refusal to ef-
> fectively respond to Iraq's actions, and now the current decision
> by the Security Council and the secretary general, backed at
> least implicitly by the United States, to seek a "diplomatic" alter-
> native to inspection-driven confrontation with Iraq, a decision
> which constitutes a surrender to the Iraqi leadership that has
> succeeded in thwarting the stated will of the United Nations.
>
> Inspections do work—too well, in fact, prompting Iraq to
> shut them down altogether. . . . The illusion of arms control is
> more dangerous than no arms control at all. What is being
> propagated by the Security Council today in relation to the
> work of the Special Commission is such an illusion, one which
> in all good faith I cannot, and will not, be a party to. I have no
> other option than to resign from my position here at the com-
> mission effective immediately.

Following my resignation, I found myself in September seated
in front of a combined session of the Senate Foreign Relations and
Armed Services committees. I was testifying about my decision to resign, which ultimately had been based on what I viewed as the failure of the United States to develop and implement a coherent
policy to effectively deal with Iraq. I still had no answer as to what
needed to be done. At that time, I saw myself as a messenger bearing
firsthand experience from seven years at the arms inspection front
rather than a strategist in the dangerous game of how to tame Saddam Hussein.

Following a warm welcome from the leaders of the two committees, I read my statement to that effect, and settled in to field
the questions. Senator Joseph Biden was first to get down to business. He asked me if I should be the one "to pull the strings" on
when the United States uses military force against Iraq. I replied that
this had not been the case, that I had had a job to do, which the U.S.

claimed it supported, but I had found the truth to be otherwise. Biden was relentless, suggesting that the question of taking the nation to war was a responsibility "slightly beyond your pay grade." Secretary of State Albright had more to consider, he said, than whether "old Scottyboy" did or didn't get into a suspect weapons site. The use of force was the kind of decision that people like Colin Powell and George Bush made, said the senator from Delaware.

I bristled but held my tongue. I fully expected this line of inquiry and had been warned in advance by Senator John McCain not to lose my temper. I had made some very serious allegations condemning the foreign policy of the Clinton administration regarding Iraq, and as such could not expect a free ride. I had an obligation to account for my actions.

Senator McCain, in his remarks, made a point that I greatly appreciated, that he "wished someone had listened to someone of your pay grade during the Vietnam War and perhaps there would not be so many names on the Wall." The U.S., he went on, was articulating one policy and doing the opposite, and that was "what was disturbing so many of us." Cut from this same cloth was Massachusetts Democratic Senator John Kerry, who said that Saddam's aim was to continue to build weapons of mass destruction at any cost. The U.S. should be prepared to use force to achieve its goals, Kerry said, though it would be ill advised to do so without mobilizing public support. But sliding into a policy of containment, he emphasized, was disastrous.

In the months that followed, I have had occasion to reflect on the words spoken by the various senators that day. I had tried to speak from the viewpoint of an arms inspector, and not a national policy expert. For this reason, I felt that my response to Biden, avoiding elaborating on the specifics of a solution regarding Iraqi obstructionism, were appropriate at the time. But it was the words of Kerry and McCain that struck home the hardest: Kerry's observation on the need for decisive military action against Iraq, and McCain's comment that if people had listened to someone of my pay grade during the Vietnam War there might be fewer dead Americans. As Senator Charles Robb, a Democrat from Virginia and a former Marine veteran of Vietnam, noted near the end of my testimony, history was replete with cases where failure to act early resulted in greater suffering later.

Events have changed the Saddam problem dramatically since then. Desert Fox, Washington's pre-Ramadan, four-day war in December 1998 to "degrade" Baghdad's weapons of mass destruction capability provided the final proof that the U.S. was fully committed to an open-ended policy of containment and little else. Precision bombardment with cruise missiles made many walls crumble. They fell precisely as targeted, but few today will argue that there was anything of substance within those walls, and cement, even in Iraq, is cheap. UNSCOM crumbled with the buildings in Baghdad. Weapons inspections ceased. And a once-mighty coalition of our allies has disintegrated.

Indeed, I have grown convinced that there has been a total breakdown in the willingness of the international community to disarm Iraq of its weapons of mass destruction. Saddam Hussein is well on the road to getting sanctions lifted and keeping his weapons in the bargain. A resurgent Iraq, reinvigorated economically and politically by standing up successfully to the United States and the United Nations, will be a very dangerous Iraq—one that sooner or later will have to be confronted by American military might. No matter how difficult stopping Saddam Hussein is today, it will become more and more difficult, and extract a higher and higher price, the longer he is left to rebuild his arsenal.

If Desert Storm and its aftermath have come to an end with the relatively puny Desert Fox, what now is the correct policy to pursue to stop Saddam Hussein? That is the subject of this book.

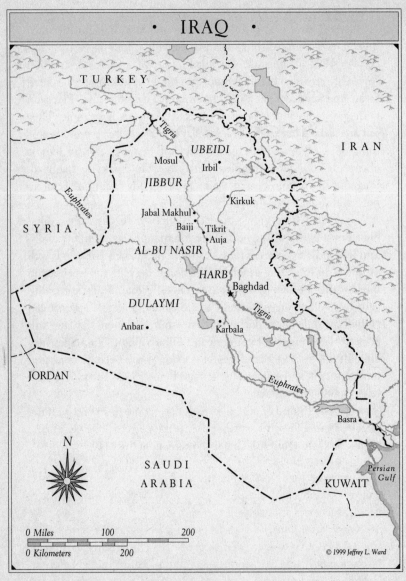

# • IRAQ •

TURKEY

*Tigris*

IRAN

*UBEIDI*

Mosul

Irbil

*JIBBUR*

Kirkuk

Jabal Makhul

Baiji  Tikrit

Auja

*AL-BU NASIR*

*Euphrates*

SYRIA

*HARB*

Baghdad

*DULAYMI*

*Tigris*

Anbar

Karbala

JORDAN

N

*Euphrates*

Basra

SAUDI
ARABIA

KUWAIT

*Persian
Gulf*

0 Miles        100        200

0 Kilometers      200

© 1999 Jeffrey L. Ward

Significant tribal groups noted in *ITALICS*

# 1

# A Journey
# of Discovery

THE JOB I resigned from on August 26, 1998, was the best job I ever had, and may ever have. I was the head of a unique organization — the UNSCOM Concealment Investigations Unit — that acted as a de facto international intelligence agency. The mission of our team was to aggressively investigate the systematic efforts of Iraq to conceal its prohibited weapons of mass destruction — chemical, biological, and nuclear — their related production facilities, and the long-range ballistic missiles used to deliver these deadly payloads.

We worked closely with the intelligence services of many nations to gather and assess sensitive information concerning Iraq's possession of these weapons and the means it employed to keep them hidden from the eyes of the world. We then used this information to build special-purpose inspection teams that were dispatched to Iraq to carry out an intricate and often dramatically confrontational game of high-stakes hide and seek. This was a grueling task, requiring months and sometimes even years of preparation, and we had our successes and failures.

Ours was a journey of discovery that should never have been. When UNSCOM was created in April 1991 by Security Council Resolution 687, Iraq was required to submit to the United Nations a declaration disclosing the totality of its stockpile of weapons of mass destruction, the components of these weapons, and their means of production. The purpose of UNSCOM and its inspections was to verify the completeness and accuracy of this Iraqi declaration, and then to oversee the destruction, rendering harmless, or removal of the material in question. Under a subsequent Security Council resolution some months later, UNSCOM was given an additional mandate of monitoring Iraqi compliance with its disarmament obligations.

Such monitoring was intended as ongoing verification following Iraq's complete disarmament of those noxious weapons. UNSCOM was thus meant to be a conventional arms control organization, based upon the principle of "trust but verify" set forth in other disarmament treaties, such as the 1987 Intermediate-Range Nuclear Forces (INF) treaty between the United States and the former Soviet Union.

There was a qualitative difference, however. This was not an arms control treaty brokered between two equal partners, but rather a disarmament agreement in which one side, Iraq—defeated on the battlefields of Kuwait in the 1991 Gulf War—was compelled to carry out the dictates of the other side, the United Nations. UNSCOM's work was an outcome of the cease-fire agreement, and Iraqi disarmament was a precondition for ending the state of war.

As the history of the intervening years has shown, Iraq had no intention of meeting its disarmament obligations. Even as the Security Council was putting the finishing touches on the creation of UNSCOM, Saddam Hussein was summoning his inner leadership for the purpose of creating a special committee to decide which weapons capabilities would be turned over and which would be kept. This committee had an additional task. It would have to devise a mechanism to conceal the weaponry retained along with related information and material from the inspectors.

The committee believed that the inspection regime would not be sustained for very long, and that if the Iraqis could pull the wool over the eyes of the inspectors—trick them into verifying a false declaration—then within a relatively short period Iraq could get back to business as usual. The crippling economic sanctions imposed by the Security Council in August 1990, following Iraq's invasion of Kuwait, had remained in place even after the liberation of Kuwait. Sanctions were the means of compelling Iraq to accept the disarmament measures and would only be lifted when UNSCOM gave Iraq a clean bill of health. All Iraq had to do was deceive the inspectors, and it would have its cake and eat it, too.

Fooling inspectors was something Saddam Hussein's Iraq had already succeeded at handily for over a decade. Baghdad had been carrying out a covert nuclear weapons program by diverting legitimate nuclear materials and disguising the true purposes of facilities that were supposedly monitored by another United Nations organization, the International Atomic Energy Agency. The IAEA inspections had been designed to prevent the very kind of activity Iraq was carrying out right under the IAEA's nose. Iraq assumed it would be able to get away with the same sleight of hand once again.

The extent of Saddam's post–Desert Storm deception, which would be assessed only much later by years of trial and error, was immense:

- Of nineteen mobile ballistic missile launchers held by Iraq at the end of the Gulf War, only ten were declared. The other nine went into hiding, part of an operational ballistic missile force that Saddam wanted desperately to keep intact;
- Of approximately 140 long-range ballistic missiles, known as the Al-Hussein or its variant, the Al-Hijara, only forty-five were declared and submitted to UNSCOM for disposition;
- While declaring its program for modifying standard, short-range Soviet-supplied Scud missiles to the 650-kilometer-range Al-Hussein, it kept secret its indigenous ballistic missile production of operational Al-Hussein missiles;
- Similarly, it declared aspects of its massive chemical weapons inventory and production capabilities, but thousands of bombs and artillery shells filled with deadly substances were hidden, including munitions and production equipment associated with the highly lethal VX—a nerve agent that Iraq never acknowledged possessing;
- Iraq did not declare any aspect of its biological weapons program in the initial declaration to UNSCOM, nor did it declare any aspects of its nuclear weapons program.

For now, at war's end, Saddam Hussein clearly believed that these capabilities were the key to his future survival. For one thing, he had to appease an internal constituency, in particular the Iraqi armed forces. They had come to regard these weapons as critical to Iraq's strategic parity with Israel. Second, Saddam sought to insure his ability to assume leadership of the Arab world as a regional super-power. These weapons and the ability to go on producing them were essential to achieving his goals.

Thus the 1991 decision to conceal set the stage for Saddam's great shell game. This time around, however, the international in-spectors were not asleep at the wheel. In June of that year, the IAEA, to its credit, doggedly pursued intelligence that led inspectors to the first clear violation of the cease-fire agreement. In a confrontation at a military barracks in western Baghdad, the inspectors attempted to intercept vehicles loaded with equipment designed to enrich ura-nium for use in a nuclear bomb. The inspection stalled when warn-ing shots were fired by the Iraqis, but the equipment was later seized and destroyed.

The discovery of this material, which included giant electro-magnetic isotope separators known as Calutrons—of the type used in the World War II Manhattan Project—and the subsequent Iraqi declaration that it indeed had an advanced nuclear enrichment pro-gram (but, it maintained, no weapons program), caused a stir in the international community. It led to a unanimous Security Council condemnation of Iraq's duplicity and the passage of a new resolution prohibiting any form of concealment. Unfortunately, it did not fun-damentally change the overall equation concerning the disarma-ment of Iraq; it merely reiterated the original requirement that Iraq had to submit a "full, final and complete" declaration so that the in-spection teams could get on with the work of verification.

For Iraq, this episode provided a respite in which to regroup and reconsider its options. What Saddam did next is a paradigm of contempt and audacity. After physically concealing the material and documentation deemed critical for reconstituting his chemical, bio-logical, nuclear, and long-range ballistic missile arsenals, he under-took a massive "cleaning up" operation, destroying most (but not all) of his missiles, munitions, and production tools, claiming that he had liquidated his arsenal—but without United Nations supervision. It was a brazen fait accompli to remove any trace of evidence of

Iraq's previous programs. This act of unilateral destruction was of course by itself a massive act of concealment, and the resultant Iraqi declarations when finally submitted were based on the "cleaned up" numbers of the cooked books. Saddam was challenging all comers to try to find his weapons. Iraq still believed that it could fool the world.

Saddam almost got away with it. In December 1991, UNSCOM, acting on a U.S. intelligence tip, began turning up the pressure. UNSCOM initiated a new series of intrusive, no-notice inspections designed to uncover an Iraqi covert ballistic missile force. The inspectors struck out time and again, though it was subsequently revealed in Iraqi statements years later how close they had come to catching the Iraqis cold. In one instance, for example, the Iraqis had evacuated ballistic missile components from a police station only days prior to the arrival of the team.

In March 1992, UNSCOM stood poised to dispatch an even larger team, this time armed with sensitive intelligence, including satellite imagery that clearly showed that Iraq had failed to declare all of its mobile missile launchers, but the Iraqis moved first and, as had become the custom, boldly. With inspectors in Bahrain about to fly into Baghdad, Iraqi authorities finally admitted to the unilateral destruction activities and invited UNSCOM to verify that all the material had indeed been destroyed.

This preventive declaration changed the dynamic of the inspection regime dramatically. All intelligence was suddenly obsolete. Any evidence that the inspectors may have had about Iraqi false statements was, literally overnight, invalidated. Iraq now claimed that all of the material of a prohibited nature no longer existed, and in fact dragged the inspectors through dozens of fields to display the wreckage of its banned weapons—crushed missile airframes and exploded warheads, rusted components and shattered bombs.

Employing a verification technique called "material balance," the inspectors set about to piece together the various parts of destroyed weapons, components, and production means jigsaw-puzzle-fashion. They sought to verify physically the Iraqi declaration of unilateral destruction. What they found was a significant shortfall.

Iraq countered with yet another innovative assertion. The debris exhibited, they said, was only part of the total; the rest had been collected and melted into ingots. The origins of the ingots were unrecognizable, but Iraq invited the inspectors to weigh them to determine whether the weight matched the weight of the missing components. Not surprisingly, the inspectors suggested another method. They asked for documents or any other record of this unilateral destruction to provide some basis for verifying the Iraqi declaration. Unfortunately, according to Baghdad, the entire affair had been top secret and carried out precipitously; there was no documentation.

The inspectors either had to accept the Iraqi declarations at face value or take action to uncover evidence of any hidden material.

The inspectors chose action. UNSCOM's first executive chairman, Rolf Ekéus, believed that documents that would refute Iraqi claims about the unilateral destruction did indeed exist. In the summer of 1992, acting on reliable intelligence, he dispatched several inspection teams into Iraq to track them down. A major confrontation, brushed with violence, erupted between the Iraqis and the United Nations weapons inspectors. I was at the center of that event. It ended in a debacle for UNSCOM but it stays with me as the first time I passed through the looking glass of Saddam Hussein's hellish netherworld.

It was the season of the maddening Middle East sun, July of 1992. For nearly a week, I had stood watch outside the Iraqi Ministry of Agriculture, part of a cordon of inspectors that kept the facility surrounded on a twenty-four-hour basis. We were trying to prevent the Iraqis from removing a cache of documents pertaining to their forbidden weapons programs. They denied that a single page even existed. But three years later, an intelligence coup would lead us to a stash of over 1.5 million pages of the very material we were now looking for. I was team operations officer. The Nissan Patrol I was riding in was parked in front of the building, alongside a large concrete block atop which was a portrait of Saddam Hussein.

Like most of the ubiquitous Iraqi paintings of their leader, it was a poorly rendered likeness, done with little regard to scale or perspective. But that wasn't what caught my eye. It was the manner in which the Iraqi president was depicted, as Sa'd bin Abi Waqqass, the great Arab warrior who defeated the Persian army in the battle of al-Qadissiyah in 633 (during the Iran-Iraq War in the 1980s, Saddam attempted to rally support by calling the war "Qadassiyaht Saddam"). Mounted on a majestic Arabian stallion and swathed in white robes, Saddam flourished a Damascus blade over his head as he led a host of Arabian warriors into battle. The portrait amused me at the time. Only eighteen months earlier, I had been stationed in Saudi Arabia, serving during Desert Storm on General Norman Schwarzkopf's staff. The thought of Saddam Hussein as an exalted military leader tickled me as much as the notion, so belied by the events of the war, of Iraqi troops assuming the offensive under his command. Suddenly, however, we inspectors became the target of a new sort of offensive, though without the direct presence of Saddam.

For over three weeks that July Iraq had refused us access, defying UNSCOM and the Security Council and threatening the safety of the inspectors. Mass demonstrations of thousands of civilians, who had been handed eggs and vegetables by the egg-and-vegetable quartermasters of the regime, had pelted us as we sat in our cars. This onslaught had failed to pry us loose from the perimeter of the ministry, and now the Iraqis tried a more direct tactic. They assaulted us with skewers and knives. Unarmed and with no mandate for self-defense, the team had no choice but to withdraw and await the outcome of the Security Council discussion of the issue.

The council failed to act decisively in defense of the rights of their inspectors, opting for a toothless compromise. We would be allowed to return to the building several days later to inspect it. That inspection, of course, found nothing, since the Iraqis in the interim had removed the documents under the cover of darkness. This fiasco put the campaign of inspections on hold, and by the fall the process was stalled, with both inspectors and the inspected engaged in a complicated dance around the arms inspections issue. UNSCOM continued to push for its right to carry out no-notice inspections while avoiding the frontal assault tactics that had left us stranded in front of the Agriculture Ministry in July.

Then in October several of us traveled to the foothills of the

Jabal Makhul mountain range about 180 miles north of Baghdad. We were outside an opulent palace complex situated high on a ridge and sweeping down the eastern slope to the edge of the Tigris. This facility had been identified by French military intelligence as a likely location for a secret nuclear reactor, rumors of which had been abundant at the end of the Gulf War. I was then deputy chief inspector of a weapons inspection team. Our convoy, a serpentine line of white vehicles stretched out on the winding road up the mountain, was suddenly stopped cold at the palace gates and surrounded by armed Special Republican Guards. The situation rapidly became quite tense.

A senior Iraqi official, Hossam Amin, informed our chief inspector, an imposing Russian named Nikita Smidovich, that the facility in question was a diplomatic entity and "out of bounds" to inspections. Both Iraq and the Special Commission were still somewhat punch-drunk after the standoff at the Agriculture Ministry and both sides sought to defuse this situation before it could get out of hand.

High-level communications between Rolf Ekéus and Tariq Aziz ensued, resulting in yet another compromise. Four inspectors would be allowed to drive through the site and look around. If Smidovich felt that a more detailed investigation were warranted, the presence of additional inspectors would be negotiated. Adhering to this agreement, Nikita, myself, and two other inspectors (a Frenchman and a German) piled into a white UNSCOM Nissan. We proceeded up the hill and into the complex, escorted by Hossam Amin and three Iraqi security officials. Oddly, the escort included Colonel Saddam Kamal, a son-in-law of Saddam Hussein and member of his personal protection detail. Saddam Kamal drove the Iraqi vehicle; clearly this facility was not one of the run-of-the-mill diplomatic variety.

What greeted us inside the complex was a sight that I'll never forget. As we wound our way up the road, we could look back on the panorama of the greater Baiji complex, with the run-down city of the same name on our left, then the sprawling Baiji oil refinery, and, on our right, the Baiji fertilizer plant, until the Jabal Makhul massif obscured our view. A prime industrial target, the Baiji area had been severely bombed during the Gulf War, and still bore melancholy scars of that campaign. And yet, as we penetrated further into the "diplomatic facility," we entered a land untouched by war, a place unlike anything I had ever seen in my extensive travels in Iraq.

The road was paved in immaculate black asphalt, with groomed white-gravel shoulders bordered by steel railings. At the top, we could look down on villas made of fine stucco and covered with red-tile roofs. There were two rows of villas, one on the ridge of the mountain and another well below along the banks of the Tigris. Between the two was a series of manmade waterfalls, cascading over the steep slope. Alongside the falls were paved paths, with benches and rest areas of brilliantly green grass and wispy shade trees. Some believe that the biblical Garden of Eden lay somewhere between the Tigris and the Euphrates; it may have been far or near from here, but this place seemed very much a paradise. It was only when we drew close to the villas that the character of this compound became apparent.

A mazelike arrangement of stone walls, some of them hundreds of yards long, screened one villa from another. Every wall was faced with fine marble, rose, white, and steel-gray. The marble had been sculpted in a most remarkable fashion with bas-relief carvings of ancient Babylonian chariots, warriors astride, bowstrings pulled back. I recognized images of the Babylonian kings Hammurabi and Nebuchadnezzar in the background. But it was the image in the forward chariot that was riveting: Saddam Hussein himself.

He was in full Babylonian battle dress, leading the forces of ancient Mesopotamia into battle against a Persian horde. Marble wall after marble wall presented itself to us with the same megalomaniacal conceit. Saddam, the warlord, Saddam, the conqueror with the vanquished enemies of Babylon prostrate at his feet, Saddam, the invincible, and, as in the fanciful portrait at the Agriculture Ministry, Saddam once again metamorphosed into Sa'd bin Abi Waqqass, routing the forces of the infidels. Everywhere we looked, we were confronted with these larger-than-life apparitions of Saddam Hussein, side by side with the vaunted leaders of ancient Iraq throughout the centuries. It was as extraordinarily garish and tasteless as it must have been extravagantly expensive. Even the Iraqis in our company, with the exception of ever-smiling Saddam Kamal, appeared mortified by this excess, cringing in their vehicle.

We found nothing relating to our disarmament mandate that day. The "nuclear reactor" turned out to be the large pumps used to move water from the river up the mountain to holding tanks that fed the lavish falls. But our brief trip to the Oz of Saddam Hussein's Iraq left us shaking our heads: what a dream case for Sigmund Freud and what a national nightmare for the people of Iraq. The delusions of grandeur that permeated the Jabal Makhul palace made me wonder if the world I occupied and the world of Saddam Hussein were on the same planet.

I resolved to know my enemy. In Desert Storm I had participated in an all-out military conflict against Saddam's Iraq. By October 1992, I found myself in a conflict of another kind. The weapons inspections process, conceived as a simple verification exercise along the lines of conventional arms control agreements, had degenerated into a complex and perilous game of hide and seek. It pitted UNSCOM weapons inspectors, armed only with the conviction that they were carrying out a legitimate mandate of the modern-day guarantors of international peace and security, the United Nations, against the forces of one of history's most devious and brutally efficient dictatorships.

In the end, I would realize that the key I was looking for was not to be found in the sagas of Nebuchadnezzar or Sa'd bin Abi Waqqass or in any of the mythical Arab leaders who grace the marble edifices to Saddam's rule known as presidential palaces, but in Saddam Hussein himself, a man with his fair share of all the strengths and weaknesses by which men rise and fall.

But this awareness would not come to me overnight. I was, after all, a weapons inspector, not a social scientist. The understanding that I sought arrived only after years of struggling to learn the nature of the Iraqi weapons program and how it was being concealed from the weapons inspectors.

# 2

# The Road to Auja

I WAS BROUGHT IN to work for UNSCOM based on two key factors: I was a seasoned intelligence officer with wartime experience in hunting down Saddam's long-range ballistic missile force, and I was a veteran arms control inspector, with two and a half years of experience in implementing the provisions of the INF treaty between the former Soviet Union and the United States. While in the Soviet Union, I learned a good deal about the technologies and principles of ballistic missiles, something that proved useful during the Gulf War when, as part of General Schwarzkopf's staff, I helped to develop specific techniques for locating and destroying scud missiles. Then Colonel Doug Englund, for whom I'd worked in the U.S.S.R., recruited me for UNSCOM, and I came on board in September of 1991.

I concentrated on Iraq's ballistic missile program from the very outset of my work with the commission. Everything that followed, in terms of investigating the Iraqi concealment mechanism, grew out of my efforts to determine the extent of Iraq's long-range missile force. I viewed the Iraqi ballistic missile capability as the key to its entire prohibited arsenal; the chemical and biological programs depended on a delivery system.

My opinion that the ballistic missile program was the key to Iraq's weapons of mass destruction was a controversial position, one that went against the grain of conventional thinking. But in my years of studying Iraq and its weapons programs, it was a position with which I grew more and more comfortable. The initial analysis that I performed for UNSCOM soon after my arrival regarding Iraq's missile inventory concluded that Iraq was not telling the truth in its weapons declarations. I was convinced that it was concealing a force of at least six missile launchers and up to eighty missiles (the actual number turned out to be eight launchers and ninety-five missiles). This represented a real military capability, one that had to be taken all the more seriously if one concluded, as I had, that many of these retained weapons would carry chemical and biological warheads. While my figures for missiles and launchers were based on my Gulf War experience, the linkage I made between retained missiles and a retained chemical and biological capability was something akin to speculation—more a gut feeling than analysis of hard data.

Why did I feel this way? My experience during the Gulf War as an analyst of Iraq's surface-to-surface missile capabilities led me to believe that this was a strategic resource that represented not only a valuable military asset for Iraq, but also a tremendous source of national pride and prestige. These missiles, named by Saddam himself Al-Hussein, had broken Iran's will to fight in 1988, and the missile force was the only branch of the Iraqi military to serve with distinction and success during the Gulf War. Not a single launcher or operational missile was lost to hostile fire during the entire Gulf War, despite the extensive allied bombing of these units.

In 1992 my pursuit of this missile connection led me to the charismatic commander of the Iraqi Al-Hussein force, Lieutenant General Hazim Abdal Razzaq Shihab Ayubi, one of his country's most innovative military minds. Nikita Smidovich and I were investigating intelligence reports that several Iraqi missile launches had been destroyed by the U.S. Special Forces during the Gulf War. Iraq had already declared the extent of its launchers to UNSCOM. If it were true that Special Forces troops had destroyed launchers, then Iraq would have had a larger inventory than declared.

I questioned General Ayubi on the performance of his units during the Gulf War. He denied that any of his launchers had been destroyed, and the pride in his eyes and the eyes of his subordinate commanders as they recounted how they successfully prosecuted their two-front campaign impressed me deeply. Later, the source of this pride hit home when I drove through the bombed-out ruins of the Taji barracks of Unit 224, the Al-Hussein force. As I entered the devastated facility, I noticed that the roads had been lined with freshly painted white rocks, and that there was a smartly attired honor guard posted at the entrance. When I drove through, the honor guard snapped to attention. I was somewhat confused about this activity, until I noticed the signs posted alongside the road, which was bordered on both sides by bombed-out buildings. In neat Arabic script, the signs read: "It was enough that we made Israel cry."

The honor guard wasn't saluting me or my inspectors; they were saluting themselves. In some strange way of looking at the world, this bombed-out facility had become a shrine to Iraqi military prowess. And those who would take the time to learn their story—as I learned it from General Ayubi—might begin to understand why.

For the people in Baghdad on the morning of January 17, 1991, the light of the new day illuminated the harsh reality of the U.S.-led coalition air strikes against Iraq. In the preceding months, an internal debate had raged within the Iraqi hierarchy. The prevailing opinion among the policymakers was that the January 15 deadline issued by the coalition for withdrawal of Iraqi troops from Kuwait should be ignored. The leadership feared nothing worse than a limited air strike against a handful of high-value targets in Iraq. Indeed, this assessment very closely paralleled initial planning that had been conducted by the U.S. Air Force in early August 1990. The air force had advocated a demonstration of U.S. power and resolve by an air campaign of gradual escalation that would be guided by political and military events. This was a game that the Iraqi leadership knew well, and one that it was more than willing to play.

However, the coalition's Instant Thunder campaign, which called for massive, all-out air strikes against a wide variety of targets, had won out over a policy of gradualism. As a result, the precision strikes of U.S. bombers dealt a knockout blow to Iraq's vaunted air defense network, and its impressive array of modern fighters were either swept from the sky by their U.S. counterparts or left impotent in hardened aircraft shelters. Indeed, Iraq appeared to be helpless before the overwhelming force brought to bear against it. So, as the sun came up over Baghdad that morning, the outcome of this new war was all too apparent in the shadows of the bombed-out buildings and the dark plumes of oily, black smoke that cloaked the city skyline.

General Ayubi, summoned to an emergency session of the Revolutionary Command Council that morning of the 17th, was notified that he was to prepare his force for an immediate attack on Israel. This was to be followed by a similar strike against targets in the Arabian peninsula.

Less than three years earlier, he had conducted the surface-to-surface missile assault against Iran, launching the barrage of Al-Hussein missiles against Iranian cities that had driven the hitherto intractable mullahs to negotiate an end to the eight-year war. Quite rightly, Ayubi had become a national hero, and the Al-Hussein force a national treasure. Now, with a new war damaging Baghdad, the force and the hero had once again been called on to deliver an Iraqi response.

That afternoon, he was ready to begin his operation. For the past several weeks he had dispersed the mobile launchers of his Al-Hussein force to hiding places north and northwest of Baghdad to protect them from any preemptive strike. In the meantime, he had prepared his men in a series of exercises in which everyone involved would work their way, step by step, through a simulated surface-to-surface missile campaign against Israel. All of this intensive preparation was soon to pay off. Now, gathered in a palm grove near the western Iraqi city of Ramadi, the officers and staff of the Al-Hussein force listened intently as General Ayubi once again walked them through a detailed battle plan—only this time it was for real.

As General Ayubi briefed his staff, the mobile launchers of the Al-Hussein force were on their way to the Ramadi area, where the force's Technical Battalion had established a site for fueling, arming, and otherwise preparing the Al-Hussein missiles for combat operations against Israel. The plan, devised by General Ayubi and his technical officers, provided for a continuous stream of missiles being readied for launch. This operation would have to avoid detection by the coalition's formidable intelligence assets.

According to Ayubi's instructions, the force was to launch immediate missile strikes against both Israel and the Arabian peninsula. To maximize their impact, Ayubi planned a single mass strike against Israel using all of his available assets, and then a shift of a significant part of his force to the south for a similar massive strike against targets in the Arabian peninsula—all the while maintaining combat operations against Israel. The goal was to increase the political pressure on the coalition—which included several Arab states—by drawing Israel into the conflict.

He then laid down the Israeli targets—eleven in the Tel Aviv area, and three in Haifa. Of the six launchers, three would fire against Tel Aviv from one location and the other three from another. This was part of a deception effort for the post-launch phase, when Ayubi anticipated that large numbers of coalition (and possibly Israeli) aircraft would attempt to destroy the launchers. Ayubi believed that coalition sensors would detect the launches as having come from launchers in fixed positions, which would buy him time for his mobile launchers to make their way to hide sites away from the launch areas and escape detection.

At three A.M. Baghdad time on January 18, the orders came down from President Saddam Hussein himself: launch. In western Iraq, at eight separate sites, the desert glowed brilliant orange as the missile fuel ignited, propelling the slender Al-Husseins into the cold night, the glow of the plume growing smaller in the sky, the deadly payload en route to Israel.

Minutes later, the calm of the Israeli seaport of Haifa was shattered. Three Al-Hussein missiles screamed down at a speed of Mach 6. Trailing a small orange flame, they could be clearly tracked as they impacted within thirty seconds of each other. The first missile plunged into the water off the city proper, exploding on contact. The second fell into the Mediterranean west of the town of Kiryat Motzkin, it, too, detonating on impact. The third missile struck a shopping mall under construction, located near the checkpoint at the north entrance to Haifa, exploding with a bright green flame.

The warhead, penetrating the roof of the mall before exploding with a force of 250 kilograms of high explosive, devastated an area about twenty-five meters in diameter. The ceilings caved in. Shards and debris scattered everywhere, damaging a hundred shops and an equal number of apartments. Fortunately, the mall was empty and there were no casualties.

Shortly after the impacts in Haifa, five more Al-Hussein missiles struck in the vicinity of Tel Aviv. The first exploded in the air, disintegrating and spreading debris over the flight path. The second struck and destroyed a civilian factory building. The city's Ezra quarter was next to be hit, with seventy-six residential apartments completely demolished and thousands more damaged. It was this missile that caused all of the casualties in this first wave of attacks, injuring sixty-eight people, several seriously. Only sheer good luck prevented many more injuries and scores of deaths. Two more missiles fell over Tel Aviv that morning, one crashing into an orchard, the other exploding in the sky. But the damage had been done. The heartland of Israel had been struck hard by Arab military forces. They had made Israel cry.

General Ayubi's insistence that his launchers remained intact was corroborated by documentation. I realized then that UNSCOM was dependent on intelligence supplied by member nations to guide us on what to inspect—in this case, U.S. military intelligence. This was not acceptable, especially in light of the 1992 incident at the Agriculture Ministry in which we were outmaneuvered by the Iraqis, who evacuated the archives while we were ordered by the Security Council to look the other way, so to speak.

We were forced to reconsider our tactics. I began formulating a concept where UNSCOM would not investigate where Iraq was hiding material and documents, but rather what Iraq was not declaring to UNSCOM about its past programs. This required a series of detailed inspections of known facilities in Iraq, where we searched for clues about what activity had taken place there prior to the Gulf War. Gradually, UNSCOM became a sort of accountant as inspectors conducted analyses that focused on the material balance, in which Iraq's unilaterally destroyed material would be checked off as no longer existing, even if confirming evidence was lacking. Based on this procedure, UNSCOM by 1995 had moved toward accepting most of the Iraqi declarations concerning past proscribed programs, and in a report to the Security Council in June of that year, Ekéus stated that once Iraq's biological weapons program declaration was verified, UNSCOM would be ready to issue its clean bill of health.

This situation, however, underwent a dramatic and clamorous turnabout a few weeks later. In August, the former supervising minister for military industry and another son-in-law of Saddam Hussein, Lieutenant General Hussein Kamal, defected to Jordan. He was accompanied by his brother, Colonel Saddam Kamal, the head of the presidential bodyguard unit (and the smiling driver of our escort at the Jabal Makhul palace), and a retinue of others, most prominent among them being two of Saddam's daughters, Raghab, the eldest and wife of Hussein Kamal, and middle child Rina, married to Saddam Kamal.

Hussein Kamal spoke openly to the media, Western intelligence agencies, and UNSCOM head Ekéus about Iraq's weapons of mass destruction programs. He revealed how Iraq was misleading the United Nations weapons inspectors through a systematic program of deception and concealment.

This revelation prompted the Baghdad government to run for cover by "discovering" a hidden trove of some 1.5 million pages of documents relating to its past proscribed weapons programs. The "discovery" was made on a chicken farm belonging to Hussein Kamal in the village of Haidar, southeast of Baghdad. Iraq attempted to shift the blame for the failure to disclose these documents to UNSCOM on the "illegal" conduct of Hussein Kamal, and pledged a new spirit of cooperation with the weapons inspectors. How such treacherous behavior by Hussein Kamal went undetected by his famously suspicious father-in-law and the whole apparatus of Saddam's police state was left to the imagination.

Hussein Kamal did not of course defect for the purpose of assisting UNSCOM. He was trying to leverage himself into a favorable position in the international community to gain support for an opposition group under his leadership to overthrow and replace Saddam. The Special Commission and the various intelligence agencies listened to Hussein Kamal's information with great interest but then kept him at arm's length. Few doubted what the more credible Iraqi dissidents had been saying about him all along—that he was a murderous thug, a war criminal whose savagery against the Iraqi people was as at least the equal of that of his mentor and father-in-law.

Four years earlier, following the military defeat of Iraq in Kuwait, Hussein Kamal had led intact elements of the Iraqi army on a brutal rampage against Shi'a rebels in southern Iraq and Kurdish rebels in the north. Saddam Kamal oversaw the torture and execution of thousands of rebels and political prisoners in the regime's hellhole prisons in Abu Ghraib and Radwaniyah. While the Kamal brothers were not alone in their barbarity, their efficiency and enthusiasm in the commission of these brutal crimes became legendary. Hussein Kamal, self-styled pretender to Saddam's throne, who had left Iraq filled with grandiose illusions, was genuinely shocked when the world community refused to shake his bloodstained hands.

Later, I had occasion to discuss Hussein Kamal with members of the Jordanian royal court. They painted a picture of a man drawn deeper and deeper into a make-believe world where he reigned supreme. This had a telling effect on Saddam Hussein's daughters, who were taken with a sudden case of homesickness and a longing for their life of privilege, particularly once the Kamal brothers had been thoroughly debriefed and their continued presence became a source of embarrassment to Jordan's King Hussein. The entire party was moved out of its luxurious accommodations at the Royal Palace to more humble surroundings, something that Hussein Kamal, for one, believed to be beneath his stature. He became increasingly despondent and given to flights of fancy that he was indispensable to Iraq and to Saddam Hussein and would be welcomed back with open arms.

Such was the state of mind of the man who then, only six months after his defection, returned to Iraq with his brother and their wives—enticed by a pardon from Saddam Hussein himself. The convoy of Mercedes sedans that departed Amman was met at the Iraq-Jordan border by Saddam's elder son, Uday, who immediately separated the Kamal brothers from their wives. The next morning, in a ceremony overseen by Saddam Hussein himself at the Republican Palace in downtown Baghdad, Raghab and Rina were divorced from their husbands, and twenty-four hours later the new bachelors were dead, gunned down by the Special Republican Guard.

Hussein Kamal's disclosures concerning the details of what Iraq had withheld from UNSCOM and the IAEA were astounding. Based on this new, firsthand information from the man who had been in charge of building these weapons, the Special Commission realized that Iraq, far from coming clean, had in fact never ceased its concealment activities. The revelations led to a decisive shift away from the hopelessly flawed material balance approach to verification and active pursuit of the concealment mechanism. Concealment-oriented inspections would in fact be at the heart of every major confrontation between UNSCOM and Iraq from that point until the December 1998 U.S. military strike, Desert Fox.

The enormity of deception was clear from virtually the first words out of Hussein Kamal's mouth. In a highly restricted meeting with UNSCOM chief Rolf Ekéus and his deputy Nikita Smidovich that first month of the defection, Hussein Kamal exposed the Iraqi lie that it had destroyed all of its operational ballistic missile capability in the summer of 1991. He revealed the existence of two hidden Russian missile launchers, one dismantled, the other completely assembled. "These two launchers," he said, "are with the Special [Republican] Guards. They are hidden in the same location where computer disks with information on nuclear programs are. If you find one you will find the other. It is difficult to pinpoint a specific location . . . [they] have a lot of information on microfiches. People who work in the MIC [Military Industrial Commission] were asked to take documents to their houses. I think you will have a new war of searches."

Those were prophetic words and weighed heavily on us that hot August day, but the UNSCOM officials were so enraptured by these and other dramatic revelations that they failed to register the significance of what happened next. There was someone in his party, Hussein Kamal said, who had a farm where molds for missiles were hidden. "I will call him," he said.

Within minutes a husky man in his late thirties was ushered into the room. Major Izz al-Din Muhammad Hassan 'Abd al-Majid, formerly of Saddam Hussein's Special Republican Guard, had defected along with Hussein Kamal, his cousin. I was not present at that meeting, but his brief testimony would affect my activities in

Iraq for a long time. "I remember there were two molds hidden in my farm," he said, according the transcript, "but they were taken away in 1992." He knew nothing about the two missile launchers, he said, and thus was given little attention. His contribution seemed trivial in the light of Hussein Kamal's debriefing. Izz al-Din was quickly dismissed from the scene.

But Izz al-Din al-Majid was not in Baghdad that fateful morning in February 1996, when the Kamal brothers were killed. When Hussein Kamal undertook his suicidal return to Iraq, Izz al-Din was in Syria, pressed into service by the U.S. Central Intelligence Agency. As a former member of the Special Republican Guard, he possessed vital information about Saddam's security system and was being courted by Western intelligence services to work with the Amman-based Iraqi National Accord, an opposition group of former Iraqi military and security officers who were emerging as the darlings of the CIA's covert action plan to depose Saddam Hussein.

On his return to Amman, Izz al-Din learned that Hussein Kamal had departed, and he found reasons not to follow in his path. This decision undoubtedly saved his life, and ultimately made him available to the Special Commission when the weapons inspectors began to scrutinize the wide discrepancies between Hussein Kamal's disclosures and Iraq's official position on the retained prohibited weapons. I was in charge of that investigation. I desperately needed some leverage to pry open the lid on Baghdad's cauldron of lies. In the few words spoken that day back in August, Izz al-Din had mentioned molds hidden on his farm, and whatever else that might lead to, it meant now that he alone bore live witness to specific acts of concealment and deception conducted by Saddam Hussein's security forces to keep retained weapons out of the hands of the inspection teams.

Over the course of several meetings, Izz al-Din told me about his farm west of Baghdad, on the outskirts of Abu Ghraib. He explained how he was ordered to receive material from a senior officer of the Special Republican Guard, and how he buried it on his farm beneath the floor of a garage. This material—production molds, tools, and dies used to produce long-range ballistic missiles, as well as the components of indigenously manufactured liquid propellant engines used in these missiles—had been brought to Baghdad from another farm, a presidential facility near Auja, a village on the Tigris just south of Tikrit.

In December 1996 an inspection team under my command was dispatched to Izz al-Din's farm, where we found remnants of the missile production tools and components still buried under the garage floor. They had been left behind by security forces that hurriedly evacuated the site in early 1992. UNSCOM now had leverage.

Faced with such incontrovertible evidence, the Iraqi authorities were compelled to confess that some material had indeed been diverted from the unilateral-destruction activity of the summer of 1991. When UNSCOM asked for records to verify this, it was provided with vehicle load manifests listing the contents of the trucks used to transport this material. Among the sites listed as hiding places was one labeled "Auja Farm."

There was that name again. Suddenly this town was taking on a certain importance for the work of the weapons inspectors. Formerly a nondescript mud village, Auja today is known to every schoolchild in Iraq as the birthplace of Saddam Hussein.

I went to Auja in the spring of 1997, following up on Izz al-Din's disclosures that this village and its surrounding area had been used as a hide site. I had read about how in the year of the birth of its most famous native son—1937—the hamlet of Auja had been nothing more than a cluster of huts nestled along the banks of the Tigris, home to poor goatherds and farmers belonging to the al-Majid household of the al-Bu Nasir tribe, a branch of the Tikriti tribal group.

When I drove through Auja in March 1997, it was a small town of broad boulevards, modern dwellings, large social buildings, and several stately villas housing Saddam's immediate relatives and friends—the clans of Saddam's own tribe, the al-Bu Nasir. The rise of Auja from an impoverished rural backwater to a modern Iraqi town parallels the rise of Saddam Hussein to power. Auja reflects the complicated tribal-based foundation of power underpinning Saddam's rule. If one wants to learn about the workings of modern day Iraq, one must go to Baghdad. However, if one seeks to understand how Saddam came to power and how he retains his power, then the journey must include Auja. One must study the al-Bu Nasir tribe, and in particular the interaction among its three clans—the al-Majid, the al-Tilfah, and the al-Muhammad. Beneath all the trappings of modern society, Iraq is still very much a tribal society and Saddam Hussein a tribal ruler.

# 3

# "He Who Confronts"

IT WAS TO HAVE BEEN a marriage between a young man and a woman from two distant clans of the al-Bu Nasir. Hussein, the groom, of the al-Majid clan, and the light of his eye, Sabha, of the al-Tilfah. Sabha's father, Tilfah al-Masallat, had arranged the marriage to draw the large al-Majid clan into his organization, a crime family. The city of Tikrit, the capital of the Salahadin Governate, was a way station on the trade route between Baghdad and Mosul, the gateway to Turkey and Europe. There was plenty of opportunity for mischief to be made by a criminal element, and Sabha's father led one of the larger gangs in the region. The addition of the al-Majid to his syndicate would give him a dominant position in the al-Bu Nasir tribe, something he hoped to extend into greater regional, even national influence.

The groom-to-be, however, had hopes of his own, and sometime before the big event Sabha discovered that she was pregnant. She tried to abort the child on her own, and when this failed, the wedding day was moved up, but Hussein was killed by a rival gang before the marriage. Sabha turned to Hussein's brother, Hassan al-Majid, and he stood in for Hussein during the birth of the child. It was Hassan who chose the newborn's name. To mark how the infant had withstood Sabha's effort to abort him, Hassan called him "Saddam," or "he who confronts." It would prove to be an apt name.

Life in rural Iraq in the 1930s was hard enough, all the more so for an unwed mother. Under tribal law, Hussein's family cared for her and her baby, but a love child and a shamed mother were no easy burden to bear. Sabha's father had been similarly humiliated by her sin, and he arranged for her to become the second wife of Ibrahim Hassan Umar Beg, a third cousin to Sabha's brother, Khayr Allah. Ibrahim took Sabha and, reluctantly, young Saddam under his roof. As a result, Saddam was now estranged from the al-Majid clan and part of a new clan, the al-Muhammad. Life in the Ibrahim household was less than tranquil and the boy apparently lived up to his name, proving to be a troublesome sort with poor academic performance. By 1947, the situation had grown untenable; Saddam ran away from home to his maternal uncle, Khayr Allah, who lived in Auja. Saddam now joined the household of a third clan of the al-Bu Nasir, the al-Tilfah. Tribal custom dictates that sons align themselves with the family of their father, but Saddam was under the sway of his mother's clan. That would prove to be critical in the future.

Uncle Khayr Allah was a former army officer who had been stripped of his commission and imprisoned for taking part in a rebellion. On his release, he embarked on a life of violent crime. He gathered fellow members of the al-Bu Nasir tribe around him in a highly efficient criminal organization built around family ties.

His political outlook put him on the side of the pan-Arab national-socialists of the Ba'ath party, and when the party expanded into Iraq in 1949, he became an early proponent. The party enjoyed little popular support, concentrating on recruiting military officers to foment insurrection in the army. Khayr Allah was an ideal member in the fledgling movement—a disgruntled military officer with fascist ambitions. The boy, Saddam, would himself be a perfect candidate for indoctrination by Ba'athist propaganda. He worked hard at it under the watchful eyes of his uncle. In 1953, Saddam was with Khayr Allah in Tikrit when Saddam murdered a fellow member of the al-Bu Nasir tribe and a distant relative, who had somehow betrayed the Ba'ath organization. Like a "made man" in the Mafia, Saddam by this killing secured his place the insular Tikriti gang. Indeed, as he later rose politically, he and his family were often referred to as the *Issaba*, or "the Gang," much in the way a Mafioso would refer to "the Family." The similarities to the Mafia were to continue. (Years later Saddam's favorite movie would be *The God-father*.)

Uncle and nephew took part in another murder a few years later, a politically motivated assassination of a civil servant. Saddam was arrested but freed on lack of evidence. Saddam's activities, and Khayr Allah's support, soon caught the party's notice, and Saddam became an associate, part of a rite of passage to full membership. Expelled from school for his role in the murder, Saddam began his new career in earnest: Ba'ath party assassin. It was 1958. At twenty-one the fatherless boy from Auja had made his mark in his world.

On July 14, 1958, two army brigade commanders, Abd al-Salam Arif and Abd al-Karim Qasim, led troops under their command in a military coup. Almost immediately, the two co-conspirators began to feud. Qasim, emerging as the victor, proceeded to suppress his political opponents, including the Ba'ath party. Dozens of Ba'athists were arrested and executed, and the party sought revenge. A six-man hit squad was assembled to assassinate Qasim, and, when one of the would-be killers fell ill, Saddam Hussein was summoned to replace him.

The assassination foray of October 7, 1959—though it failed—has gone down in contemporary Iraqi history as an example of their great leader's courage and steadfastness under fire. In reality, it was a comedy of errors. The assassins were unable to carry off their initial plan to ambush Qasim outside his office, then failed to get him when his car got stuck in traffic, instead killing his driver and wounding his bodyguard, but leaving Qasim unharmed. Saddam himself was wounded along with one of his accomplices, and the head of the squad was killed, all by their own guns.

Saddam and his injured comrade were spirited off to Syria, where they were placed under the protection of Syrian intelligence officials, supporters of the Ba'ath party. Saddam spent six months in Syria. It is said that he was befriended by Ba'ath party founder Michel A'flaq. The Syrians arranged passage for Saddam to Cairo, where he attended the university for the next two years.

The Ba'athists, in bloody street fighting in February 1963, finally ousted Qasim, killing him and many of his supporters. Ahmad Hassan al-Bakr, a cousin of Khayr Allah and a fellow member of the al-Bu Nasir tribe, was installed as the president of Iraq. Saddam Hussein returned to Iraq.

Nominated at last for full membership in the party, Saddam was, however, rejected. Undeterred, he went on to attempt to prove his mettle as an effective tool of Ba'athist repression. Saddam personally participated in the rounding up, torture, and murder of thousands of Iraqis who dared oppose Ba'athist rule. Nevertheless full status in the party continued to elude him and it was not until he married Khayr Allah's daughter, cousin Sajida—which sealed his relationship with his uncle and, through family ties, with Ahmad Hassan al-Bakr, the new president—that the coveted standing was granted. The lesson that he had reaped his reward through family ties and not party loyalty did not escape Saddam. Moreover, he was given time to reflect on this lesson when in November 1963, less than ten months after the Ba'athists had seized power, another military coup ousted the ferocious al-Bakr regime.

Besides following up on the Izz al-Din intelligence, one of the reasons for my visit to Auja was to investigate a French intelligence report. It had placed hidden missile components on the premises of a presidential palace along a bluff overlooking the Tigris on the outskirts of the village. The report was several years old and had lain dormant because it lacked corroboration and also because there was concern about trespassing on sensitive ground without corroboration. Now, apart from the French report, Izz al-Din had led us to the Iraqi documents listing Auja as a hide site. Moreover, we possessed highly sensitive information from mid-1996 indicating that prohibited material was being transported from Baghdad to the Auja-Tikrit area for concealment—all of which made Saddam's hometown a valid inspection target.

High-altitude U-2 surveillance photographs had provided us with two plausible locations for inspection, both within the grounds of Saddam's main Auja residence. One appeared to be a camouflaged road and the other was a strip of disturbed earth in an orchard fitting the description of a site being used to bury material. The U-2 images had also indicated that all access to the area was cut off by roadblocks and checkpoints except one. This was a long, tortuous detour through farm fields and orchards along the bank of the Tigris. Skirting a roadblock, it would take us to a rear entrance of the presidential site. We were accompanied by a single Iraqi vehicle carrying Iraqi engineers from the National Monitoring Directorate. None of them was a native of Tikrit and all were a little in awe of what was happening.

Tikrit and Auja were the seat of power for Saddam Hussein, and the area was treated as highly privileged. Foreigners were especially excluded. So it was somewhat amusing to observe the reaction of the Iraqis we passed on our way to the inspection site: the stares of Special Republican Guard air defense gunners standing beside their cannons as we went by; the confused faces of other Special Republican Guard soldiers, infantry, manning a roadblock, when we turned into the orchard; and surprisingly, the warm smiles and heartfelt waves of farmers and their families as our white vehicle with unmistakable U.N. markings made its way past them while they worked their land or stood outside their homes.

The dirt path was our little secret. It gave us access to a sanctuary closed to all but a select few, the tribal elite of the al-Bu Nasir. The path brought us back onto a two-lane asphalt road and at that point we had violated sacred ground. Heading north, we drove by a tan Chevrolet Suburban coming out of the gate of a large, fenced-off farm. Four men were in the truck dressed in elegant white robes, wearing flowing white kafiyas crowned with gold braiding. The robes themselves were trimmed in gold embroidery. The men were visibly startled when they saw us, and started shouting as we went by. They chased us at high speed until they drew up alongside, gesticulating and shouting all the while. The two men in the rear were brandishing shiny new Kalashnikov rifles. Fortunately, by then we had arrived at the scene of the checkpoint, manned by Special Republican Guard soldiers. Assessing the situation, the driver of the Suburban stopped and the passengers got out.

They were resplendent in their finery, looking every bit like Arab royalty. Each one had a long ceremonial dagger thrust into a sash tied around his waist. If it were not for their vehicle and automatic weapons, it would have been easy to imagine having been transported back into history, to the time of another famous Tikriti,

# Saddam Hussein's Family Tree

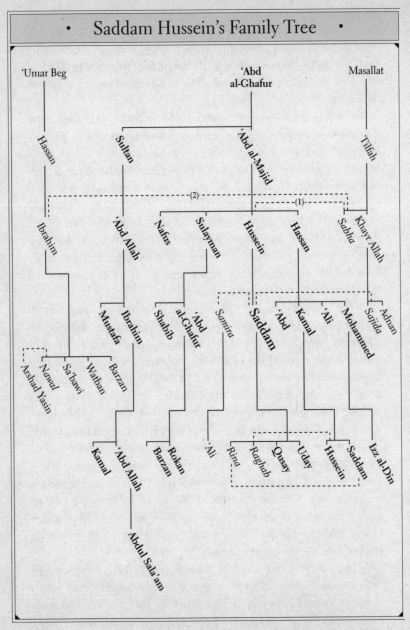

Note: Member's of Saddam Hussein's *khams* (five generation family unit, counting back from Saddam's sons) are indicated in **bold**. Females are indicated in *italics*. This family tree is not all inclusive and is limited to those characters who have a significant role in the narrative.

Saladin. As the discussions regarding access proceeded, our little gathering was visited repeatedly by a stream of similarly clad men, all of whom stared in amazement at us intruders. We had stumbled on an aspect of Iraqi life not readily visible to the rest of the country or the world: the tribal society of the al-Bu Nasir of Tikrit and Auja.

These distinguished-looking Arab men were a far cry from the hardscrabble criminals who had cast their lot with Khayr Allah and the original *Issaba* of the 1950s. The long climb of the al-Bu Nasir tribe from regional gang to dominant family in Iraq was not an easy one in the light of the turbulent events of revolutionary Iraq.

In the aftermath of the November 1963 coup that ousted al-Bakr, Saddam Hussein was arrested. While in prison, he was named deputy leader of the party. A largely symbolic title, it nonetheless established him as a party leader. He was either released or escaped shortly after his incarceration, and in any case, began the life of an underground revolutionary. He lobbied hard for a position of real responsibility within the new Ba'ath party, and in 1966 was finally given such a position: director of the Organization of Yearning for the Homeland, the Jihaz Hanin.

The Jihaz Hanin was created as a paramilitary apparatus with security and counterintelligence functions. Saddam began by gathering only the most trusted persons around him — which meant fellow members of the al-Bu Nasir tribe. He chose carefully, bringing in his cousin 'Ali Hassan al-Majid and his three half-brothers (the sons of Sabha and Ibrahim), Barzan, Sa'bawi, and Watban.

By murder and terror, Saddam gradually eliminated those in the party who did not support al-Bakr and, by extension, himself. When in July 1968 the Ba'athists regained power through a coup, Jihaz Hanin became the infamous, euphemistically titled Public Relations Bureau with Saddam at the helm. Al-Bakr, returned to the presidency, formed the Revolutionary Command Council (RCC) of the Ba'ath party, which he headed as its secretary general. Saddam secured a seat on the RCC in his role as party deputy.

From 1968 to 1979, Saddam continued to reinforce his position, rising from the most feared to the most powerful man in Iraq. He was responsible for several massive purges, including those of

Iraqi Jews in 1969, Iraqi Shiʻa from 1970 to 1972, and the Iraqi communists in 1974. Along with the victims of each purge inevitably a cell of their sympathizers was discovered within the Baʼath party and liquidated by Saddam, eliminating internal enemies and strengthening his grip on Iraq.

By 1973, he had become the de facto ruler of Iraq, with President al-Bakr reduced to the role of figurehead. Saddam, known widely as "Mr. Deputy" (al-Saʼid al ʼNaʼeb), came to dominate every aspect of the country's political and economic life. On July 17, 1979, Saddam declared himself al-Bakr's successor, exposing a huge Syrian "conspiracy" involving the president and senior Baʼath party officials. More than 200 Baʼathists, including twenty-one high party functionaries, were summarily executed. At last Saddam had removed all opposition to his rule. In the power vacuum he had created, he now inserted those he trusted most—the staunchly faithful family and friends of the al-Bu Nasir tribe.

Saddam had maintained close ties with both Auja and Tikrit, where his mother still resided. Sabha played an important role in her son's life until her death in 1982. It was through Sabha, either directly or indirectly, that Saddam drew continually closer to the al-Bu Nasir tribe as the most influential posts were distributed through the age-old practice of nepotism. Three families in particular of the al-Bu Nasir—the al-Majid, the al-Muhammad, and the al-Tilfah—were to play a particularly significant role.

Saddam's father, Hussein, was an al-Majid. Hussein's brother Hassan—who supported Sabha after Hussein's death—had remained a powerful member of the family. Saddam, indebted to the Hassan household, granted favors to Hassan's son, ʻAli Hassan al-Majid, who had gained notoriety as a man utterly without scruples. In 1975, Saddam put him in charge of suppressing the Kurdish rebellion in the north. In 1979, he was made governor of Najaf province in the south with the mission to destroy the Shiʻa opposition. Through ʻAli Hassan al-Majid, the al-Majid clan gained a reputation as the strongest arm of Saddam's rule.

Even more lavish were the privileges extended to Saddam's half-brothers—Barzan, Watban, and Saʼbawi—a reward for the tenacity of their mother, Sabha. Barzan became director general of the Iraqi intelligence service, the Mukhabarat. Sa'bawi was appointed deputy director of the Directorate for General Security (the DGS, or Amn al-Amm, Iraq's political security force), and Watban was named minister of the interior.

The final dispensation to the al-Bu Nasir was saved for the al-Tilfah clan, notably Saddam's lifelong mentor, Uncle Khayr Allah, and his son, Saddam's best friend, Adnan. During his purge of 1979, Saddam had the governor of Baghdad executed for corruption, and he named his uncle governor. The lifelong criminal now had the richest city in Iraq laid at his feet, ripe for picking. Saddam had not only surrounded himself with friends and family loyal to his authority, but had also created a powerful support base that was separate from and superior to the traditional constituencies of the party, the security services, and the military. Saddam and the al-Bu Nasir now controlled them all.

In a remarkable perversion of Ba'athist doctrine rejecting tribalism as a remnant of colonialism, Iraqi society found itself by the end of the 1970s under the near total domination of one tribe. In a lame attempt to mask the extent to which the al-Bu Nasir had taken control, Saddam decreed that Iraqi men use only their first two names, which prevented easy tribal identification. But everyone knew who was in charge. So many Tikriti men and families began to move to Baghdad that the colloquial Arabic spoken in Tikrit became the language of power, with even non-Tikritis speaking it in an effort to be seen as insiders.

Now that he controlled the Ba'ath party, Saddam turned his attention to the road to absolute power—the army and the powerful Amn al-Amm, or Directorate for General Security, the Iraqi secret police. Since the birth of the modern Iraqi state, the army had shown a propensity for political action. A string of failed insurrections and successful coups marked the historical landscape of Iraq, a fact that Saddam Hussein was only too aware of.

Saddam and al-Bakr understood that if Iraq was going to be a great regional power, it required powerful armed forces. In the mid-1970s, taking advantage of a windfall created by high oil prices, they enlarged and rearmed the army. Iraq signed a strategic agreement with the Soviet Union in 1974, and began receiving new tanks, armored fighting vehicles, helicopters, and aircraft. It also looked to Europe, especially France, and soon military hardware was flowing in from that direction. While the expansion of the army boosted the morale of its officers and men, diminishing the likelihood of a coup, Saddam knew the recent history of Iraq, and so augmented both the Popular Army and the elite Republican Guard. The latter had become the exclusive turf of the al-Bu Nasir, dedicated to protecting Saddam Hussein. To offset the increased size of the army, Saddam doubled the ranks of the Republican Guard from one to two brigades, and added a special forces battalion as well. The new recruits for these units were drawn exclusively from the Tikrit area.

But as the regular army grew, it acquired a sense of prestige that Saddam found threatening. Beginning in 1977, he began purging members of the Iraqi high command on an annual basis, replacing them with his own supporters. By the time he took over the presidency in 1979, he and his men *were* the high command, running the armed forces despite their total lack of military experience. But this meant nothing to Saddam. What was important was that the politically emasculated army no longer represented a threat to his presidency. The appointment of Adnan Khayr Allah, Saddam's cousin and best friend, as defense minister, capped this achievement.

At the same time Saddam was taming the army, he turned his attention to the powerful Amn al-Amm, the Directorate for General Security. In 1973 the DGS had attempted to mount a coup against Saddam and President al-Bakr. Intelligence provided by the Public Relations Bureau allowed Saddam to thwart the move by employing Republican Guard units. He then transferred the DGS's intelligence and security functions to the Public Relations Bureau, renaming it the Directorate of General Intelligence, or Mukhabarat.

Saddam's moves to defang the army and the DGS, along with his purge of the old-time Ba'ath party leadership, made him responsible only to his own al-Bu Nasir tribe. It was to the al-Bu Nasir that Saddam looked for support of his presidency, and in turn the al-Bu Nasir looked to Saddam for power and prestige. The rise of Saddam Hussein was a triumph of tribal politics unseen since the ascension of the house of Saud in Arabia.

•

Saddam's Iraq of 1979, however, remained full of complexities, domestic and international. Aside from his consolidation of power through repression of the Ba'ath party, reorganization of Iraqi secu-rity services, and appeasement of the armed forces, two other major threats were looming on the domestic front: Kurdish separatists in the north and Shi'a fundamentalists in the south.

A key international issue was directly linked to these internal ethnic rivalries. Prior to World War I, Ottoman Turkey ruled what is now modern-day Iraq. The Ottomans never formally demarcated the border with Iran, and with the discovery of oil in Iran in 1908, this took on strategic significance. Great Britain and Russia intervened and negotiated the Constantinople Protocol of 1913, which gave Iran navigation rights on the Shatt al-Arab waterway—a vital ship-ping route for inland oil-producing areas to the Persian Gulf. The end of World War I and dissolution of the Ottoman empire saw the creation of modern Iraq in 1920 and the coming to power in Iran of Riza Shah in 1923. Neither of the two new governments had signed the Constantinople Protocol, and the contentious matter was re-ferred to the newly formed League of Nations. A settlement treaty, signed in 1937, remained in force until 1969, when the Ba'ath gov-ernment renewed its claims to the Shatt al-Arab waterway, leading Iran to denounce the treaty. The resulting tensions engendered acts of mutual subversion in support of various coup and assassination at-tempts and other destabilization efforts.

Both Iran and Iraq had sizable Kurdish minorities that aspired for either increased autonomy or independence. Iran began to sup-port a Kurdish nationalist movement in northern Iraq, and by 1974 the Iraqi Kurds had grown from a nuisance into a viable threat to Ba'athist rule in Baghdad.

The Iran-Iraq situation was serious enough to have attracted the attention of the OPEC countries, which believed a general war be-tween Iran and Iraq would be disastrous. The shah took advantage of Iran's superior military position to pressure Iraq to accept a mediated settlement, which was signed by the shah and Saddam Hussein at the conclusion of an OPEC meeting in Algiers on March 6, 1975.

Two elements of the Algiers accord were not as obvious as the territorial issues but in many ways more important. On one hand, the shah agreed to stop financing and supplying the Iraqi Kurdish groups, and on the other, Iraq agreed to curtail the efforts of the Ayatollah Khomeini, an influential Iranian Shi'a cleric expelled by the shah in 1965 for preaching against his rule. Khomeini had taken refuge in Iraq, at Najaf, the site of an important Shi'a shrine. Iraq had funded the ayatollah, allowing him to use Najaf as a base from which to destabilize the shah's regime. However, after the Algiers accord, Iraq placed Khomeini under house arrest and expelled him in 1978. The scheme backfired with the sudden downfall of the shah and Khomeini's return from exile in early 1979 to take power. The ayatollah not only intended to bring Islamic revolution to Iran, but also wanted to export it to Iraq and elsewhere. He immediately contacted influential Iraqi Shi'a clergy in an effort to mobilize against Iraq.

Khomeini proved to be as opposed to Kurdish separatism as the shah. Taking advantage of the ongoing factionalism among the Kurds, he formed an alliance with the Iraqi Kurdish Democratic Party (KDP), providing money and weapons for its war against Baghdad in exchange for assistance in fighting the Kurdish Democratic Party of Iran (KDPI) and Patriotic Union of Kurdistan (PUK). By June 1979 the covert war being waged between Khomeini's Iran and Saddam's Iraq reached overt proportions. Iraqi aircraft began flying combat missions against KDP positions in Iran, while Khomeini urged Shi'a activists in Karbala and Najaf to riot. This prompted a massive crackdown on Iraq's Shi'a population by Saddam Hussein, leading to the arrests of thousands and scores of executions.*

Fear of Shi'a unrest was exploited by Saddam to justify his 1979

---

* Saddam was well-versed in the reality of Iraq's demographics. Sunni Arabs, such as the al-Bu Nasir, account for less than 20 percent of Iraq's population. Kurds make up around 20 percent. Small minority elements, such as Christians, account for only 2 percent of Iraq's population. The remaining 60 percent are Shi'a. The split between the Sunni and the Shi'a goes back to the seventh century and is rooted primarily in the question of succession of leadership in the Islamic world. While 90 percent of the Shi'a are concentrated in the southern provinces of Iraq, internal migration since the discovery of oil early in the twentieth century has changed Baghdad itself from a Sunni stronghold to a predominantly Shi'a city.

purge of internal opposition, but the threat was to some extent real. Khomeini not only dispatched agents into Iraq to foment Islamic revolution, he sponsored organizations such as the Islamic Call, or the Da'awa party, a highly disciplined Shi'a cadre that proved itself capable of carrying out impressive attacks, including the attempted assassination of Tariq Aziz, even then an influential member of Saddam's inner circle.

In December 1979 Saddam declared the Algiers accord null and void. He began actively supporting Iranian opposition forces, prompting Khomeini to redouble his efforts among Iraq's Kurdish and Shi'a populations to oust his nemesis in Iraq. Saddam responded by increasing suppression of the Kurds and Shi'a, but he also set about coopting them by providing job opportunities in the government in Baghdad.

In the midst of all this strife, Saddam held the first general elections for the Iraqi National Assembly since the coup of 1958. Not surprisingly, he was given a sweeping endorsement of his presidency, and some 250 handpicked supporters took their place as the representative members of the Iraqi people, including large numbers of Shi'a. Seeking to pacify Kurdish separatists, Saddam then authorized elections for a fifty-member Kurdish Legislative Council. Powerless and indebted to Saddam for their continued survival, the existence of these elected officials created the illusion of a democratic process, which had been absent in Iraq for two decades. They also served to divide the Shi'a and Kurdish communities into two camps, one that sought to advance its cause by removing Saddam Hussein, and the other that saw autonomy better served by a beneficial relationship with the president.

Having initiated measures to shore up his authority with the domestic Kurdish and Shi'a populations, Saddam again turned his attention to the military. The Iraqi army was a conscript force, representative of the country's ethnic diversity. Dissent expressed in the civilian population was therefore likely to be reflected by the army. Saddam was in the process of purging and redefining the Ba'ath party to better prop up the rule of the al-Bu Nasir tribe, and the army was in a state of flux. It is at this point that the strange duality of Saddam Hussein's personality first emerges: Saddam the godfather from Auja, carefully playing one side off against the other to keep the center of power squarely on himself, and Saddam the man of destiny ever ready to compare himself to the great figures of the past.

Because Saddam had put so much power in the hands of the al-Bu Nasir, he had to be careful. Given the multitribal makeup of the armed forces, and the deep underlying tribal character of Iraq, no officer or group of officers outside the al-Bu Nasir tribe would easily accept usurpation by a single tribal entity. Saddam needed a grand unifying cause and, in the tradition of his Mesopotamian and Arab forebears, looked east to the mountains of Persia. He needed to metamorphose into Sa'd bin Abi Waqqass, the conqueror of Persia in the battle of al-Qadissiyah in 633. Thus the eight-year nightmare that was the Iran-Iraq War, the "Qadassiyaht Saddam," began.

# 4

# School for Weapons of Mass Destruction

IN 1980 I WAS A PRIVATE in the army. Like most Americans, I viewed Iran as the domain of the wild-eyed ayatollahs who had stormed our embassy in Teheran, taken scores of our citizens hostage, and had rendered us confused and powerless. I was shattered on the morning of April 24 to awaken to the news that eight Americans had gone down in an Iranian wasteland, attempting to rescue those hostages. The television images sent back of mullahs poking knives into the charred remains of our servicemen made my blood boil. To my mind the mullahs and their ilk were evil personified, and when Iraq invaded Iran in September, I silently cheered on the Iraqis, hoping that somehow the tanks of Baghdad could strike the blows that my nation seemed impotent to deliver.

There was little to cheer, however. A simple border conflict would escalate into a war that threatened the world's supply of oil. Less recognized, then and even now, was what the Iran-Iraq War would mean in the development of Iraq's weapons of mass destruction. It would contain the seed of the Iraqi problem as it faces us today: a launchable chemical, biological, and, potentially, nuclear warfare threat in the hands of a terrorist state.

It was Saddam's desire to better or at least match the time frame of the stunning 1967 Israeli-Arab Six Day War. The Iraqi army sent in four divisions along a 700-kilometer front opposite Khuzistan, overrunning some forty-five kilometers in three days. Three more divisions struck along the central front. The fall of Khuzistan seemed at hand, but after five days of unopposed advance, the Iraqi army was stopped dead in its tracks by its own doing—having exhausted its own ability to wage war.

Command and control had collapsed; movements of units, supply, and logistics crumbled. More than anything else, this failure pointed to the foolhardiness of the commander-in-chief, Saddam Hussein, having ordered an attack while woefully lacking in preparation. After six days, Saddam had not achieved victory; instead, he was caught fast in a quagmire.

On the other hand, the relatively easy going until the logistical breakdown may have prompted Saddam to feel he had achieved his conquest. Hoping to snatch victory from the jaws of self-defeat, he welcomed the intervention of the United Nations on September 28, and accepted the provisions of the Security Council resolution calling for a cease-fire. It soon became apparent, however, how badly Iraq had miscalculated. Iran's ruler, Ayatollah Khomeini, rejecting the cease-fire offer, made it clear that Iran was girding for a battle whose objective was nothing less than the total defeat of Iraq.

Saddam had clearly bitten off more than he had intended. At the time of the invasion, Iraq had huge cash reserves. Saddam was busy investing the nation's oil wealth not only in the military, but also in a remarkable civilian development plan in an attempt to improve Iraqi living standards. But by the end of September Iranian military action had totally disrupted Iraq's oil export infrastructure in the south. An Iranian blockade of the Persian Gulf made securing access to the Gulf a strategic requirement. The loss of the Gulf oil terminals created a major economic crisis for Saddam. The need to stabilize the situation in Iraq was almost immediately recognized by Saudi Arabia and Kuwait, which agreed to increase their own oil output and market the sales on behalf of Iraq. Iraq was obligated to repay this debt once the war ended, with the result that eight years later Iraq would be saddled with a crippling economic burden. The oil war also caught the attention of the United States, which initiated a military buildup in the Gulf that would be maintained until today. The pieces were being assembled for the puzzle that is still vexing U.S. policymakers.

In 1982, an Iranian offensive battered Iraqi forces all along the front, creating a sense of fury in Saddam Hussein. Saddam had taken over direct command of the fighting. He ordered a series of massive counterattacks that repeatedly faltered in the face of the Iranian defenses. Whatever his frustrations then, they paled when a new onslaught of Iranian offensives in the spring of 1982 totally routed the Iraqi army in Khuzistan. In the eighteen months that had passed since Iraq invaded Iran, Saddam Hussein had done little to increase the capabilities of his army and less to win their loyalty.

Instead he turned to expanding the counterforce to the regular army, the Ba'athist paramilitary Popular Army. Introducing a paramilitary force to the realities of modern war produced a predictable result: slaughter. By the end of May, Iraq's battle casualties reached intolerable proportions—30,000 dead and wounded, 20,000 prisoners taken in a two-month period. Saddam was in a quandary—and Iran knew it. Khomeini played his trump card—a diplomatic offensive that succeeded in inducing Syria to close down and seize all Iraqi oil in its pipeline and reservoirs located in Syria.

Suddenly, the entire future of Iraq rested on one pipeline, the Turkish, which ran through a region that was as unstable as any in Iraq—Kurdistan. Worse, the massive drop in oil-derived income brought the Iraqi economy to a screeching halt. Iraq could no longer pay for the war, let alone finance its domestic economy. Saddam was now in the fight of his life.

The front began to collapse. Iranian human-wave assaults, which threw masses of children against Iraqi defenses, overwhelming them at unimaginable cost, demoralized the Iraqi army. Saddam tried in vain to stabilize the situation, and in early June announced a unilateral cease-fire, but Khomeini ignored it. Peace could only be had, the Iranian leader made it clear, through the removal of Saddam Hussein.

Saddam had never appeared more vulnerable than now, his army wrecked, blood drenching the deserts of Khuzistan, his generals bitter and angry. The Ba'ath party, too, was in disarray, with so many of its members either dead or captured as a result of the disastrous use of the political Popular Army at the front. The economy was in ruins, dependent solely on the benevolence of the weaker

Gulf Arab states that Saddam Hussein had dreamed of dominating one day. In his darkest moment, the street-fighter in Saddam took over, and he reacted as he always had—ordering the purge of all dissent, real or perceived.

In June, he dismissed the seventeen-member Revolutionary Command Council, replacing it with a smaller group to his liking. He dismissed almost half the membership of the Ba'ath party. He revamped his cabinet. He executed one minister for suggesting that he step down, and in a display designed to further cow the army, he executed a dozen generals for poor battlefield performance. But the deep-seated paranoia remained irrepressible, and he continued looking for new ways to crush his enemies.

The Syrian shutdown of the pipeline forced Iraq to reexamine its options. First priority went to securing and expanding the Turkish pipeline. Iraq also began discussions with Saudi Arabia to hook up with Saudi pipelines running to the Red Sea. But these were long-term projects, designed to offset the loss of the Gulf oil-loading capacity. The need to rebuild the Iraqi army was paramount, and Saddam spent Iraq's entire cash reserve of $36 billion to do this. Much of the matériel came from Egypt, which sold $4 billion of its aging Soviet equipment to Iraq to replace its battlefield losses. But Saddam wanted new and better weapons, and for these he had to go to the West.

France was a major beneficiary of this shopping spree, as was the Soviet Union. The Iraqi army was rebuilt, bankrupting the nation. Prior to the Iran-Iraq War, average per capita income in Iraq was around $3,000, significantly less than that of the Gulf Arab states, but a big advance from earlier years. Saddam desperately sought to maintain this level, but he had to borrow heavily to do so.

Swallowing his pride, Saddam sent his intermediaries hat in hand around the Gulf begging for money. This was a major loss of face to the man who dreamed of being the leader of the Arab world. But Saddam had to endure the humiliation if he was to survive.

When I first started inspecting units belonging to the Special Republican Guard, I noticed a board hanging just inside the main entrance to the barracks citing the combat record of that particular unit. I was surprised to find that these units had been involved in more than presidential security. The 4th Battalion, for example, proudly lists its first combat experience as "The Battle for Kurdistan, 1983." The 2nd and the 5th records "Panjwin, 1983" as their baptism by fire. The fact that the situation on the Panjwin battlefront warranted the emergency commitment of Saddam's personal protection force highlights the urgency of the situation that faced Iraq in the fall of 1983. The battle of Panjwin, high in the mountainous terrain of northeastern Iraq, witnessed two key events that deeply influenced Saddam Hussein, shaping the Iraqi crisis of the 1990s.

Months earlier, Iraq had employed chemical agents for the first time in an effort to stem the Iranian advance, although with little luck. The use of chemical weapons was proof that the Iraqis were in a desperate search for anything that could help offset the Iranian human-wave attacks that were so demoralizing and costly to defeat.

Allied with anti-Iraqi Kurdish forces, the Iranians threatened Panjwin. If they were to take Panjwin the Iranians would be in a position to threaten the oil fields of Kirkuk, the vital Iraqi-Turkish oil pipeline, and important population centers as well. The psychological value of such a victory might have been enough to promote massive unrest in Kurdistan at a time when Saddam Hussein could ill afford to dispatch troops to counter it.

Thus, in the first half of October, Iraqi army helicopters, together with air force ground-attack fighters, dropped bombs filled with mustard agent on Iranian troop positions. Killing and wounding thousands, the chemical weapons succeeded in turning the tide on the battlefield at a time when further Iraqi combat casualties were becoming untenable for the regime in Baghdad. And yet these weapons only stalled the Iranian attack. By November 4 the Iranians were back on the offensive, driving toward Panjwin. The Iraqi 1st Corps was still regrouping from its earlier defeat, and the situation again seemed dire.

Then Saddam's personal shock troops, the newly formed Special Republican Guard, arrived. Founded a few months earlier, ostensibly a birthday gift from a grateful Iraqi people, the SRG was recruited almost exclusively from the ranks of young men from the tribal areas loyal to Saddam. Transported by helicopter from Baghdad, the guard changed the course of that fight, and its success insured its position as Saddam Hussein's personal intervention force.

But the guard's deployment also highlighted the distress facing Iraq in terms of manpower. Something had to be done to relieve the pressure on the army. Saddam, together with the Defense Minister Adnan Khayr Allah (son of Saddam's favorite uncle), decided to augment the Republican Guard from two brigades to ten in order to exhaust the attacking Iranian forces through attrition, and then repel them with sharp counterattacks delivered by the Republican Guard brigades.

Expanding the Republican Guard so dramatically posed a problem for the Iraqi leadership. The al-Bu Nasir was incapable of providing that much manpower, even if one took into account the non–al-Bu Nasir tribes that were directly allied with Saddam, such as the Khazraj and Harb. The Republican Guard in its new mode was going to be a combat unit, and would be expected to sustain significant casualties. If the pain of war were to hit too close to home, Saddam could not expect to remain in power very long.

A new coalition was required, and Saddam again demonstrated his deft touch in selecting an effective mix, turning to three prominent Sunni tribes, the Jibbur, the Dulaym, and the 'Ubeidi. All three tribes were fiercely proud people, and to be selected by the leader of Iraq to defend the country was an honor that made them willing to send their sons into battle against the national enemy. For Saddam, the choice took in geographic considerations as well. The Jibbur occupied territory in the vicinity of Tikrit and Mosul, Saddam's two most strategic areas. The large and powerful Dulaym tribal federation is located in western Iraq, between Anbar and Ramadi. And the 'Ubeidi are concentrated to the north of Baghdad, neighbors of the Harb tribe. In coopting these tribes, Saddam could keep war's hardships out of Baghdad and secure his flanks.

While Saddam began rebuilding his Republican Guard, the army focused on improving its defensive posture. Iraq had slowly adapted to the Iranian human-wave assaults by learning to concentrate firepower into a massive killing field. New tactics were also employed, such as rapid counterattacks with armor, as well as the widespread use of electrified water barriers to slow and channelize the Iranian attacks. The result was that by March 1985, Iran had bled itself dry.

Iraq also began to make effective use of its chemical weapons, employing a mustard agent against Iranian troop concentrations, breaking up many attacks before they got started. In the end, however, heavy fighting gained little more than thousands of new casualties on both sides.

Escalating the fighting, Iraq and Iran struck deep into one another's territory, with Iraq launching hundreds of air raids against Iranian cities, including Teheran. Iran responded by raining Scud surface-to-surface missiles on Baghdad, killing hundreds. But this set in motion a project that would become a symbol of Iraqi military and industrial capability: the Al-Hussein missile.

I had been commissioned as an intelligence officer in the United States Marine Corps in May 1984, and after completing my basic officer's course at Quantico, Virginia, in May 1985, I was sent to Twenty-nine Palms, California. This was the home of the Marine Corps Air Ground Combat Center and the 7th Marine Amphibious Brigade — the Marine Corps ground combat element of the rapid reaction force. I quickly became involved in the updating of intelligence contingency plans for operations in the Persian Gulf, and the ongoing war between Iran and Iraq provided plenty of data to be collected and analyzed.

At the beginning of 1986, I was in Little Creek, Virginia, undergoing my formal intelligence officer's training. The Iran-Iraq War was a major focus (as was the war in Afghanistan between the Soviet Army and the mujahadeen). On January 6, early in the course, we started receiving intelligence reports about an Iraqi offensive aimed at liberating some strategic islands in the marshlands of the Shatt al-Arab. Begun on Iraqi Army Day, the three-day offensive was the most impressive piece of Iraqi offensive combat witnessed up to that time, involving a multibrigade attack that overwhelmed the Iranian defenders and drove them off the island. The student body at the intelligence school was about evenly split on the significance of this action, with some believing it signaled a turn in the war in favor of

Iraq, and others, including myself, arguing that Iran wasn't finished yet. Within a month Iran made its case—initiating broad attacks that staggered Saddam and his generals. Nevertheless, the turn in this remote and seemingly perpetual war was about to occur and no amount of intelligence could tell us, nor for that matter anyone else, how its ripple effect would one day reach our own shores and circle the entire globe.

The Iranian Scud attacks on Baghdad prompted Iraqi authorities to seek a means of retaliation in kind against Teheran. Initial efforts centered on aircraft, but the Iranians had increased their surface-to-air missile defenses around their capital, making this tactic impractical. The next option was to strike Teheran with surface-to-surface missiles. Having no weapon in its arsenal capable of the required 600–650-kilometer range, Iraq attempted to procure intermediate-range missiles from the Soviet Union, as well as to acquire Soviet technical assistance in increasing the range of Iraq's existing arsenal of Scud missiles. The Soviet Union turned down the Iraqi government on both requests. In the face of these rejections, Iraq sought to acquire an indigenous capability for extending the range of the Scud missile.

The Al-Hussein missile program provides an ideal case study of the complicated interplay of personalities and organizations that ran Iraq's military-industrial complex.

As the war broadened in scope and intensity, the Iraqi army by the end of 1986 had grown to nearly 800,000 men serving in the regular army with another 650,000 organized reserves in the Popular Army. Iraq had doubled its tank force to over 4,000, and because of the need to improve its defensive capabilities had invested heavily in artillery of all types. But there was an Achilles' heel. Iraq was totally dependent on other countries for weapons and ammunition.

Iraq had already begun upgrading its domestic arms industry, building huge explosives plants south of Baghdad. Heavy industrial capabilities were expanded at the Nasr State Establishment, near Taji, north of the capital, and a huge industrial complex was built in Amariyah, due west. Iraqi chemical weapons production facilities were expanded greatly, with the Muthanna State Establishment, west of Sammara, expanding both its research and development capabilities as well as its manufacturing plant.

Saddam and the Iraqi leadership had been profoundly shaken when in June 1981 Israeli fighter-bombers launched a devastating attack on the Iraqi nuclear research facility at Tuwaitha, destroying a reactor the Israelis believed to be involved in covert nuclear weaponization efforts. The Israeli attack, and the continued threat of Iranian air strikes against Iraqi strategic targets, prompted Iraqi officials to seek a system of countermeasures.

The Iran-Iraq War led to the increased influence of the Iraqi military intelligence, or Istachbarat, which was given the task of safeguarding Iraq's nascent military-industrial infrastructure from Israel-like attacks. The Istachbarat, in turn, sought assistance from its Soviet counterpart organization, the KGB.

The KGB's contribution would be long-lasting. From 1982 through 1985 it provided the Istachbarat and its civilian sister service, the Mukhabarat, detailed instruction on strategic camouflage, concealment, and deception operations that were designed to safeguard Iraq's military programs and operations, as well as its strategic industrial programs. The KGB brought with it a wealth of information about the strategic reconnaissance capabilities of the Western world, especially those of the United States. The Iraqis were schooled in how to situate industrial sites to minimize their vulnerability to air attack, and how to reduce identifiable features (from the air) of each facility through deception and practical measures such as shielding heat sources.

More important, the Iraqis were taught the value of early warning and rapid evacuation of a site subject to attack. In addition, new Iraqi facilities were designed to absorb the destructive power of a bomb, making extensive use of "blow-away" walls that left the frame of the structure relatively intact, allowing for speedy reconstruction.

What could not be reconstructed was the critical equipment and the personnel working in the facility. Iraq integrated into all of its military-industrial plants a plan for rapid evacuation, even if the facility had already been bombed. The KGB taught that conventional air attacks did not normally achieve the desired results on the first strike, and that the process of battle damage assessment by the enemy provided a window of opportunity for the facility managers to remove undamaged equipment before a second strike. Later, precision-guided munitions would render these tactics obsolete, but not the preparedness training.

In 1985 the Iraqis curtailed military cooperation with the Russians, in protest over the failure of the Soviets to deliver munitions and weapons in the quantities requested. However, the joint Istachbarat and Mukhabarat committee continued to meet to discuss and coordinate strategic concealment and deception efforts.

Against this background, the one man in the right place at the right time was Saddam's son-in-law, the future calamitous defector Hussein Kamal.

A member of the al-Majid clan of the al-Bu Nasir, Hussein Kamal had been a former police sergeant recruited into the palace security apparatus, becoming personal chauffeur to President al-Bakr and, more important, Saddam's informant on al-Bakr's comings and goings. After Saddam disposed of al-Bakr, Hussein Kamal's loyalty—which may even have extended to a role in al-Bakr's sudden death by poison—was rewarded with assignment to Sajida's protection detail. As bodyguard to Saddam's wife, Hussein Kamal appears to have brought romance into the life of Saddam's daughter Raghab, and in what would be one of the most fateful moves of his presidency, Saddam in 1983 gave his consent to their marriage, further unifying the al-Majid clan. This union, however, caused a deep rift in the al-Bu Nasir tribal family because another suitor from another clan, the nephew of Saddam's half-brother Barzan, had been jilted. But Saddam appears to have been seeking a return to tribal roots in a tradition called the *khams*, or five-generation family unit. The concept of the *khams*, which continues today to influence Saddam's decisions, resembles a blood oath in which every male member of the circle of relatives encompassing five generations around the person at the center is responsible for avenging the life and honor of that person, and vice versa. Raghab's marriage to Hussein Kamal brought the *khams* even closer together. He was a member of Saddam's *khams*, while Barzan's nephew was not.

The marriage in fact catapulted Hussein Kamal to the rank of lieutenant colonel, in spite of a total lack of military training, and the chief of the Himayet al-Rais, the precursor of the Special Repub-

lican Guard. His rapid rise notwithstanding, Hussein Kamal was an
~~~~~~~ ~~~~~~~ character and so was soon champing at the bit

l security, he proposed
with expanded duties,
Saddam, it would man-
and the Special Repub-
curity and intelligence
hus arose the SSO, or
s), with Hussein Kamal
Mukhabarat and Istach-
ntelligence and security
ervice. Only six months
SSO scored its first vic-
officers dissatisfied with
in the arrest and execu-
Hussein Kamal's relation-

Hussein missile program
when the SSO, in its watchdog role, beg   sitting in on the camouflage, concealment, and deception coordination meetings between
the KGB and the Istachbarat and the Mukhabarat. After the 1985
disengagement with the Soviet Union, Hussein Kamal and the SSO
stepped in to take the lead in concealing Iraq's indigenous military
industry.

To enable the SSO to manage this new concealment and deception responsibility—and continue to build his empire—Hussein
Kamal created yet another entity, the Special Office for Technical
Industry, or SOTI. This was headed by a highly capable and charismatic engineer, Lieutenant General Amer al-Sa'adi. A handsome
man, educated in England and Germany, Amer al-Sa'adi, who
spoke English without a trace of accent, had a gift for logical analysis
as well as unquestionable loyalty to the regime. Also a man of ambition, Sa'adi developed a good working relationship with Hussein
Kamal, serving as his deputy in the SSO.

As of 1985, Iraq possessed little in the way of a ballistic missile
research and development capability. Most of its experience lay in

battlefield artillery rockets. It had expended massive quantities of these rockets during the early period of the Iran-Iraq War, quickly depleting its stocks. Between 1984 and 1987, approximately 100 Iraqi engineers received training in ballistic engineering concepts in Brazil, and Amer al-Sa'adi turned to them when he made his first large-scale move in the military industrial field. They formed the Research and Development Group (RDG) of SOTI to initiate the program for the development of missile technology and weapons systems.

Following the Iranian Scud attacks on Baghdad, Sa'adi pooled his RDG with personnel from the Ministry of Defense's Scientific Research and Technical Development Organization (SRTDO). The Defense Ministry was, of course, the domain of Saddam's cousin and boyhood friend Adnan Khayr Allah, Hussein Kamal's archrival. But the missile program forced them together. Along with others, their units formed an ad hoc group responsible for the development of a surface-to-surface missile that was to be derived from the Scud-B and be capable of achieving ranges of approximating 600 kilometers. The range required to strike Teheran was 580 kilometers.

Based on analysis of the Scud-B training missile and technical literature surveys (with its emphasis on the World War II German V-2 missile program data), the ad hoc group opted for an incremental approach to development of the extended-range missile. Within a couple of months, trial-and-error failures gave way to a successful test launch in April 1987 that extended the Scud's range to 450 kilometers. In August, a further modified, elongated version flew 650 kilometers, enough to reach Teheran.

Although this prototype showed signs of breaking up in flight, the basic design was judged to have been validated. General Amer al-Sa'adi immediately communicated the good news to Saddam Hussein. Saddam would dub it the Al-Hussein, in honor of Imam Hussein, a Shi'a martyr.

The successful test of the one-of-a-kind Al-Hussein was a far cry from developing a reliable home-grown production capability. The responsible organizations were restructured, with Hussein Kamal taking on ministerial rank to head the newly created Ministry of Industry and Military Industrialization (MIMI), a tension-heightening shuffle that meant all the credit would redound to him and his deputy, Amer al-Sa'adi, at the expense of Defense Minister Adnan Khayr Allah.

A new endeavor—known as Project 144—was created in September 1987 to oversee the development of the Al-Hussein. Seven more prototype missiles were constructed; three were set aside to verify the results of the August test and all three were successfully launched in September. After a series of further testing, in which it was discovered how to correct the angle of attack, and improve the speed and accuracy of the earlier prototypes, a test firing in December revealed that the problems had been solved.

Initially, Project 144 was able to produce a single Al-Hussein by cannibalizing Scud-B missiles at a ratio of 3:2, that is, three Scuds were needed to manufacture two Al-Hussein missiles. By year's end, Project 144 was able to improve the modification ratio to 4:3, and by the spring of 1988, production had risen from one missile every three days to three missiles a day.

The pressures to produce and use the missiles in combat against Iran had grown enormously. The people of Iraq, since learning of the success of the Al-Hussein back in August, had seen no evidence of this miracle weapon, but were very much aware of the continual Iranian missile attacks on Baghdad. Project 144 was being badgered by Saddam Hussein and Hussein Kamal to provide enough missiles for a sustained campaign against Teheran. At the start of September 1987, Iraq had only 360 Scud-B missiles in its inventory. Repeated visits to Moscow by Tariq Aziz and Adnan Khayr Allah persuaded the Soviet Union in 1987 to resume the delivery of weapons to Iraq. The Soviets promised 118 additional Scud-Bs, which were finally delivered in January and February of 1988. This gave Iraq enough Scud-Bs to convert to more than 250 Al-Husseins. The Iraqi high command had determined that it required 110 operational Al-Husseins before it could begin the projected strikes against Iranian cities.

For two months the engineers and technicians of Project 144 worked day and night to modify missiles; in the later stages of this effort, missiles were being delivered to the army unpainted, but that did nothing to reduce Saddam Hussein's newfound capability to strike deep into the heart of Iran—courtesy of son-in-law Hussein Kamal and his new super-ministry, MIMI.

On February 29, 1988, Iraq fired nine Al-Hussein missiles against Teheran. At last Saddam could issue the announcement he had been longing to make since the first successful test back in August 1987:

> Oh, Heroic Iraqis! Iraqi missiles pounded Teheran, capital of the imposters, the oppressors, and the aggressors, three times today. Your missiles have reached their targets, over the heads of the Khomeinists and into their capital with the required precision to rend apart the body of depravity, destroy the dens of the Satans, and avenge our innocent martyrs. We announce publicly that our missiles will continue throughout the night to bombard Teheran until it is demolished. . . . The Iraqi missiles . . . embody the success of our country in the field of advanced military manufacturing, as in other fields, by grace of God, under the guidance of the directives of our Leader, the beloved Saddam Hussein, and owing to the dedication of the men of the military industries.

Thus was the War of the Cities resumed. It was to be an affair that became increasingly one-sided. Between February 29 and the end of April 1988, Iraq fired 189 Al-Hussein missiles against Teheran and five other Iranian cities.

At first Iran and the world were completely perplexed. The warheads carried by the Al-Hussein did not pack much of a destructive wallop, but they had an eerie howl as they passed overhead, then exploded very loudly. This caused panic in the streets of Teheran. Civilians, accustomed to the sirens that signaled the approach of the Iraqi air force in conventional bombings, had no advance warning to take shelter and brace themselves for the explosions. Speculation arose that the Soviets had sold Iraq SS-12 intermediate range ballistic missiles, or some advanced model of the Scud. The Soviets vehemently denied this.

Oddly, I was in a position at that time to vouch for the Russians—though of course no one asked me. I had just been assigned to the On-Site Inspection Agency, a U.S. Department of Defense organization formed to oversee implementation of the Intermediate Nuclear Forces (INF) treaty, which had been signed by Presidents Reagan and Gorbachev in December 1987. The SS-12 was an accountable item under the INF treaty, and the reports coming out of Teheran raised some eyebrows. The question was brought up at a special intelligence briefing concerning Soviet production of missiles affected by the treaty, including the SS-12. I was preparing to go to the Soviet Union as part of an inspection group with the task of monitoring missile production at the Votkinsk Machine Building Plant, a large enterprise in the city of Votkinsk, about 700 miles east of Moscow. The SS-12 was one of the missiles produced there.

The Iraqis kept the siege going. By March 10, they had launched forty-eight Al-Husseins at Iran, forty-five of them on Teheran, and on the 11th they unleashed a salvo designed to send a clear signal to Khomeini and the Iranian government that the only way to stop the missile strikes was to accept a United Nations cease-fire.

The devastating impact on the citizens of Teheran played a major role in ending the war. Although these were conventional missile attacks, the terror of chemical warheads reigned from the outset. The Iraqi air force had actually killed more people and destroyed more property than the Al-Hussein attacks, but the psychological effect on a population exhausted by nearly eight years of revolution, war, and economic turmoil was immense. By April 1988 Iran was a beaten nation.

On the other side of the border, the Al-Hussein missile attacks had a remarkably uplifting effect on the Iraqi population. The Project 144 leadership and the engineers were regarded as national heroes. This adulation heavily influenced postwar ballistic missile development.

Saddam had created a new legend in which he had grown larger than life. After years of misadventure at the front, he was now exalted as the great warrior and wise leader.

The story of the Al-Hussein missile reflected the struggle between Hussein Kamal and Adnan Khayr Allah, and in the end showed how the tribal and familial quest for power shaped politics in Iraq.

# 5

# "Dr. Germ" and "The Chemist"— A Family Business

MAY 1996.     It was cool and drizzly outside the Marriott Hotel lobby in Amman, Jordan. I was in Jordan together with Charles Duelfer, UNSCOM's deputy executive chairman, and Nikita Smidovich, deputy director for operations. We had traveled to this corner of the Arab world for the opportunity to peer into the inner workings of Saddam's Iraq. We were to debrief several high-level defectors from Baghdad. The three of us had spent the better part of the morning waiting in vain for unreturned phone calls or some signal of any kind from the Jordanian authorities that the meeting was on. Suddenly two black Mercedes sedans pulled up outside. They were carrying men dressed in the open-collared white shirts and black leather jackets that mark the intelligence and security services of many Arab countries, so we had an answer of sorts.

We were taken to the large granite and limestone headquarters of the General Intelligence Directorate, where we met the chain-smoking head of Jordanian foreign intelligence. He coaxed us through a long explanation of our mission before finally ushering us to two separate defectors, one from the Special Republican Guard and the other a former senior official in Iraqi military intelligence.

Three hours later, after hearing them out, we were driven through an elegant residential neighborhood in downtown Amman. The drivers carried out some rudimentary maneuvers to check whether we were being followed. The reason for all the cloak-and-dagger stuff became apparent when we circled one particular villa before parking down a back street about 200 yards away. The leather-jacketed men signaled one another, and we quickly made our way through the gates of the villa.

We soon found ourselves in a large living room furnished quite lavishly. We sat down and waited, but no more than a minute later we were joined by a middle-aged, stocky man sporting the standard mustache of an Iraqi official. His expensive-looking business suit, though it fit well, was obviously worn with unease, probably because he was a man more at home in the green fatigues of the Iraqi army, most recently in the uniform of the chief of staff of the Iraqi Ministry of Defense. Offering a gracious smile and the direct gaze of a senior officer used to being in command, Lieutenant General Nizar 'Abd al-Karim al-Khazraji took a seat on a sofa opposite ours.

We questioned General Khazraji for several hours, breaking now and then for tea and cookies. Although we covered several matters, the one that I, in particular, bore down on was that of the relationship between Saddam, the Iraqi army, and weapons of mass destruction. On this topic General Khazraji was most enlightening.

According to Khazraji, the Iraqi military had a long history of involvement in chemical weaponry, dating back to the mid-1970s. Iraqi chemical warfare doctrine was largely drawn from that of the former Soviet Union. It was based on the concept of chemical weapons employed by artillery and aircraft on the battlefield.

The Iraqi army, the general said, had been trained since the 1960s to operate in a chemical warfare environment. The Iraqi Chemical Corps was organized along the lines of its Soviet counterpart, and indeed many of its personnel received their training in the Soviet Union. In 1975 the Chemical Corps was heavily involved in the formation of the Al Hazen Ibn al-Haytham Institute, the predecessor of the offensive biological and chemical weapons programs of the 1980s. The Al Hazen Institute was closed in 1978, and the chemical weapons development programs transferred to new projects at Al Rashad and a new site in the desert west of Sammara, the Muthanna State Establishment. From 1978 until 1986, the Iraqi Chemical Corps ran the Muthanna State Establishment, a huge chemical agent manufacturing concern. The chemical weapons program was run by a Defense Ministry commission composed of the Chemical Corps, the Muthanna State Establishment, and military intelligence.

The Al Rashad and Muthanna produced significant amounts of mustard agent, and operated a research and development location for developing more advanced nerve agents, such as tabun and sarin.

These weapons were available in limited amounts when war broke out with Iran in 1980, but do not appear to have been used meaningfully until 1983. By 1986, however, the poor experience of the Iraqis in the battlefield employment of chemical weapons had soured many in the military on their use, notably Defense Minister Adnan Khayr Allah.

Despite effective use by the Iraqis in Panjwin, chemical weapons by the end of 1986 had produced only a relatively small number of casualties. Most battles were fought on wet or mountainous terrain, which severely degraded the mustard agents used by Iraq. The Chemical Corps had not perfected the employment of these weapons, and sometimes fired them when wind conditions pushed the gas back on Iraqi troops, or fired them into mountain slopes so that the agent flowed into the path of onrushing Iraqi soldiers.

Adnan and the Iraqi officers knew that they were killing far more Iranians using conventional weapons, and acted accordingly. In 1983 Adnan Khayr Allah formed a research facility, the SRDTO, under his ministry. Air force Lieutenant General Amer Rashid was appointed director, and he brought in Amer al-Sa'adi as his deputy as well as an entire team of highly capable scientists and engineers. The goal of the SRDTO was to develop Iraq's domestic manufacture of conventional weaponry as well as give Iraq independence from its foreign suppliers, who since the start of the war with Iran had grown increasingly fickle.

There was another angle: as minister of defense, Adnan had made a fortune in kickbacks from the multibillion dollar weapons procurement program from these same foreigners. With the cutback in foreign purchases, he needed a new source of revenue, and control of Iraq's military industry would provide just that.

What he could not foresee, however, was that Hussein Kamal had set his sights on his turf. Both men were near the pinnacle of power, Saddam's son-in-law versus Saddam's closest cousin and childhood chum. As an intimate of Saddam, Hussein Kamal was well aware of his father-in-law's infidelities. One such dalliance was his affair with Samira al-Shahbander, the wife of a financial adviser to Uday, Saddam's elder son. Rewarding Saddam's love, Samira divorced her husband and married him as his second wife, second to Sajida. In 1985, Samira gave birth to their son, 'Ali, and she and the infant were moved into a separate villa of the presidential palace. This caused a huge scandal within the Saddam family. Sajida's father, Khayr Allah, instructed his daughter to leave Saddam, and she moved out of the palace into a complex of villas occupied by her daughters.

The Samira scandal created a schism in the clans. On one side stood Saddam, supported by the powerful al-Majid clan. On the other was Sajida, supported by her son Uday, and the influential al-Tilfah clan, including Khayr Allah and his son Adnan. The estranged al-Muhammad clan—Saddam's half-brothers, Barzan, Sabawi, and Watban—were somewhere in the shadows, undoubtedly ready to move, and into these shifting sands stepped surefooted Hussein Kamal.

An early clash between the two rivals emerged over the chemical weapons issue. The research and development department of the Muthanna State Establishment was campaigning for advances in chemical weapons technology, including branching out into biological weapons research. Adnan opposed this on the grounds that such weapons were meaningless on the Iranian front and would never be used against Israel because such an action would be suicidal. He was also convinced that if Iraq were to possess large-scale chemical and biological warfare capabilities, it would be challenged by the Western nations, particularly the United States, which challenge it could not win.

Informed of Adnan's opposition, Hussein Kamal went directly to Saddam and convinced him of the need to possess a vigorous chemical warfare capability. If Adnan was not willing to underwrite such a project, he said, then the responsibility should be given to the Special Security Organization, SSO, and its technical arm, Special Office for Technical Industry, SOTI, both of which reported to Hussein Kamal. Saddam concurred, and in 1986 administration of the Muthanna State Establishment was transferred from Adnan's Chemical Corps to Hussein Kamal's SOTI.

No sooner had he moved in on the chemical and biological weapons programs than Hussein Kamal eyed the embryonic Iraqi ballistic missile program. Again according to my debriefing of General Khazraji, Hussein Kamal approached Saddam Hussein with a grandiose plan. Emphasizing the difficulties Iraq was facing in producing much needed war matériel, Hussein Kamal proposed that if Iraqi scientists and engineers were liberated from the constraints of existing bureaucracies, then they could compete with the rest of the world. Such were the origins of the unification of military and civilian industry under a single organization. When this plan was adopted in the August 1987 Law of Military Industrialization, Hussein Kamal had completed his coup, trumping Adnan Khayr Allah, and opening a wound that would never heal.

Despite Adnan's reservations about the use of chemical weapons, he worked closely with Hussein Kamal. The Chemical Corps played a key role at Muthanna, providing most of the manpower. Muthanna began experimentation on the production of VX nerve agent, by far the most lethal such chemical. The Chemical Corps pressed for the production of sarin and tabun. As short-lived agents, they could be employed in relative proximity to Iraqi troops, enabling the assault formations to exploit the panic and casualties resulting from a gas attack.

Work continued on biological agent development as well. In 1983 an Iraqi biologist, Abdul Nassir al-Hindawi, had written a classified study on the potential applications of biological agents in battle. This paper had been criticized by the Ministry of Defense, but revived by Hussein Kamal to pressure Adnan to accept a SOTI team of biologists headed by the notorious Rihab Taha, the woman who would become known in the Western media as "Dr. Germ." Taha set out to explore biological warfare options. Within a year, she and her fellow scientists were experimenting with a wide range of biological agents, including pathogenic bacteria (anthrax, plague, and *Clostridium perfringens*, which causes gaseous gangrene) and toxins (botulinum, aflatoxin, ricin, and mycotoxins).

However, in March 1987, when Saddam ordered the increase in chemical agent research and production, Adnan drew the line on biological agents. He had strong views concerning the wisdom of embarking on such a path, and refused to allow this work to take place at Muthanna. Hussein Kamal fought Adnan on this issue and lost. As a result, Taha and her team joined a special unit run by the SSO called the Technical Research Center, or TRC. The TRC was involved in a wide number of intelligence support activities, including the use of biological agents in covert operations. Hussein Kamal now had control of Iraq's biological weapons program, and began large-scale construction to build new research facilities to the likings of Rihab Taha.

The Al-Hussein blitz of Teheran had broken Iran's spirit but had not yet ended the war. By 1987 Saddam had added his advanced chemical weapons arsenal to the equation and he was determined to end the hostilities once and for all.

He understood that to win you did not necessarily have to kill your opponent; in fact, the death of an enemy would often be used to rally support for the cause of the vanquished. While he would never balk at killing, he was a master at terror, and prefered brutal intimidation over death. A thoroughly broken foe was putty in his hands.

He had acquired these skills as the Ba'ath party's chief enforcer, learning to break a man's (and woman's) spirit in the torture chambers of the Qasr al-Nihayyat, the Palace of the End. One of the features of this particular prison was its red rooms. Every thing in a red room would be just that, red: the walls, the furniture, the light bulbs. This was done to disorient the prisoner and when he or she was brought into the sunlight, the results were invariably crushing.

I had heard about this prison, both in written accounts from former Iraqi officials who had been incarcerated there as well as in my debriefings of Iraqi defectors. In April 1998, during the inspections of the Republican Palace, our inspectors finally got to see that this was not just a place of fantasy, but a horrible reality. As the inspectors walked through the empty building and the red cells (everything considered sensitive had been evacuated by the Iraqi government prior to the inspection), they saw graffiti on the walls, either scratched in with a stick, or painted in blood.

"To my wife and children: Tomorrow I die. I will miss you."

"To whoever reads this and lives, please tell my mother that I have perished and not to worry, for I am with God."

Many of the prisoners had signed their names, and most of them were from Tikrit. Later, Saddam constructed a larger prison in Radwaniyah, adjacent to his presidential complex. This prison was particularly horrific. Those sent there very rarely emerged. Through his control of the security system, Saddam also ran the large DGS prison at Abu Ghraib, as well as the Al Rasafah prison of the Mukhabarat in downtown Baghdad. Whether Saddam was going to kill you or not, you had first to be stripped of your humanity. This often meant arresting and torturing the prisoner's family. Wives and daughters would be gang-raped by guards, often while the husband or father was forced to watch. Children would be cruelly tortured in front of their parents. The ways of inflicting pain were many. Saddam would then kill the prisoner, or let him go, depending on the effect desired. The message to his people was that to challenge him meant swift and inescapable retribution.

This was the brand of terror Saddam brought to solving the Iranian problem. Saddam needed to break his enemy's will to fight. He turned to chemical weapons.

Coordinated by Adnan and Hussein Kamal, special tactical units were developed to use these weapons. Saddam began his experiment with innovative chemical weapons tactics when he vested the commander of the 3rd Corps, Lieutenant General Maher 'Abd Rashid, with the authority to release chemical weapons without first going to the general command for approval. As with the Al-Hussein missile offensive, where Saddam delegated the conduct of the day-to-day battle, chemical weapons were authorized to be used in massive quantities at the discretion of the field commander.

Saddam and his lieutenants began by turning their attention to Iraqi Kurdistan. Saddam sent his cousin 'Ali Hassan al-Majid, who was serving as the minister of interior, to Kurdistan to oversee this operation.

Two Kurdish villages were selected, Dojaila and Hallabja. On

March 24, 1988, as Iraqi troops pulled out, bombers appeared over-head and dropped a number of cannisters containing a mix of mus-tard and nerve agents. In Hallabja over 5,000 civilians perished, about a sixth of the population. The atrocious images of dead Kurd-ish mothers and babies grew sadly familiar around the world. In Dojaila, with a population of some 20,000, the casualties were fewer but no less ghastly. 'Ali Hassan al-Majid would earn the title "The Chemist," an appellation he would welcome with perverse pride. Saddam had made his point.

As this fighting unfolded, Adnan and his generals prepared their own major attack. The April 17 offensive against Iran named "Blessed Ramadan" (it was the first day of the Muslim holy month) unleashed both mustard and nerve agents along with the largest ar-tillery barrage since World War II. Retreating, the Iranians ran right into the mustard agent while the Iraqis came barreling in, slaughter-ing the exposed Iranian troops. Within thirty-five hours, the Iranians were defeated. Saddam had reclaimed his southern border.

On July 20, the Ayatollah Khomeini accepted the latest United Nations cease-fire resolution, announcing over the radio, "taking this decision was more deadly than taking poison." On August 8, the documents were signed. The sweet-tasting brew of victory belonged to Saddam, praised widely as a great leader. The streets of Baghdad were filled with celebration. Saddam's portrait hung at every street corner. They hang there still in Baghdad today, a beaming Saddam Hussein, in full military dress, leading the forces of Iraq to victory over the bearded fanatics of the ayatollah.

But victory over Iran did little for the breach wrought by Saddam's having taken Samira as a second wife. Saddam's troubles with the al-Tilfah clan of Khayr Allah and Adnan were mounting. Adnan was a national hero, with the support of the generals. Saddam had alienated the generals. During the war, Saddam had sought to win them over, as well as expand his coalition inside the al-Bu Nasir, by marrying his younger son, Qusay, to Zainab 'Abd Rashid, the daughter of Lieutenant General Maher 'Abd Rashid. Rashid was a member of the al-Bu Nasir and a war hero, and immensely popular. The marriage of Qusay to Zainab was Saddam's insurance policy against a military coup, and also had the added benefit of linking Saddam to the popular general. However, when Rashid and Adnan challenged Saddam over choices he had made in awarding medals for the decisive victories over the Iranians, Saddam was incensed. He had Rashid placed under house arrest in Mosul, and ordered Qusay to divorce Zainab. Saddam moved quickly to purge hundreds of officers loyal to Rashid.

Qusay was becoming increasingly important to his father. After graduating from university in 1988, he was appointed deputy director of the SSO, keeping presidential security within the family. On the other hand, Saddam's elder son, Uday, was growing increasingly difficult. In October 1988, Uday killed a close friend and associate of his father at a party in downtown Baghdad. The particularly brutal murder of Kamel Hana Jojo occurred in front of a number of witnesses, including the wife of President Hosni Mubarak of Egypt. Uday had apparently been enraged by the role of Kamel Hana in the seduction of Samira by Saddam, and was strongly influenced by his mother, Sajida, who had let it be known that she wanted Kamel Hana punished. Uday also had concerns of his own. Now that Saddam had a second wife and a son by that marriage, there was a real risk that Saddam would repudiate his marriage with Sajida, and thus Uday would lose his position as heir apparent.

Uday's actions pushed the family squabble into an open fight. Adnan made a public show of meeting with Sajida to side with her over Samira, as did Khayr Allah. Uday's murder of Kamel Hana made no secret of where he stood. The marital strife between Saddam and Sajida had spread to the entire clan, with Saddam and Qusay on one side, Sajida and Uday on the other.

With the marriage of daughter Raghab to Hussein Kamal and daughter Rina to Sadam Kamal, Saddam had secured the loyalty of the al-Majid. Sajida had the al-Tilfah clan on her side. Saddam had to act quickly to redress the balance of power, and he did so through the rehabilitation of the al-Muhammad clan. Sa'bawi Ibrahim, who had been dismissed from the DGS, or political police, was reinstated in early 1989 and immediately assigned by Saddam to take action against the al-Tilfah, which he did.

Meanwhile the parvenu chauffeur-bodyguard son-in-law Hussein Kamal, climbed higher. Hussein Kamal and the scientists of MIMI had been paraded before the Iraqi public as heroes equal to their combat-hardened brethren in the army and air force. It had been Hussein Kamal's MIMI organization that built the Al-Hussein missiles and produced the poison gas as well as the conventional weapons that had won the war.

On the other hand, Hussein Kamal had spent billions of dollars on Iraq's military industrial infrastructure, continuing to spend billions more in a massive reconstruction to repair the ravages of war. At war's end, Iraq was deeply in debt, to the tune of about $70 billion, including oil debts to Saudi Arabia and Kuwait. And yet there was no effort to rein in spending. Indeed, it was dramatically increased. In 1988, for example, Hussein Kamal and MIMI signed close to $830 million in high technology contracts with German companies, including deals involving ballistic missile, chemical, and biotechnology related equipment. In 1989, such contracts grew to over $1 billion. Italy had agreements worth hundreds of millions of dollars; France, Russia, the U.K., and the U.S. all boasted deals worth billions.

In early 1988 Hussein Kamal's MIMI was renamed the Military Industrial Commission (MIC), and took over all major industrial enterprises in Iraq. But with postwar Iraq on the verge of bankruptcy, Adnan argued for cutbacks, particularly a demobilization program. Iraq had, by this time, almost 1.2 million men in uniform. Thus the two rivals found themselves again at loggerheads.

Hussein Kamal now regarded Iraq's next number-one enemy as Israel (the "Zionist entity"). He argued that Israel possessed weapons of mass destruction and the means of delivering them to Iraq, and that if Iraq did not develop its own capability, it would never be the regional leader among Arab nations that it aspired to be. Adnan, consenting to a major buildup of strategic capabilities, ordered the expansion of Iraq's chemical and biological weapons capabilities, but remained opposed to Hussein Kamal's strategy.

Adnan expressed his doubts to Saddam. He was convinced that should Iraq try to match Israel weapon for weapon, then Iraq would lose. Hussein Kamal argued the opposite: such a buildup was the only way to keep Israel at bay. The two adversaries argued their respective positions, Adnan urging a low military profile and Hussein Kamal a vigorous weapons of mass destruction program. Saddam decided to develop a strategic deterrent.

A letter went out from the presidential council, the text of which is published here for the first time:

Presidential Council letter No. A/4/99/32573,
17 *September* 1988

The principle of deterrence is the best means for defense against the Zionist entity and we suggest in this respect the following: to continue to develop the chemical weapons with an attempt to acquire more lethal types of munitions in large quantities;

1.  to develop the means to carry chemical warheads on long-range missiles for the purposes of confronting any threat;

2.  to prepare special storage areas for chemical weapons in the western region, provided that these areas are within the impact range of the missiles available at present, as well as other means of delivery to the active Zionist targets in order to secure our ability to launch surprise attacks and to respond quickly to deter the enemy.

This letter was signed by Hussein Kamal, in both his role as director of the SSO and the supervisor of the MIC.

Thus Iraq embarked on the path of developing advanced chemical and biological weapons.

According to my 1996 debriefing of Lieutenant General Khazraji, Adnan thought this to be folly. Hussein Kamal was an expert in the politics of palace intrigue, and was soon able to convince Saddam that Adnan was behaving in a manner that violated Iraq's interests. Adnan was in favor of a smaller, more professional military. As Hussein Kamal saw it, this meant developing a strong base of support that could then be used to threaten the presidency. Adnan was very popular; a smaller military where he was able to select the key officers would pose a serious threat. Hussein Kamal could see no useful purpose for such a small military other than strengthening Adnan's internal posture.

Hussein Kamal argued in favor of weapons of mass destruction as a deterrent to Iran and Israel. Adnan's opposition to these programs meant that they must remain secret, under the protection of the SSO. These were the president's programs, the guarantors of Saddam's greatness, power, and prestige. And he, Hussein Kamal, was the man the president could trust with these programs. Saddam agreed.

When Adnan heard rumors of a nuclear weapons program, he confronted Hussein Kamal and then Saddam himself, but was told nothing. Adnan became more and more isolated, both because of the dispute over weapons of mass destruction as well as the ongoing family crisis.

On May 5, 1989, Adnan was killed. He had been piloting a helicopter that allegedly crashed in a sandstorm in the northern city of Mosul. Opposition sources stated that Adnan was murdered by Saddam himself in the midst of an argument at a presidential retreat north of Mosul. Others point to Hussein Kamal as the culprit, following orders from Saddam. At Adnan's funeral, his father, Khayr Allah, shouted that Saddam had murdered his son and dishonored his daugher, Sajida. He claimed that he had information that a bomb had been placed aboard Adnan's helicopter by Hussein Kamal's henchmen. No autopsy was performed; the body was returned to the al-Tilfah in a sealed coffin. Adnan was buried with state honors in Baghdad and his villa in the Republican Palace remains unoccupied as a memorial. However he died, by the spring of 1989 the sphere of influence of the al-Tilfah had been considerably reduced, and the star of Hussein Kamal had risen higher.

Unrivaled now, Hussein Kamal continued to build his empire.

# 6

# The Two-Day War

IN THE AFTERMATH of Saddam's victory over Iran the Iraqi economy was in terrible shape. Everywhere he turned to purchase weapons and technology, Saddam was confronted with a stark reality: Iraq had no credit. The oil wealth that Saddam was sitting on was heavily mortgaged, not the least of which was the oil debt to Kuwait of $14 billion. One of Iraq's goals was to become a net exporter of military equipment but Saddam first had to build up his military-industrial base, and this required substantial infrastructure-related expenditures. Saddam held grand military fairs in Baghdad, and the world flocked to the displays of Iraqi military hardware. The now famous Al-Hussein was being marketed as a complete missile system, including the Al-Walid mobile launcher, Iraqi fuel, and oxidizer trucks. There were few buyers however; businessmen came trying to sell and intelligence personnel came for a firsthand look at the Iraqi military machine.

The situation only worsened when the major Western suppliers of military weapons and technology to Iraq—Britain, France, Germany, and Italy—agreed to sell to Baghdad, but that only put Iraq deeper in debt. Something had to give.

Having won the war with Iran, Iraqis expected a return to normal, the good life of the late 1970s, when the oil boom improved living standards. Saddam began feeling the pressure, and in typical fashion started looking around for a new enemy against whom he could mobilize support for keeping Iraq on a war footing. He found it in Israel.

Saddam Hussein and Hussein Kamal dreamed of becoming the regional superpower, the one Arab nation above all others that could stand up to and confront successfully the state of Israel. Saddam's pride still stung from the humiliation of having to beg for assistance from nations he viewed as beneath him. Now that he had emerged a victor, he believed his time had come.

In February 1989 he invited Egyptian President Hosni Mubarak, King Hussein of Jordan, and President Ali 'Abd Allah Saleh of Yemen to Baghdad, where they formed an ambitious economic alliance known as the Arab Cooperation Council (ACC). This grouping was meant to counter the GCC (the Gulf Cooperation Council)—the Gulf states council formed in the 1980s in response to the threats posed by the Iran-Iraq War. Unlike that organization, however, the ACC had no real economic power; indeed, with the exception of Yemen, the ACC countries were all beneficiaries of GCC wealth in the form of loans and grants, and were regarded coolly by them.

The ACC was a deft political maneuver that boosted Saddam's stature in the Arab world. A general Arab nationalist mobilization against Israel, keeping Iraq on a war footing, would divert attention from his troubles at home. But his long-range strategy, the one that would yield the most in terms of economic recovery, was to build a strong Arab alliance to support Iraq against the ultimate target of his military ambition: Kuwait.

Historically, the territory that encompasses modern-day Kuwait had been a part of the Ottoman province of Basra, one of three provinces (the other two being Mosul and Baghdad) that formed Iraq. Kuwait became an important British port in 1889, and after World War I gained its independence. Baghdad refused to accept the separation of Kuwait, and Iraqi attempts to seize it in 1958 and 1961 were thwarted by international intervention. Although Iraq treated Kuwait as an independent nation after its admission to the U.N. in 1963, it never formally recognized the Kuwait-Iraq border. This border in part stood astride the Rumaila oil fields, one of the richest in Iraq. Because of the dispute, Iraq and Kuwait agreed that an ill-defined strip of territory separating the two countries would be considered the border. During the Iran-Iraq War, Kuwait began to expand its oil production in the Rumaila oil fields, moving drilling equipment into the no-man's-territory of the strip. (Iraq later accused Kuwait of stealing over $2.4 billion in oil from the Rumaila fields, including oil taken from Iraqi fields through the practice of slant drilling.) Iraq remained quiet about this intrusion because of the support Kuwait was providing during the Iran-Iraq War. When Saddam was faced with the crushing postwar economic burdens, however, the Kuwait issue took on new importance.

Kuwait, seeing an opportunity to solve the matter with Baghdad in dire straits, followed U.S. advice and proposed writing off Iraq's war debt of $14 billion in exchange for recognition of the border as it stood. Iraq countered with a demand for an additional $10 billion loan—a $24 billion package—and there the negotiation froze.

Inside Iraq, Saddam's family split continued to worsen. Saddam by this time had become more and more dependent on Hussein Kamal as both adviser and friend. His alliance with the al-Majid was stronger than ever, but that was hardly the case elsewhere. Despite the significant economic hardships experienced by the rest of Iraq, the *Issaba* remained as wealthy as ever. An indication of the immense wealth generated by the graft and corruption managed by the family is the fact that at the time of his death in 1989 Adnan had a personal fortune estimated at $3 billion.

But now, as 1990 arrived the economy was grinding to a halt. Hussein Kamal's expensive weapons programs and the costs of keeping an army of 1.2 million men in the field was ruining Iraq regardless of Saddam's ambitions. The economic hardship was especially unwelcome to a population weary of years of struggle.

The first signs of unrest came from a most unlikely source—the Jibbur, a tribe allied to Saddam's al-Bu Nasir that had provided so many of its sons for conscription when Saddam was in need. Many of them had risen to positions of authority in the Republican Guard and other security services, and were getting an insider's look at Saddam's government, not liking what they saw. Among their grievances was a program Saddam had initiated to expropriate tribal lands, The Jibbur had been targeted. A group of tribesmen, headed by a Republican Guard officer named Sattam Ghanim al-Jibburi, planned to take matters into its own hands, hatching a scheme to assassinate Saddam Hussein in January 1990 at Army Day celebrations in Baghdad. Hussein Kamal's SSO exposed the plot, and hundreds were rounded up for interrogation. Twenty-six Jibbur were executed. The Jibbur had not acted alone. Members of by the 'Ubeidi tribe who served in Saddam's security forces and the Republican Guard were arrested, too.

The attempted coup forced postponement of the Army Day celebrations for the first time since the 1968 Ba'ath revolution, and sent shock waves throughout the Iraqi leadership. Saddam began to see plots everywhere, at home and abroad. He began portraying himself and Iraq as victims of a vast conspiracy being perpetrated by Israel and the United States.

Repercussions of his 1988 repression of the Kurds plagued him, too. The massive use of chemical weapons against the village of Hallabja had become an international cause célèbre, but the slaughter had not ended with the war. Saddam had given his interior minister, 'Ali Hassan al-Majid (The Chemist), carte blanche to subdue the Kurds. Making extensive use of special-purpose chemical battalions, 'Ali Hassan al-Majid poured 60,000 Iraqi troops into Kurdistan and, supported by helicopter gunships and chemical agent, depopulated huge swaths of Kurdish territory to subdue the Kurds once and for all. Tens of thousands of Kurdish civilians were forcibly evacuated from their villages, which were then razed, and tens of thousands more were forced to flee for their lives into Turkey and Iran. Thousands of Kurds were tortured and executed by the Iraqis. Any members or sympathizers of the KDP and PUK unfortunate enough to be captured were summarily put to death.

Saddam may have succeeded in pacifying the KDP and PUK, but the extreme measures, especially the use of chemical agent against civilians, caught the attention of the United States Senate. Pressure was brought to bear on the Bush administration to sanction Iraq. The move was resisted by State Department officials, who thought a policy of constructive engagement could work with Saddam's Iraq. By early 1990, it was clear that such a policy was futile, and the U.S. reduced its level of cooperation with Iraq. The Voice of America denounced Iraq's human rights record in its Arab-language broadcasts, signaling a new direction in U.S.-Iraqi relations, which did not escape Baghdad's notice.

In February, Israel sounded an alarm over the deployment of the "All Arab Squadron," a joint Jordanian-Iraqi air force unit based in Jordan. French-made Mirage F-1 fighters with sophisticated photoreconnaissance pods enabled the Iraqis to take high-resolution photographs deep inside Israel as the aircraft flew along the Jordan-Israel border. The Israelis were concerned that the Iraqis were using these photographs to develop targets for their air force and missile forces. The purpose of this joint unit became clearer a few days later during the summit meeting of the ACC in Amman. Saddam condemned the world's disregard of the plight of the Palestinians and called for the creation of "one Palestine, from the river to the sea."

Such harsh rhetoric had to be taken seriously by all who were listening, Palestinian and Israeli alike. Saddam also lashed out against the United States and the Arab countries that were on friendly terms with America. In early March, the U.S. detected the installation in western Iraq of missile launch sites oriented toward Israel. Suddenly the rhetoric was becoming very real.

Saddam's comments at the ACC summit sent a wave of concern through Israel, and caused the release of classified Israeli intelligence assessments about the existence of an Iraqi nuclear weapons project in an advanced stage of development. Israel would not stand idle while Iraqi built such a weapon, it said. If Iraq were to launch a nuclear weapon, there was little Israel could do to stop it once the attack had been initiated. Only a preemptive strike could neutralize such a threat, and Prime Minister Yitzhak Shamir made an announcement to that effect. On April 2 Saddam escalated the exchange of threats, warning of a chemical weapons attack. Then on April 18, Saddam told Israel that an attack on Iraq's missile arsenal would trigger a war that would not end until Israel was eliminated.

In March a British journalist, Farzad Bazoft, was hanged in Baghdad on charges of spying at a missile fuel facility, and a few days later, British officials announced the seizure of electronic switches, or krytons, that, according to London, were in transit to Iraq for use as triggers for an Iraqi nuclear weapon. Another interception of Iraq-bound advanced military hardware was made public shortly afterward, this time of high-grade steel tubes to build a "supergun" designed to lob 500-kilogram warheads to ranges of 1,000 kilometers. The entire world was suddenly buzzing over international support for Iraq's military programs, many of which had weapons of mass destruction associations.

The nuclear trigger incident fed Saddam's growing paranoia about tribal enemies. A highly placed member of the al-Bu Musa Faraj, a clan of the al-Bu Nasir, had fallen under suspicion of having spied for the British. As a member of the Mukhabarat, he had personally managed the covert operation in London to procure the krytons. He and his deputy were arrested on charges of plotting a coup. Both men were tortured, tried, and executed on orders of Saddam.

Crisis loomed. During the proceedings of the Arab League summit, held in Baghdad May 28–30, Saddam gave expression to his frustrations. He blasted those who were engaging in a systematic campaign of economic, psychological, and military isolation of Iraq, lashing out in particular at the U.S. and Kuwait, both of whom, according to Saddam, were engaged in economic warfare against his nation. In this atmosphere, Saddam again approached Kuwait concerning the $10 billion loan. Kuwait vacillated, then balked again.

Saddam had nowhere else to turn; he was weeks away from default on all of Iraq's loans, which would be the beginning of economic collapse. Worse, oil prices suddenly plunged, signaling absolute ruin for Iraq.

At an emergency meeting of OPEC on July 10, Saddam got nowhere seeking an increase in Iraq's output quota; instead, disarray among OPEC producers led to an even further dip in the price of oil, $14 to $11 per barrel—untenable for Saddam.

On July 17, the anniversary of the Ba'athist revolution, Saddam issued a fiery speech, in which he said that Iraq was losing $14 billion a year, something that was leading to its financial ruin. Saddam was vehement in his warning to Kuwait to halt overproduction (in fact, Kuwait was abiding by its OPEC limits).

On the 18th, Deputy Prime Minister Tariq Aziz, at a meeting of Arab League foreign ministers, laid out Iraq's case concerning a

Kuwaiti conspiracy. No one seemed to take notice, prompting Tariq Aziz to scold them: "I am talking to you about a state of war, and you are not moving."

On the 19th Saddam began moving his army toward the Kuwait border. Last-minute diplomatic activities by the United States and the Gulf Cooperation Council were to no avail.

Saddam Hussein invaded Kuwait on August 2.

The decision to invade Kuwait, like the decision to invade Iran, was taken quickly, immediately prior to the July 17 speech. Saddam consulted with only three advisers: Hussein Kamal, 'Ali Hassan al-Majid, and Lieutenant General Ayad Futayih al-Rawi, the commander of the Republican Guard. Hussein Kamal and 'Ali Hassan al-Majid were told to prepare for the occupation of Kuwait; Hussein Kamal was to organize the interim government, and 'Ali Hassan al-Majid was to take emergency measures in southern Iraq and Kuwait to forestall any possible civil unrest among the Shi'a populations of southern Iraq or Kuwait.

General al-Rawi was to move the entire Republican Guard, over 100,000 men, to Kuwait, to have his forces assembled on the border by July 31, and to carry out the total occupation of that country within a forty-eight-hour period, a two-day war. The Republican Guard by now was a huge organization, the best trained and best equipped of all the Iraqi armed forces. It was composed of two armored divisions, the Hammurabi and the Medinah; two mechanized divisions, the Nida and the Tawalkana; four infantry divisions, the Adnan, the Nebuchadnezzar, the Baghdadi, and the Al-Faw; and four special forces brigades. General al-Rawi would use the bulk of these forces in his attack.

At two A.M. August 2, the Tawalkana and Hammurabi divisions crossed the border and raced for Kuwait City nearly unopposed. Three special forces brigades launched heliborne assaults on Kuwait at first light, sealing off the avenues of retreat for the government of Kuwait, which Saddam hoped to capture intact. The Medinah division guarded the exposed western flank of this attack, in case of the unlikely intervention by GCC forces. The four Republican Guard infantry divisions followed on the heels of the armored thrust to occupy Kuwait. After consolidating Kuwait City, the three heavy divisions moved to the Saudi-Kuwait border, occupying the entire country. Saddam had his forty-eight-hour victory.

Saddam never intended to move his forces on into Saudi Arabia. His goal was the annexation of Kuwait so he could acquire that nation's great wealth as his own. He sincerely believed that the Arab world would understand his position, and that no concerted action would be taken to reverse his action. He, of course, seriously miscalculated.

The story of Iraq's barbarous occupation of Kuwait, the mobilization by the United States together with the Arab world of an international coalition to liberate Kuwait, and the brief but violent Gulf War has been told many times, and does not need repeating here. Saddam looted Kuwait of billions of dollars (over $45 billion, according to some estimates), much of it in goods brought into Baghdad and sold at reduced prices, a payoff of sorts for the Iraqi people. Even after the Gulf War, when UNSCOM inspectors entered Baghdad, the local souks were awash in new watches, cameras, and other expensive consumer goods, all of a 1990 vintage.

After Saddam looted Kuwait, he raped and brutalized it, under the expert supervision of 'Ali Hassan al-Majid. And, when it became clear that he was not going to be permitted to keep his prize, Saddam attempted to raze it, ordering the destruction of Kuwait's oil wells in one of the most flagrant acts of economic terror in the history of the modern world.

Saddam had alienated a large part of the Arab world by his invasion of a fellow Arab nation. Once Iraq's occupation was challenged so vociferously by the world community, especially the Arab community, then Saddam's hands were tied. He could not withdraw from Iraq without losing face, especially among the military, which he had just won over with his lightning invasion.

Prior to the invasion of Kuwait, there was a growing consensus among the military elite in Iraq that Saddam, regardless of his earlier mistakes, had matured into a military leader of strategic vision. This maturity rested on three foundations: the most powerful army in the Arab world, a powerful military industrial base, and a strategic deterrent to Israel's nuclear arsenal. Following his invasion of Kuwait,

Saddam's stock within the military was even higher. Gradually, as the U.S.-led coalition grew in size, Saddam sought more and more to link the issue of Kuwait with the issue of Palestine. It took its ultimate form on January 9, 1991, following a meeting between U.S. Secretary of State James Baker and Iraqi Foreign Minister Tariq Aziz in Geneva, Switzerland. The meeting had not gone well, and when queried by a reporter whether if war started, Iraq would attack Israel, Tariq Aziz responded without hesitation, "Yes, absolutely yes."

The key to any such attack was Iraq's surface-to-surface Al-Hussein missile force. Iraq had two delivery vehicles for attack: mobile launchers and fixed-arm launchers. In August Iraq deployed to western Iraq seven of its nine Soviet-made mobile launchers, called TELs. They were spread out in tree groves and other sites selected to conceal them from allied coalition or Israeli reconnaissance resources. Seven fully fueled missiles were also dispatched to western Iraq, complete with chemical warheads. These missiles were under the control of an SSO special weapons handling unit, and were kept separate from the launchers. They were made ready, if needed, as an emergency response to any preemptive nuclear attack by Israel.

Since a fueled missile has a shelf life of only sixty days, seven new missiles were prepared in November to replace the seven already deployed, which were then sent back to Taji for refurbishment by Project 144. This rotation was repeated in January 1991. These were not missiles in remote storage; these were ready-to-launch missiles, capable of striking heavily populated regions of Israel if the order to launch came down or, of even greater concern, if the missile force commander lost communications with the Iraqi high command. The presence in western Iraq of such hair-trigger missiles, so to speak, throughout the period of buildup and actual conflict demonstrates the significance of the Iraqi ballistic missile force. Derided by many as an obsolete capability having the military significance of a "mosquito," the critical role that the Iraqi Al-Hussein missile played in the psychology of Iraq and its neighbors during the Gulf War cannot be ignored. By the middle of January 1991, Iraq was ready to fight a missile war.

During this time Iraq was developing another payload for its ballistic missiles, the product of an extensive effort on the part of the

Iraqi government and the Iraqi Atomic Energy Commission to develop an atomic bomb. The actual weaponization program (known as PC-3), however, was directly related to its primary delivery system, the ballistic missile. The facility dedicated to the production of the Iraqi atomic weapon was located at Al Atheer, near the town of Musayyib. At this site PC-3, by this time under MIC, established Group 4 of Project 190, an elite group of scientists and technicians dedicated to the development and production of a nuclear weapon. Group 4's mission for the development of an atomic weapon was successful. By the end of 1989, the Al Atheer scientists submitted their Basic Design Report, proposing an atomic weapon based on an implosion mechanism using uranium as its fissile material and having an energy yield of twenty kilotons, about the size of the Hiroshima bomb. The Iraqis were working on a crash program to convert highly enriched uranium from the safeguarded fuel at Tuwaitha (because of the invasion of Kuwait, the IAEA was unable to continue its safeguarding inspections) into a fissile core for use on a nuclear device. Additionally, Group 4 asked for, and received, an empty Scud-B warhead, which was used to develop mounting concepts for fitting the nuclear device into the warhead. In the end, the Iraqis may have run out of time. They were unable to produce both the fissile core and the actual physical implosion device for the nuclear warhead prior to the Gulf War.

# 7

# Burying Treasure

To be sure, the Gulf War was a major disaster for Saddam Hussein and Iraq. At the end of the conflict, Saddam announced to the people of Iraq that they had emerged victorious and heroic from the 'umm al-Ma'arik, the Mother of All Battles. But that was a whistle in the dark. Saddam, according to eyewitness accounts, was left enfeebled, depressed, and forlorn. If Hussein Kamal is to be believed, Saddam turned to him on one of the dark days in March 1991 and muttered, "We are finished, sonny boy." He had taken on the look of a hunted man, and in the end trusted only his closest advisers.

The walls of his cities had tumbled. His army lay in tatters in the deserts of Kuwait and southern Iraq. In the south, the Shi'a had erupted in a general revolt against the regime. In the north, the Kurds had taken advantage of a weakened Iraqi military presence to reemerge and liberate much of Iraqi Kurdistan. In Baghdad and throughout central Iraq there was a sense of near-anarchy, with armed gangs roaming the streets.

On April 4, 1991, the Security Council adopted Resolution 687, requiring the certified destruction of Iraq's weapons of mass destruction as a condition for ending economic sanctions. Saddam was in no position to challenge the will of the United Nations, especially with the American-led coalition still overseeing southern Iraq. U.S. reconnaissance flights were overflying Baghdad several times a day, deliberately breaking the sound barrier so that the sonic boom might remind the citizens of the capital that their country had been whipped.

But psychological warfare was a game that Saddam could still play as well as anyone else; and when the fire and brimstone of Desert Storm subsided, he grew stronger as the coalition dissipated and he consolidated his domestic and international positions.

From the outset he decided to outwit the disarmament provisions of the Security Council resolution. Immediately after the adoption of 687, an emergency committee, chaired by Tariq Aziz and loosely based on the SSO-run Weapons Control and Maintenance Committee, met in Baghdad to craft Iraq's response. The model was at hand. For years, Iraq had carried out a clandestine nuclear weapons program—code-named PC-3—while the United Nations watchdog, the IAEA, remained none the wiser. The International Atomic Energy Agency inspectors had been easily hoodwinked, and Iraq's nuclear weapons PC-3 leadership, headed by Jafar Dhia Jafar, said it could deceive the United Nations Special Commission UNSCOM inspectors in the same way. The committee had clear instructions from Saddam Hussein: save as much of the Iraqi weapons of mass destruction capability as possible.

Broad guidelines were established from the start. Iraq would not declare any aspect of its nuclear weapons program, nor would it admit to any violation of the nonproliferation treaty. It would not declare any aspect of its biological weapons program. Dr. Germ notwithstanding, it would maintain that it had never had such a program. With regard to the Iraqi chemical weapons program, the well-known activities of the Muthanna State Establishment could not be concealed, but that facility had been reduced to rubble by Desert Storm. Stocks of chemical agent and weapons were to be declared to UNSCOM, but the extensive research and development activities as well as a residual supply of chemical munitions were to be retained. Iraq's most advanced chemical weapon, VX, was to be totally hidden from the inspection teams. The Al-Hussein missile manufacturing capabilities undertaken in the past would be declared, as well as a portion of the operational capabilities of the Al-Hussein force. Concealed, however, would be all prohibited domestic manufacturing, especially the ambitious missile programs. In short, Iraq would go through the motions of disarmament, but not disarm.

Tariq Aziz's committee issued instructions for what was in effect an emergency evacuation of all weapons-related materials not to be turned over to the United Nations. A plan was put in place to make an inventory of the relevant equipment of each project, listing the items that would and would not be declared to UNSCOM. Each project was to establish a system of evacuation and dispersal of the material to be retained. Plans for how to deal with inspections were also drawn. Responsibility for this activity was delegated to the various emergency committees of each project. The physical layout of facilities was altered to hide evidence of prohibited activity. Elaborate exercises were conducted complete with mock inspections. Special teams played the role of inspectors and the site personnel were coached on how to respond to a wide range of anticipated questioning. On April 18, 1991, Iraq submitted its declaration to the United Nations, initiating the process of sham and deception that would never cease.

For all its foresight and planning, the one thing that Iraq had not counted on was the professionalism and tenacity of the first executive chairman of UNSCOM, Sweden's Rolf Ekéus. The Tariq Aziz committee had been briefed on what to expect based on the experience of the Iraqi nuclear program with IAEA inspections. However, it soon became clear that there was, so to speak, a new sheriff in town, who would brook no violations of the law as set forth in Security Council resolutions. On April 30, Ekéus dispatched a letter to the Iraqi government in which he outlined significant shortfalls in the Iraqi declaration. This included Iraq's failure to declare much of the industrial infrastructure related to the research and development activities of the prohibited programs. Ekéus put Baghdad on notice that UNSCOM was conducting a comprehensive assessment of Iraq's weapons of mass destruction capabilities, and that on-site inspections would begin shortly, not only of facilities declared by Iraq, but also of undeclared locations.

This correspondence was received by Iraq with great concern. Saddam's presidential secretariat convened a coordinating body called the Joint Committee (or Joint Board) in early May and Tariq

Aziz reported on preparations undertaken for the inspections. The Presidential secretary determined that the preparations were insufficient, and advised Saddam that new, extraordinary measures would have to be implemented.

Saddam instructed that a new committee be formed—the Concealment Operations Committee—under the direction of his son, the director of the SSO, Qusay Saddam Hussein. This committee, he directed, would oversee the collection and safeguarding of information and material that was prohibited by Security Council resolutions.

Qusay's concealment committee met regularly in the Republican Palace. He and his senior lieutenants from the SSO and Special Republican Guard decided that the SRG and other agencies and organizations form task forces responsible for the material to be kept from UNSCOM and the IAEA. In coordination with the commander of the SRG, Staff Brigadier Kamal Mustafa, scores of SRG officers were chosen for these duties, primarily based on their tribal and familial relationship with Saddam. Operations began late in May of 1991. With the assistance of technical personnel from the Military Industrial Commission, and logistical support from the Republican Guard, regular army, and several ministries, the task forces began to assemble the material to be concealed and safeguarded. The initial phase, involving the actual receipt of the relevant material by the concealment forces from the responsible MIC organizations, was completed by June 20. All that remained was for the inspectors to enter Iraq, do their jobs, find nothing, submit their reports, and get out.

It had been the dream of Hussein Kamal to keep intact the weapons of mass destruction programs—the fruit of years of hard labor and billions of dollars of funding. Hussein Kamal knew that these programs were the key to his future; they represented the one lever with Saddam Hussein that no one else could pull but he. But when Qusay was handed the assignment to form the Concealment Operations Committee, Hussein Kamal was not invited to participate; he was brought in only to advise on logistical and technical matters. Nevertheless, Qusay's committee was concerned only about the actual hardware, and made no effort to take control of the massive quantities of documentation in the possession of the MIC and its security service, the Amn al-Tasnia. The SRG and SSO personnel had little inkling as to what they were receiving from the various production groups and the military. The MIC enterprises and projects simply turned over the boxes and crates of material to the Special Republican Guard soldiers who showed up to collect them. MIC technicians were appalled by the rough manner in which the SRG soldiers handled delicate equipment. I was told by one missile engineer that after watching the soldiers toss specially tooled instruments into the back of a truck, he knew that the material would be useless for any future work. According to the plan put forward by the concealment committee, the SRG task groups, after loading, would drive these vehicles to military camps and remote farms, hiding them until the inspectors had finished their work. No one expected the inspection process to take more than a few months at the most.

An aggressive IAEA chief inspector named David Kay was the first to demolish Iraqi expectations. In late June 1991 Kay's inspection team, surveying Iraqi declared nuclear facilities, visited a military camp west of Baghdad, Abu Ghraib. Unknown to the team at that time, the camp was actually the barracks facility of the 8th Battalion of the SRG. This unit had been tasked by the SRG Commander, Kamal Mustafa, to form a concealment cell and be prepared to receive for safekeeping material that would be delivered by Jafar Dhia Jafar, the father of the Iraqi nuclear program and the director of PC-3, the nuclear weapons project. Jafar had collected the material from the evacuation sites prepared by PC-3 in accordance with the emergency plan and delivered them to the Abu Ghraib barracks. Unfortunately for the Iraqis, among the material being transported were huge electromagnetic isotope separators known as Calutrons. These devices had to be transported on heavy tractor-trailers. They were easily identified by U.S. photographic interpreters who had been reviewing satellite imagery for clues such as this. The location of the vehicle convoy was passed on to UNSCOM and the IAEA. After four days of cat-and-mouse pursuit, Kay was able to run the vehicles to ground (but not until the Iraqis fired shots over the heads of the inspectors in a futile effort to intimidate them). The Iraqis drove the vehicles away in full view of the inspectors, who filmed the incident along with the unmistakable forms of the Calutrons. The Iraqis had been caught in the act, and now the Concealment Operations Committee was in a bind.

The fallout from the Abu Ghraib episode was severe. The Security Council condemned the Iraqi actions, and dispatched a senior delegation, including UNSCOM's chief and the director general of the IAEA, Hans Blix, to clarify the situation. The Concealment Operations Committee met in emergency session with the Joint Committee on June 29, two days before the scheduled arrival in Baghdad of the U.N. delegation. Until now, Iraq's weapons of mass destruction capability had been kept secret from everyone but a small group surrounding the president.

The Joint Committee decided that Iraq would have to reveal certain aspects of its nuclear program, specifically those involving the enrichment of uranium, but would continue to deny the existence of a nuclear weaponization effort. Moreover, it concluded that the concealment committee would no longer be able to continue hiding its operations; U.S. intelligence satellites would be scouring Iraq for evidence of such activity, and inspection teams would be dispatched, prompting a repeat of the Kay incident. It would only be a matter of time before the inspectors got lucky, and Iraq could ill-afford to be caught again in such a massive lie.

All concealment task forces were directed to initiate emergency procedures for the identification of critical components and material that would continue to be hidden by the Concealment Operations Committee. The unilateral destruction of the remaining material was also decided at this meeting.

When the U.N. delegation arrived, the Iraqis worked hard to explain away the problems, all the while waiting for news from the Concealment Operations Committee regarding progress on the next set of deceptions. In the aftermath of the Kay incident, the task force had repaired to a remote area near Lake Tharthar, where the critical components of the nuclear enrichment project were assembled. These included specialized laboratory equipment, samples of centrifuges, centrifuge components, and critical valves. This material was loaded into several trucks and dispatched to an emergency site north of Tikrit. That was where Colonel Muzzahim Suleiman al-Latif, of SRG operations, was receiving material for hiding at the numerous presidential farms and villas in the area. The nonessential material was either later turned over to the IAEA or destroyed at Tharthar.

Other task forces were doing the same throughout Iraq. The missile production group, a convoy of about a dozen vehicles loaded with engines, engine parts, and the production tools and molds, drove to a rendezvous at Al Alam. The Al-Hussein force turned over at least seven missiles and two mobile launchers to the Concealment Operations Committee. The Chemical Corps dispatched several truckloads of chemical artillery shells and aerial bombs filled with chemical and biological agent, along with over a dozen Al-Hussein warheads filled with anthrax and VX nerve agent. Drums of VX agent precursors were sent to Al Alam, as were tons of growth media used to cultivate biological agent. Several trucks containing mobile laboratories used to make biological agent were retained and sent to Al Alam, as were crates containing equipment intended to be installed at a pesticide plant that would be converted into a VX production facility.

In the first week of July about 100 trucks of all shapes and sizes arrived at Al Alam. Muzzahim al-Latif spent the next three days sorting and deciding which material would be retained and which destroyed. Number one priority was to get it stashed away, and by July 10 vehicles started rolling to their hide sites in and around Tikrit. The farms chosen belonged to senior SRG and SSO officials. Muzzahim also made use of presidential farms. By July 18 the last of the trucks, escorted by SRG guards, departed to their hideouts. Muzzahim, exhausted by his work, returned to Baghdad and reported to Qusay. All that Qusay could do now was wait until the storm passed over.

The Security Council received the report of the high-level delegation to Iraq with concern and alarm. It passed a new resolution, reiterating Iraq's obligation to disarm and submit new "full, final and complete" declarations, prohibiting concealment from the weapons inspectors. But even as the resolution was being voted on, Iraq was putting the finishing touches on its massive deception effort: the unilateral destruction effort to deceive the inspectors about the true scope and nature of the weapons programs, based on the premise that if UNSCOM and the IAEA did not suspect a program's existance, then they would not look for it. By the end of July the bulk of the unilateral destruction activity was finished. The blown-up material and equipment was either buried underground or carted away to smelters and melted into large indistinguishable ingots, which in turn were either buried or thrown into a river.

By September 1991, the Concealment Operations Committee was in a standby mode, its retained materials secreted away in remote hide sites. In the minds of the Iraqi leadership, the threat had passed; UNSCOM and the IAEA had been left to tilt at windmills. When they tired, they would go home. Thus Baghdad was taken by complete surprise in mid-September when it learned that the redoubtable David Kay had struck pay dirt again. Leading a joint team of UNSCOM and IAEA inspectors, he and his men had arrived at Iraqi nuclear headquarters in the early morning hours and, catching the personnel off guard, scaled the fences, burst into the building, and discovered millions of pages of documentation pertaining to Iraq's nuclear weapons programs, including evidence that proved that Iraq had a nuclear weapons design.

The Concealment Operations Committee was doubly surprised. It had been ordered to secure prohibited hardware, but no mention had been made of documentation. Until then, responsibility for the paperwork of the proscribed programs had been left to the organizations involved.

The original guidelines had called for the evacuation of documents and their placement under MIC security. However, there were no other provisions beyond disposing of loose papers scattered about at sites that had been struck during the war. Despite the Concealment Operations Committee's rapid-fire mobilization and containment of the Kay team inspectors (ending a four-day standoff in the parking lot of the facility with the Iraqi security services forcibly removing the documents from the hands of the inspectors), the damage had been done. Iraq knew that from now on every inspection team would be looking for similar document caches.

The concealment committee was given new orders to gather all remaining documentation of weapons of mass destruction, and re-move it to safe houses, where it would be evaluated. Certain docu-ments were culled and the rest microfilmed. The hard-copy originals were sorted by discipline for use by MIC scientists for their continuing work. This library was maintained by the SSO, which se-cured the microfilms as a strategic reserve. Although microfilming continued through 1992, the safeguard system was in place by the end of 1991. The library was moved to an inconspicuous location at the Ministry of Agriculture in downtown Baghdad, very near the site of the parking lot incident. Apparently the Iraqis believed that light-ning could not strike twice.

When it did, in the July 1992 standoff that I participated in, in which inspectors were attacked by civilians organized by the SSO, the archives were removed from the Agriculture Ministry by the SSO, most probably to a presidential area in or around Tikrit. The SSO has since moved the document library on a regular basis to pre-vent UNSCOM inspectors from gaining access to it. The bulk of this library were turned over to the Special Commission and the IAEA after the defection of Hussein Kamal in August 1995. How-ever, UNSCOM believes that portions of it remain under the con-trol of the SSO for ongoing use by the MIC.

# 8

# The Year of the Gun

ON THE NIGHT of August 3, 1995, a violent argument erupted between Saddam's son Uday and Saddam's half-brother Watban. Uday's bodyguards opened fire, killing a number of Watban's bodyguards and wounding Watban in the leg. After hearing of the shooting, Saddam in a rage set fire to a garage containing over a dozen of Uday's sports cars. Saddam was still in a rage when only hours later the earth-shaking news of his son-in-law Hussein Kamal's flight to Jordan arrived. Eventually, of course, Hussein Kamal convinced himself that his father-in-law would welcome his return, so he made his suicidal trip back to Iraq.

All had been forgiven, Saddam had assured him, but when Uday received the returning party at the border, instead of a fond embrace, he slapped Hussein Kamal across the face. He removed his sisters from their husbands' Mercedes. Raghab and Rina were driven to the Republican Palace, where they were reunited with their father. Hussein Kamal and his brother were taken to a family villa in the suburbs of Baghdad, where their father, Kamal, had been waiting for them. After talking the matter over with his daughters, Saddam sent word to the Kamal brothers that he wanted the marriages ended. Hussein Kamal refused. Saddam became very angry, and he summoned the clan to a meeting at the palace.

Saddam called upon his *khams* to authorize, and then implement, tribal authority to spill blood—the *hadr al-dam*. No one dissented, although an uncle who had met with Hussein Kamal in Amman is said to have questioned the proceedings because the head of the al-Majid family—Hussein Kamal's father—was not present for such important deliberations. But Saddam had had enough of the formalities, and the next morning the al-Majid villa was surrounded by forces of the Special Republican Guard, accompanied by at least sixteen members of the *khams*.

'Ali Hassan al-Majid (The Chemist) was in charge. He called on Hussein Kamal, his nephew, to come out. Kamal, the father of Hussein and 'Ali Hassan's brother, emerged instead. He wanted to discuss the presidential pardon that had lured his sons home. There was nothing to be discussed. Tribal justice had to be given its due. 'Ali Hassan al-Majid begged his brother not to go back into the villa. Kamal refused. The Special Republican Guard opened fire, entering the villa and killing everyone inside—Kamal, Saddam Kamal, Hussein Kamal, and several women and children. Some say that Hussein Kamal survived the hail of bullets but was shot dead in an escape, and spat on by 'Ali Hassan al-Majid—and Uday, who along with Qusay was observing the massacre.

Again, a schism arose in the family. Killing the Kamal brothers left Saddam alienated from all three of the major clans of the al-Bu Nasir—the al-Tilfah, the al-Muhammad, and now the al-Majid. Resentment grew among the *khams* for being used this way. A code had been broken by Saddam in meting out his punishment. Even under the harshest application of the *hadr al-dam*, it was understood that women and children would be spared. In the end, Saddam atoned. 'Ali Hassan al-Majid lobbied hard to have Hussein Kamal rehabilitated, and Saddam found the way, elevating all those whom he had ordered slain to the perverse distinction of "martyrs of tribal wrath." The al-Majid clan was showered with money to build elaborate dwellings in Tikrit, many located on the grounds of the presidential palace.

No sooner had Saddam quieted the Hussein Kamal affair when another tribal issue confronted him—dissatisfaction among the Dulaym tribe, one of the sources of manpower for the security services. With their bedouin heritage, the Dulaym, once they had joined with Saddam, had gravitated to warriorlike positions, swelling the ranks of the military, intelligence, and security services. They formed mutually beneficial relationships with the other major tribes. Sometime after the end of the Gulf War these alliances began to unravel, however.

Early in 1996 the leader of the al-Bu Nimr clan of the Dulaym, Air Force Major General Muhammad Mazlum al-Dulaymi, was arrested by Saddam's security forces on suspicion of plotting against the regime. He was tortured to death, his body dumped by Saddam's security service on the streets of Ramadi, and his family was forced to compensate the government for the cost of his execution. This proved too much for the al-Bu Nimr clan. On May 17, 1996, the streets of Ramadi erupted in violent demonstrations against the regime, and soon the entire region was in general revolt. It took three weeks for the Special Republican Guard and the Emergency Forces (Quwat al-Tawari) of the dreaded Amn al-Amm, Iraq's political police, to quell all resistance.

Exactly one Islamic year after their revolt, Saddam was warmly received by a clearly repentant Dulaym leadership. Saddam suggested that the Dulaym cleanse themselves of their shame by the blood of their own kind. Despite the harsh crackdown, there were still echoes of dissent. Addressing the assembled leadership, Saddam alluded to the *hadr al-dam* blood code implemented against Hussein Kamal. The message was clear: the Dulaym were to kill any member of the tribe who had acted against Saddam. The Dulaym, in their desire to ingratiate themselves with the president, exacted an awful retribution on the men, women, and children of the al-Bu Nimr. Those closest to the family of Muhammad Mazlum al-Dulaymi paid the highest price. Anyone who had been associated with the revolt was rounded up, often by Dulaym from the ranks of the Amn al-Amm or the Mukhabarat. Women were raped, their husbands, brothers, and sons forced to watch. Children were beaten to death, and infants were suffocated in plastic bags and thrown into canals and rivers.

Then in June 1996 Saddam was informed by his son Qusay that the security services had exposed an incipient coup set for July. Most disturbing was that it was to be carried out by Special Republican

Guard officers of the 3rd Battalion (special forces) of the elite 1st Brigade. This was a CIA-backed effort in support of the Jordan-based opposition group, the Iraqi National Accord. The INA was composed of former military personnel who had defected from Iraq and who were hoping to take advantage of their old contacts at home. Unfortunately for the plotters, the Mukhabarat had penetrated their organization with spies and false defectors, and all of the plans fell into the hands of Baghdad.

Striking preemptively, Qusay arrested hundreds of Special Republican Guard and Republican Guard officers and soldiers, including the entire 3rd Battalion. Dozens were subsequently executed, while others were discharged from service. The involvement of an SRG unit in a plot of this nature was a heavy blow to Saddam and Qusay. The SRG had been enlarged twice since the end of the Gulf War. Now, in 1996, Saddam and Qusay realized that this expansion had been too big and too fast.

After thwarting the July 1996 attempted coup, Saddam rallied the military to an impressive victory over the CIA-led Iraqi National Congress in Irbil. The army destroyed the INC's military capability along with the other Kurdish militaries, driving out the CIA. This was a tremendous morale booster for the Iraqi military, restoring a sense of pride and accomplishment to a service that had, for the past six years, known only mortification and defeat.

Qusay had saved his father from the CIA, but Uday had become dangerous to both men. The split between Saddam and Sajida over the Samira affair had put Uday at odds with Qusay; in addition, Qusay had led an investigation into his criminal activities after Uday had murdered Kamel Hana in 1988. Uday had formed his own paramilitary organization, the Martyrs of Saddam, or the Fidayeen. Some 20,000 volunteers had enrolled in what had become Uday's private army. They served as guards for his many business activities and, more important, provided security services to the family of Khayr Allah, including Uday's mother. Qusay and Uday now commanded competing armies, the Special Republican Guard and the Fidayeen. Baghdad was their battleground.

It was common knowledge that every Thursday night Uday

would cruise the neighborhood of Al Mansur looking for women. One such Thursday in December 1996, five men or more were waiting at a traffic light as Uday came driving up in his Porsche. In a well-choreographed ambush, the assailants fired their AK-47 rifles into the armor-plated door of the driver's side until they were able to penetrate. The bullets struck Uday's lower body, saving his life but causing serious injury to his groin, lower back, and legs. The attackers escaped.

Although the assault was publicly blamed on Iranian terrorists, the actual would-be assassins may have been affiliated with the al-Bu Nasir's Hazza' clan, who were exacting revenge on a symbol of Saddam's excesses and an easy target. The episode changed Saddam's perspective. He considered it a direct attack against the family, brought on by its own weaknesses. Saddam undertook two strategies to alter this situation.

First, he sought reconciliation with Uday. By all accounts, he was truly grief-stricken. He was a frequent visitor to his son's bedside. In an effort to placate Uday's outrage over the Samira affair, Saddam agreed to spend more time with Sajida, and made several television appearances with her at his side. Saddam also restored Uday to positions he had stripped him of. Saddam was clearly trying to induce his elder son to start preparing himself to assume the mantle of leadership. This reassured Uday and Sajida, and helped initiate a healing process with the al-Tilfah. Uday recovered from his injuries—and returned to his same rapacious, thuggish ways.

Second, Saddam relied more heavily than ever on Qusay to improve the security of the regime. In the end, the paramount objective was protecting the president.

# 9

# Fortress Saddam and the Concealment Mechanism

FOLLOWING THE TURMOIL OF 1996, Qusay constructed a series of circular shields to protect his father from any physical threat, foreign or domestic. The outermost ring is manned by the Iraqi intelligence service, or Mukhabarat. The Mukhabarat has a mandate for conducting intelligence operations abroad to gather information or perform special tasks (such as assassination and covert procurement on behalf of weapons of mass destruction programs). The Mukhabarat also monitors the activities of foreigners inside Iraq.

I had many encounters with the Mukhabarat during my years in Iraq, probably many more than I'm aware of. One has stuck with me over the years as a defining illustration of institutionalized terror. It happened in June 1996. A heat wave had settled on the Baghdad area, with the temperature often topping 120 degrees Fahrenheit. It was the first day of an inspection, and the team was scheduled to investigate ten sites in the Abu Ghraib area. Half the men were arrayed along the old Jordan Highway, which bisected the Abu Ghraib Military Camp. They were sealing off the exits to encampments suspected of belonging to the Special Republican Guard. The other half, operating under my command, was investigating two separate sites. One was a secured facility thought to be housing the security directorate of the Military Industrial Commission (the Amn al-Tasnia), which was responsible for concealment activities in the effort to hide prohibited material from UNSCOM.

This facility was first on our list, and as we approached it half the vehicles turned off at the main entrance and the other half went around the perimeter to seal off any rear exits. Almost immediately, our path was blocked by armed soldiers dressed in camouflage uniforms and red berets — the garb of the elite regiment of special forces used by the Mukhabarat to protect its facilities. The situation was tense, and the Iraqis let it be known that they would not allow us to enter this facility. I radioed the other half of the team, learning that they, too, had been denied access.

This inspection team, UNSCOM 150, had been assembled and trained in great secrecy. Breaking from the standard practice of mission preparation at the UNSCOM Field Operations Base in Bahrain, UNSCOM 150 had trained at a remote British military facility near Basingstoke. Each subteam had received many hours of instruction followed by realistic exercises, drilled into the inspectors until they had become second nature. We would be looking for critical documents, and one of the tactics concerned how to proceed if we found them. The team making such a discovery was to radio a signal, which would allow the chief inspector or his deputy to respond to the event without tipping off the Iraqis that something had been found. For UNSCOM 150, it was agreed that this signal would contain the phrase "get a message to Charles."

About fifteen minutes after we had been stopped at the gate, I received a call over the radio. There it was: a request to "get a message to Charles." I jumped in my Nissan Patrol and moved out at high speed to the location of the incident, a checkpoint set up by the inspectors on the outskirts of a village that bordered the inspection site on its western side.

I arrived to find a large cluster of inspectors and Iraqis huddled around a couple of Iraqi men, dressed in civilian clothes. Each of the Iraqis carried a large bundle of documents under his arms. The men looked more embarrassed than worried. I queried one of our men, a French colonel, for a quick situation report. His subteam, he said, had arrived at its assigned location, a crossroads in the center of the village, and had seen the two men walking toward them from the place we wanted to inspect. The UNSCOM colonel got the attention of his Iraqi minders, and together they apprehended the men.

They claimed to be students taking a shortcut home by cutting through the village. The colonel, insisting on examining the documents, had got one in his hands and was reading it before the Iraqis took it back.

The document was marked "Top Secret" and made reference to high explosives. The Iraqi minders became nervous, and questioned the two men, concluding that they had indeed taken the documents from the facility. The "students" stated that they had acted on their own. When the UNSCOM inspectors showed up, they said, they instinctively grabbed the classified documents and climbed over the wall to elude the inspection team. They acknowledged that they had made a mistake, and indicated that all they wanted to do was to go back to their facility and wait for the situation to be resolved.

From a procedural standpoint alone, this was a serious issue. While the Iraqis had clearly indicated that they had no intention of letting us in, on the grounds that the site related to national security, they did understand the implications of having weapons inspectors catch personnel fleeing with thousands of highly classified documents. One of the stated objectives of the inspection was to expose Iraqi concealment practices, and it appeared that this in fact was what had happened.

Major General Hossam Amin arrived and was briefed by his colleagues. The look on his face indicated that he understood the gravity of the situation. He suggested that the two men be permitted to return to the facility before continuing our discussion, a suggestion I refused. If the documents were important enough to remove from an inspection site in violation of Security Council resolutions, then they would need to be examined. After going off for several minutes to make a secure phone call from inside the facility, he returned.

"The Iraqi side has made a mistake here," he said, "and we must not give you any excuse to report to the Security Council that we are hiding anything." Hossam Amin invited us into the site to carry out an inspection and to examine in more detail the documents in question. I asked him what kind of facility this was, and he looked at me with grave eyes. "You will find out in due course."

We entered the main headquarters building. I was introduced to the director of the facility, who said it was an anti-terrorism school run by the Mukhabarat. Sending the bulk of my men to survey the entire facility, I sat down with the director and a British translator from my team to examine the documents at the center of the controversy. They were extraordinary.

The first thing we established was that this was not just any anti-terrorist school, but one under the auspices of Directorate M-21 of the Mukhabarat, the directorate for special operations. M-21 reported directly to the secret office of Directorate M-4, covert operations. Next, we learned that while it was true that they taught many subjects at this school, none related to anti-terrorism. In classic doublespeak, the "anti-terrorist" school was a school *for* terrorists and terrorism.

Page after page revealed plans for terrorist operations—many, for example, against the Kurds. A requisition to the army asked for Iranian land mines so that the high explosive could be removed and used in booby traps overseas—the purpose being to dupe any forensic examiner into concluding that the culprit was Iran not Iraq. There were designs for mines configured as toys. Plans for ambushing moving convoys. A primer on how to wiretap.

Document after document outlined an international program of terror. By the time we had finished, the room was filled with over thirty Iraqis from the M-21 Directorate, each of whom hovered over me and the translator as we plowed through thousands of pages. The Iraqis were not overjoyed about our seeing these papers, and I couldn't blame them. These documents had nothing to do with our mandate and would not have been examined at all had the Iraqis not tried to sneak them off. They were an indictment of a regime that would authorize such an organization to exist, and that was what was apparently upsetting even these hardened professionals (most of the minders who normally accompanied us had left the room, fearful of being exposed to the kind of information contained in the documents). These were state-sanctioned assassins, who did not shrink from shedding the blood of innocent civilians, including women and children. It was all justifiable to them, in the name of defending the regime. It was no wonder people referred to the Mukhabarat as the "Long Arm of Saddam." As for our team, we were no closer to the weapon we were searching for, but we left M-21 somewhat wiser in the ways of the Iraqi regime.

As a Baghdad landmark, the next ring of security around Saddam cannot be missed. Rising in the Balidiyat neighborhood in the eastern part of the city, its brown buildings are encircled by a double wall of fancy brick, less for decoration than as a means of obscuring anything within. Machine guns mounted on trucks stand at each corner, and guard towers ring the complex of buildings, which cover the equivalent of six city blocks. All this was within view of UNSCOM headquarters at the Canal Hotel. Our work often carried us into the late hours of night, and as we drove back to our lodgings downtown, we could see the walls of the complex lit up with garish strings of red and white bulbs, its interior glowing a soft yellow from the light of the lampposts in its courtyards. Many of the offices were invariably lit as well, as those inside worked harder and later than anyone else. Indeed, the work of the Directorate for General Security, the DGS or Amn al-Amm, never stops.

Ostensibly reporting to the Ministry of the Interior, the Amn al-Amm functions as a political police force. The Amn al-Amm also fights banditry and insurrection, and has its own paramilitary arm (the Quwat al-Tawari, or Emergency Forces), created in 1991 in response to the breakdown of law and order following the Gulf War. Amn al-Amm's reputation for brutality is legendary, with torture, rape, and murder commonly used to control and intimidate the Iraqi people. Its thousands of officers monitor the day-to-day lives of the population of Iraq, dogging and tracking down every scent of dissension.

The reach of the Amn al-Amm is impressive. As with the Mukhabarat, I had many occasions to interact with the Amn al-Amm. In Tikrit in June 1997, I was inspecting sites believed to be used to hide ballistic missile components. We had received information that linked the Salahadin Company of the Emergency Forces of the Amn al-Amm to such activity, and had moved on Amn al-Amm's Tikrit headquarters to investigate further. But it was other activities of the Amn al-Amm in Tikrit that caught my attention.

# Iraqi Concealment Mechanism Chain of Command

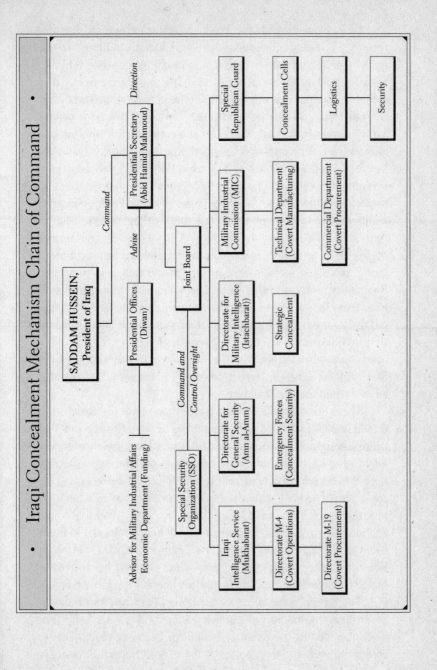

We walked through the headquarters, searching for damning records. The task was daunting: there were literally millions of documents stuffed into every nook and cranny of this three-story building. Only by random sampling could we hope to get a picture of their contents. The vast majority of the documents were reports on the citizens of Tikrit and Salahadin province, of which Tikrit is the capital. They dated back well into the 1970s and covered every minor aspect of their lives. Births, schools attended, marriages, friends made and lost. No detail was too trivial to escape these files, and apparently everyone was willing to talk in depth about his or her neighbor. In the Investigations Department, we found rooms full of files on informants, and by the size of it everyone in Tikrit had to have been an Amn al-Amm informant. Its Technical Directorate was another eye-opener. True to its title, it carried out sophisticated technical monitoring, including monitoring every telephone and radio frequency. Room after room was filled with cassette tapes of ordinary conversations recorded in homes, restaurants, hotels, and cars. It reminded me of East Germany's notorious secret police, the Stasi. After the Berlin Wall came down and the Stasi files were exposed, East Germans were dumbfounded by the monumental snitching they had lived with for decades. Here in Saddam's home area, this was Stasi all over again, maybe Stasi plus.

The Mukhabarat and Amn al-Amm combine to provide their president with an intimidating array of security—but apparently not nearly enough. Paradoxically, no matter how loyal these institutions might be to the regime, their personnel is drawn from too wide a circle not to be regarded as suspect by the president and the inner circle. Ultimately, final responsibility for protecting Saddam lies with, first, the Special Security Organization, the SSO or Amn al-Khass, and second—under the the Amn al-Khass Office of Special Republican Guard Affairs—the Special Republican Guard, or Haris al-Khass. Together, these two organizations represent the innermost protective shields around the president and his immediate family.

The Special Republican Guard is organized into four brigades, an artillery command, an air defense command, and force-level units managed by the Special Republican Guard headquarters. According to written orders posted at the various Special Republican

Guard headquarters, its stated mission is fourfold: 1) protect the president; 2) conduct any other duty that may be ordered; 3) protect presidential facilities; and 4) prepare for combat duties. To carry out this mission, the Special Republican Guard is organized into two basic structures: the combat battalion and the security battalion. Tellingly, the security battalion was the larger of the two.

The innermost circle of protection is the SSO or Amn al-Khass. As a security organization, its powers are absolute. Its eye is also trained on the Mukhabarat, the Amn al-Amm, the armed forces, the Republican Guard, and even the Special Republican Guard.

Within the SSO itself the circle becomes a kind of spiral, winding closer and closer to the president in the flesh. Closest to Saddam in the spiral is the Murafaqin, or Companions of Saddam.

The Murafaqin are the only persons in Iraq allowed to approach the president alone, unescorted, and armed. They are exclusively al-Bu Nasir, evenly divided among the family subclans. The Murafaqin consist of approximately forty persons, in two main groups and a third minor group. The first is the Special Location Group, responsible for Saddam's safety in places used by him or his immediate family. The second group is known as the Salih, or Mobile Group, responsible for the security of the president and his immediate cordon of bodyguards. The third group, the smallest, is the Kulyab, made up of Saddam's personal cook and butcher, and swimming and fishing companions.

Crossing the moat surrounding Fortress Saddam is all but unthinkable. And it is this same security structure that protects his weapons of mass destruction.

The concealment mechanism operated by Iraq against UN-SCOM remained unchanged until the August 1995 defection of Hussein Kamal. The SSO arrested over 600 persons within days of the defection and conducted a rapid appraisal of the situation. It recommended shifting all blame to Hussein Kamal, and a major restructuring of the concealment mechanism itself was undertaken.

In October 1996 the Joint Committee reexamined concealment in conjunction with the entire issue of presidential security. The extension of the no-fly zone in the south, together with attempted coups from within the Special Republican Guard and a large number of defections from within the ranks of both the SRG and the SSO, prompted a relocation of operations away from Baghdad to the Tikrit region. In addition, organizational restructuring in terms of personnel and agencies involved in the concealment mechanism occurred, it seems, with a greater reliance being placed on sites and personnel within the presidential *diwan*, or presidential office and which are affiliated with the Tikrit area. This shift was implemented by February 1997, and is still in force.

The concealment mechanism in place today is believed to be shaped by the Weapons Control and Maintenance Committee of the SSO, which provides guidance on camouflage, concealment, and deception, and the Office of the Presidential Adviser for Military Industry, which provides input on how to manage the information flow to UNSCOM and the IAEA while maintaining a credible cover story concerning the disposition of retained material and activities.

The heart of the concealment mechanism is the Concealment Operations Room, run by the SSO from a location either in or near its main headquarters in downtown Baghdad. This operations center coordinates with the SSO to implement concealment measures for past programs, covert procurement, and covert manufacturing.

Several organizations are believed to have a supporting role in the concealment mechanism, among them the Military Industrial Commission (MIC), responsible for retained manufacturing capability as well as the covert procurement efforts that support it; the Mukhabarat; the air force and army, most probably represented by the offices of the *Istachbarat*, or military intelligence; the SSO, the central coordinating body for this activity, safeguards the retained material while supervising access to it by the preceding organizations.

The concealment mechanism was the most difficult issue facing UNSCOM in its work in Iraq. It was UNSCOM chief Richard Butler's frustrations over the continued acts of concealment that prompted his report to the Security Council of December 16, 1998, that led the United States to unleash Operation Desert Fox. The seventy-hour aerial attack was largely directed against over 100 targets in Iraq involved in concealment.

What Iraq tried for seven years to conceal from UNSCOM was a weapons of mass destruction program that is little more than the bare bones of the massive projects undertaken prior to Operation Desert Storm. This reduced capability reflects the effectiveness of the UNSCOM and IAEA inspection process, which, despite all of Iraq's efforts to conceal, obfuscate, and distort the truth, managed to dispose of the vast majority of the prohibited weapons programs.

In 1991 the Iraqis were in a position to rain down death and destruction on the heads of their neighbors in the form of long-range ballistic missiles and aerial bombs filled with chemical and biological agent, and, if the war had not taken place when it did, nuclear weapons.

Iraq was a nation ruled by an expansionistic megalomaniac, filled with fantasies of regional domination. Saddam's power, both domestic and foreign, rested on these weapons, which placed Iraq (in its own mind) on the same strategic plane as Israel—a parity no other Arab nation could claim. This perception, or self-delusion, allowed Saddam to place himself in the pantheon of the great leaders of ancient Mesopotamia and his near-contemporary pan-Arabist visionary President Gamal Abdel Nasser of Egypt. Of course, Saddam falls short, but such pompous aspirations suggest how important his weapons program is to his stature, both real and self-perceived.

Against the movable backdrop of Saddam's complicated and ever-changing power relationships the one constant since 1988 has been his weapons of mass destruction. Saddam will not readily relinquish them. No one really knows the true extent of Iraq's prohibited weapons holdings today. Iraq never provided a full accounting of its past programs to UNSCOM or the IAEA. But enough is known about what it received prior to the Gulf War, and what it has procured and hidden away from UNSCOM in the years since, to put together a fairly comprehensive picture of the state of Iraq's weapons of mass destruction program today (see Appendix).

Under the pressure of constant monitoring and inspections, whatever material Iraq retained has been kept hidden and on the move, unable to be reconstituted in any meaningful form for fear of exposure to the international watchdogs. And despite eight years of crippling sanctions, Saddam still maintains a large base of support in

Iraq, among the tribal coalitions he has built, torn down, and rebuilt, the military he has constantly purged and abused, and the leadership structures he commands.

In many ways, he is stronger and more stable than ever. The continuous series of crises he faced since the end of the Gulf War have galvanized the security of his regime. He has struck an uneasy balance between tribal politics and the need for professionalism in the management of Iraq, in both civilian and military spheres. Saddam's inner circle of domestic and foreign affairs advisers are all old-time friends and colleagues in whom he places trust and confidence. His recent appointments to ministerial positions reflect the growing professionalism in the current difficult economic and political conditions. All of them are, of course, absolutely loyal to the regime, but were selected based upon their professional qualifications as well as their political reliability.

Saddam appears to have come full circle in terms of his relationships with people. The need for a foundation of beliefs for the lower and middle echelons of leadership has led him to resurrect, at least to some extent, the basic principles of the Ba'ath party, which had been allowed to crumble over the past decade as he pursued a confused mixture of Ba'athist nationalism, Arab tribalism, and Islamic fundamentalism in defining an Iraqi ethos.

But in the end, it still boils down to whom Saddam trusts with his life. He may approach his kitchen cabinet of close advisers from the regional leadership and Revolutionary Command Council concerning matters of state, but there are only four persons who have his unconditional trust—'Ali Hassan al-Majid, Rokan 'Abd al-Ghafur Suleiman al-Majid, Abid Hamid Mahmoud, and his son Qusay.

Despite his removal from the Defense Ministry, 'Ali Hassan al-Majid has remained Saddam's chief troubleshooter. Indeed, when Iraq was broken down into four administrative zones in anticipation of a loss of command and control during Operation Desert Fox, Saddam appointed 'Ali Hassan al-Majid director of the southern zone. Given the history of revolt in the south, this was a very important position. Rokan 'Abd al-Ghafur remains Saddam's personal bodyguard. He has assumed responsibility for overseeing Saddam's relationship with the al-Majid clan. With the ongoing instability of Uday, Qusay continues as the bastion of support for Saddam. In Qusay, he has entrusted the entire security infrastructure that maintains power in Iraq. Qusay's record of high performance under duress compared with the erratic and unpredictable nature of his older brother had made Qusay a suitable candidate to replace Saddam if Uday cannot be brought into line.

Of these four individuals, three are from the al-Majid clan, proving that tribal loyalties stand above all else. The fourth person, Abid Hamid Mahmoud, belongs to the al-Khatib clan but still a member of the al-Bu Nasir tribe. Abid Hamid Mahmoud, in his role as presidential secretary, is the most influential and powerful person after Saddam. Himself a former bodyguard, Abid Hamid Mahmoud serves as the gatekeeper to Saddam, through whom all others, including Saddam's sons and 'Ali Hassan al-Majid must pass. He alone is empowered to act on presidential authority. He is the second most powerful person in Iraq today.

Saddam's durability is puzzling to outside observers. Militarily battered, his economy in ruins and his oil sales controlled by outside parties, his country torn apart by ethnic and religious factionalism, his territory under constant aerial surveillance and frequent bombardment, his weapons industry subjected to the most comprehensive inspection regime in the history of arms control, Saddam, some might conclude, has never been weaker. But this is not true.

He has created a uniquely Iraqi identity, based on the years of confrontation with the West and the world. There is a perverse pride in Iraq today for having stood up to the West for so long and, to their surprise, remaining standing. The Iraqi people see Saddam as a symbol of hope in their world of despair.

Saddam Hussein has a vision of Iraq in the next decade. The goal of ridding itself of the economic sanctions without disarmament seems nearer today than ever. Expansion of Iraq's severely diminished weapons of mass destruction capabilities will begin the moment Saddam decides that the pendulum has swung his way. In the wake of Operation Desert Fox, with no UNSCOM inspectors in his way, the road is open. Feeding off its massive oil wealth, a resurgent Iraq, strengthened by its retained weapons capability and a perceived victory over the United States, the Gulf War coalition, and the United Nations, is bound to reemerge in a few years as a force to be reckoned with.

For Saddam Hussein the stakes are very personal. Victory means power and glory, defeat means ignominy and death. How then do the United States and the world deal with the vexing and dangerous problem of Saddam Hussein's Iraq?

# 10

# The Ghost
# in the Machine

A MAN WHO represented a new face on how the United States was dealing with Saddam's post–Gulf War Iraq was a senior operative with the Central Intelligence Agency. He was a member of the CIA's Special Activities Staff, responsible for covert paramilitary operations on behalf of the Directorate for Operations. I will call him Moe Dobbs.

Dobbs was a veteran of the U.S. Army Special Forces, as were so many of his colleagues. He had started his service in Laos, working covert operations on behalf of the CIA. Lured from the military by the intelligence agency, Dobbs became a master of covert warfare, and played a critical role in support of the contras in Nicaragua. During the Gulf War he was based in Syria, directing a covert operation that used Arab agents inside Iraq. They assisted him in setting up escape and evasion areas for downed U.S. pilots. Later, he conducted operations in northern Iraq, running Kurdish agents who would collect military intelligence. During Operation Provide Comfort—the humanitarian effort to create a safe haven for the Kurds under siege by the Iraqis—Dobbs and his team would operate under U.S. Army cover, assisting special forces units with unique intelligence capabilities.

I would get to know Moe Dobbs as a resourceful but shadowy figure, who, as will be seen, would come in and out of my life during my tenure at UNSCOM.

The CIA, prevented from carrying out active covert paramilitary operations inside Iraq during Desert Storm, was at a disadvantage when ordered by President Bush in late 1991 to develop a plan to overthrow Saddam Hussein. The agency put together a $30 million package to destabilize the regime. It combined anti-Saddam propaganda with active support for a political opposition group. The CIA chose the Iraqi National Congress to serve as its front. The INC is an umbrella organization open to all other anti-regime parties. It was set up in the fall of 1992 after various opposition groups held two conferences, the first in Vienna and then in Iraqi Kurdistan, in the city of Salahadin. Its support for democratic principles made it acceptable in Washington and was thus an easy sell for the CIA.

The INC has a three-man presidential council consisting of Mustafa Barzani, the leader of the KDP, Muhammad Bahr al-Ulum, a Shi'a cleric with few ties to the Iraqi Islamic parties and head of Ahl al-Bait, a charitable religious endowment, and General Hassan al-Naqib, a Sunni from a prominent family who was a senior military Ba'athist in the 1960s and 1970s. He defected in 1978 and led resistance forces operating out of Iraqi Kurdistan.

The INC also formed a twenty-seven-member executive committee, headed by Achmed Chalabi, and representing seventeen political parties.

It was hard to imagine the INC, with its complex leadership, as a serious contender against Saddam Hussein, but the CIA had no choice. The alternative of supporting Shi'a rebellion in southern Iraq raised the fear of stirring up fundamentalist Islamic forces that could strengthen Iran and undermine U.S. allies in the Gulf region. With Operation Provide Comfort in the north, the U.S. had a secure base of operations close to Baghdad from which it could directly influence affairs. No one really believed that Chalabi could ever pull together a functional military organization, and people doubted his ability to manage the Kurds. However, Chalabi was soon recruiting an independent INC army, and had succeeded in uniting the KDP and PUK into a trilateral alliance that was preparing to take on Saddam's army in northern Iraq.

This was more or less the situation when President Clinton and his national security team took office in January 1993. In all fairness, the Clinton administration had inherited a hot potato. Under two consecutive Republican administrations, America's Iraqi policy had grown from no policy at all, to one of open embrace, to containment, to confrontation, and back to containment.

During the Gulf War there had been several attempts to track and kill Saddam in air strikes. In one such case, for example, I was summoned by General Calvin Waller, deputy commander of U.S. forces in Desert Storm, to a meeting with Prince Turki bin-Faisal, head of Saudi intelligence. Saudi agents operating in Kuwait and Iraq had reported that Saddam was due to go to Basra to meet with his commanders and had provided a description of the building where he would be staying, in a remote location north of the city. Using this description, I worked with photographic interpreters scanning recent imagery in an attempt to identify the location. Three candidates were selected and I submitted them to the target planners. Two, I learned later, had actually been bombed. In the end, of course, Saddam survived everything the coalition could throw at him, and the United States was faced with the prospect of finding a way to deal with him by other means.

President Bush decided not to exceed his mandated mission of liberating Kuwait. This was undoubtedly the correct decision. The coalition would never have tolerated a march on Baghdad, and the U.S. would have been left with an unmanageable military occupation for which there was neither military preparation nor support back home. Bush had fought hard for congressional approval of military action in the Gulf, and to expand the scope of the American involvement was unthinkable.

Moreover, many believed that it was merely a matter of time—less than six months, it was thought—before Saddam would be overthrown as the price of his ruinous Kuwaiti adventure. The U.S. had predicted Saddam's demise at the outbreak of the war, and assumed that it would shortly come true. But assumptions are not an endgame, and all hope of the "quick and clean" exit was dashed in a quagmire for which Washington had no plan. In many ways, the war-ending 1991 Security Council Resolution 687 with its economic sanctions was supported as much for the pressure it would exert on Saddam's regime as for its disarmament benefits.

By the end of 1991 it was apparent to the Bush administration that Saddam was more durable than the experts had predicted. Fishing for policy, Washington stood by almost passively throughout the summer of 1991 as Iraq challenged the United Nations weapons inspectors. By late fall the realization that Iraq was not going to fully comply with its disarmament obligations had set in, and a decision was made by the Bush team to support the inspection effort more vigorously than before. But there was still no sense of purpose in the American approach to UNSCOM. In the 1992 confrontation between Iraq and UNSCOM outside the Agriculture Ministry, the U.S. took days to react. The end result was that American policy toward Iraq evolved into one of containment through sanctions, with just enough support for UNSCOM to keep it alive.

The new Clinton administration accepted the Iraqi containment policy in 1993 as a fait accompli. It was soon tested when Iraq suspended the flights of the UNSCOM air shuttle between Bahrain and Baghdad, leaving the majority of inspectors stranded in Bahrain after the Christmas holiday. A strong U.S. response, with cruise missiles clobbering a known military industrial facility, prompted Saddam to back down, and later that year, in June, Clinton continued to punish Iraq by launching a similar strike against the Mukhabarat headquarters in Baghdad because of Iraq's involvement in a plot to kill former President Bush during a visit to Kuwait earlier in the year. But there were few policy options available that would resolve the Iraqi situation. Faced with Iraqi acts of provocation and confrontation, the Clinton team opted to continue the Bush program of covert action targeted against Saddam Hussein and his regime.

The CIA was compelled to provide active support to the INC—beyond funding—when in 1994 a visit by senior staff members of the Senate Select Intelligence Committee to the INC stronghold in northern Iraq convinced the staffers that the INC was a viable opposition group. By late 1994 the CIA had set up a paramilitary base in northern Iraq and begun the active training and direction of an INC military force. The feuding between the KDP and the PUK continued, however, and soured the CIA on the prospects of INC success. More and more, the CIA was being wooed by the British Secret Intelligence Service, or MI6, which proposed a quick, simple coup, orchestrated from within by military officers close to Saddam. Such was the offer being presented by the rival opposition group, the Iraqi National Accord. The CIA began supporting both factions, but putting the bulk of its effort behind the INA.

By 1995 the INC had recruited a 10,000-man army, and was poised to launch large-scale military action against Iraqi troops in northern Iraq. The goal of the operation was to establish a sanctuary, with U.S. airpower operating in the no-fly zone providing cover, where Iraqi troops could defect and organize armed resistance to Saddam Hussein. On the eve of the battle, in March 1995, the U.S. changed its policy, and the CIA was ordered to inform INC head Achmed Chalabi that no military assistance would be forthcoming. Chalabi launched his attack anyway, making minor gains until the Kurdish coalition broke apart and a concerted Iraqi counterattack routed his forces. Thus in early 1996 the CIA was ordered to develop a quick-fix solution that would get rid of Saddam before the 1996 presidential election campaign. The only option available was the INA.

I first began working with the CIA's Moe Dobbs in the spring of 1992, when he and his team of paramilitary operatives were made available to UNSCOM as inspectors. Dobbs and his men provided seasoned personnel who could operate vehicles, organize logistics, run communications—simply put, the kind of people you want around you in a difficult situation. They were not weapons experts, but we had enough of those. From the spring of 1992 until November 1993, my relationship with Dobbs was very close. We worked together to plan the operational and intelligence support for the largest and most complex inspections ever undertaken by UNSCOM, including the UNSCOM 63 inspection, which operated in Iraq for close to two months and involved over 100 inspectors. The UNSCOM 63 inspection made use of innovative airborne radar to scour thousands of square kilometers of Iraqi territory in an effort to find buried Scud missiles. In the end none was found—a fact that forced the CIA to reassess the number of Scud missiles retained by Iraq from over 200 to a few dozen.

I had the full authority of Executive Chairman Rolf Ekéus

when carrying out this coordination, and the results of our inspections spoke for themselves. Between Nikita Smidovich, Moe Dobbs, and me, some of the most difficult disarmament issues were reconciled, such as the Scud missile reassessment, and by the end of 1993 UNSCOM was well on the road toward setting up a functional monitoring system, signaling the end of the confrontational intrusive-discovery-type inspections.

As I've already explained, all this changed with the August 1995 Hussein Kamal defection. Suddenly the concealment issue required new large-scale intrusive inspections, and once again Nikita and I were scrambling to reconstitute a dormant capability. I queried the U.S. government about the availability of Dobbs and his men, and by September 1995 we were back in contact.

The Moe Dobbs team was involved in the UNSCOM 143 inspection in March 1996. UNSCOM 143 was the first of a series of large-scale inspections in Iraq designed to elicit a detectable Iraqi response from the organization that was hiding Iraq's secret arsenal. These inspections, controversial and confrontational by design, were supported by an elaborate information collection plan. The plan integrated the work of the inspectors on the ground, surveillance aircraft overhead, and a new element—sensitive communications scanners. These instruments were manned by UNSCOM linguists and technical personnel who would search for Iraqi communications related to the inspection and monitor Iraq's reaction. I was the architect of this strategy, heading the planning and analytical phases back in New York and participating in the inspections in Iraq.

As foreseen, UNSCOM 143 was resisted by the Iraqis, who obstructed, harassed, and delayed the work of the inspectors. This prompted the passage of a new Security Council resolution and, when the Iraqis continued to hinder the work of UNSCOM, a statement from the president of the Security Council reiterated UNSCOM's right to carry out such inspections and demanded that the inspectors be accorded immediate and unrestricted access. The inspection turned up no direct evidence of Iraqi wrongdoing, but rather enabled UNSCOM to establish a comprehensive baseline of data demonstrating how Iraq responded to help narrow the range of our efforts to monitor Saddam's security apparatus, with particular emphasis on the Special Republican Guard.

In June we followed up UNSCOM 143 with UNSCOM 150—a more comprehensive inspection of Special Republican Guard facilities believed to be protecting weapons of mass destruction related material and documentation. Moe Dobbs and his men played their biggest role in support of UNSCOM 150. Including Dobbs there were nine CIA paramilitary covert operators on the inspection team. They served as regular team members as well as the team communicators. They had nothing whatsoever to do with the UNSCOM mission of intercepting Iraqi communications. This was a separate operation run by British operatives. I never observed Dobbs or any member of his team behave in an inappropriate manner during the course of an inspection. Further, when UNSCOM 150 ended, I never saw Dobbs again. He and his team simply vanished—though their presence would come back to haunt me soon enough.

Iraq refused to permit UNSCOM 150 to inspect the SRG facilities. We engaged in a standoff lasting several days with inspectors surrounding three barracks on a twenty-four-hour basis. I was the deputy chief inspector on this mission, and in addition to coordinating the efforts of the entire team, I was responsible for our stakeout of a Special Republican Guard warehouse facility and commando training base on the northern edge of Saddam International Airport. We were parked in the open on a blazing stretch of desert sand in 120-degree temperatures.

Back in the U.S. this inspection was creating quite a stir. Senior staff members of the National Security Council were scurrying between Washington and New York, trying to elicit the strongest possible reaction from the Security Council. A concerted effort was underway to ensure that a Security Council resolution would find the Iraqis in "material breach" of council resolutions. Those were the magic words that would permit the use of military force to bring Iraq back into compliance, i.e., cooperation with the UNSCOM inspectors.

But some members of the Security Council, Russia and France in particular, wanted one last diplomatic initiative, urging Ekéus to reason with the Iraqis. The U.S. was hesitant, fearing that the Iraqis would find a way to wiggle out. Instructions were sent to Ekéus to go

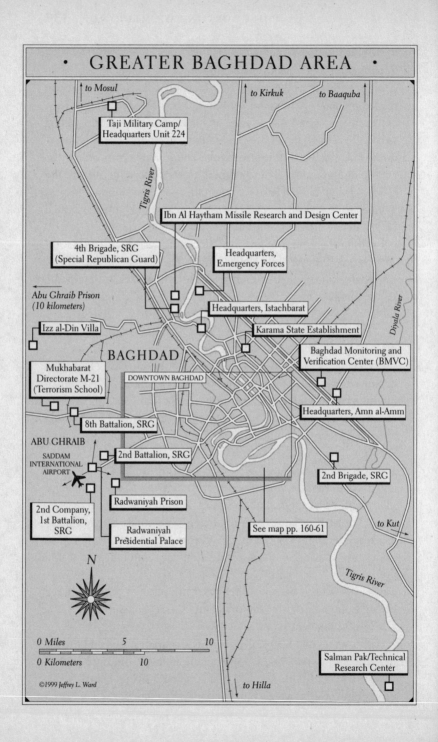

# • GREATER BAGHDAD AREA •

to Mosul

to Kirkuk

to Baaquba

Taji Military Camp/
Headquarters Unit 224

Tigris River

Ibn Al Haytham Missile Research and Design Center

4th Brigade, SRG
(Special Republican Guard)

Headquarters,
Emergency Forces

Abu Ghraib Prison
(10 kilometers)

Headquarters, Istachbarat

Karama State Establishment

Izz al-Din Villa

Diyala River

BAGHDAD

Baghdad Monitoring and
Verification Center (BMVC)

Mukhabarat
Directorate M-21
(Terrorism School)

DOWNTOWN BAGHDAD

8th Battalion, SRG

Headquarters, Amn al-Amm

ABU GHRAIB

SADDAM
INTERNATIONAL
AIRPORT

2nd Battalion, SRG

2nd Brigade, SRG

2nd Company,
1st Battalion,
SRG

Radwaniyah Prison

See map pp. 160-61

to Kut

Radwaniyah
Presidential Palace

N

Tigris River

0 Miles          5          10

0 Kilometers          10

©1999 Jeffrey L. Ward

Salman Pak/Technical
Research Center

to Hilla

to Baghdad to deliver a warning that the Iraqis had to comply with the Security Council resolutions in full.

Meanwhile, in Baghdad, the mood of the inspectors was grim but professional. "Wall watching" was a very tedious task, and the excitement of the standoff soon wore off as the drudgery of standing eight-hour shifts took its toll. The inspectors expected to be backed up by the Security Council. Then word came down for the team to be withdrawn, and a major military strike seemed about to take place as soon as our plane left Iraqi airspace. The Iraqis obviously thought so, too: as we drove out of Baghdad we could observe a huge deployment of air defense artillery into the area.

Ekéus met with Tariq Aziz and other senior Iraqi officials at the Iraqi Foreign Ministry in downtown Baghdad on the evening of June 19, 1996. The atmosphere was distinctly cold. The transcript of the exchange that took place between Ekéus and Tariq Aziz allows a rare look into negotiations under the approaching storm clouds of war. Here are some excerpts:

> ROLF EKÉUS: There are different views and policies on this issue among the various members of the council, but our two sides should grasp this new opportunity and move forward soon so that it might lead to a situation where the council could address [the lifting of sanctions]. . . . Iraq's behavior had tested the commission's patience and that of the council. This should end. I hope that our two sides can organize our work in a way that would achieve this. The key is for us to look forward in a constructive manner.

Ekéus had an agenda, and he set it out. Iraq would reaffirm its intent to comply and UNSCOM would carry out its mandate without harming the national interests of Iraq. The sovereignty issue was the touchiest.

> TARIQ AZIZ: Iraq asserts that it has all the rights to protect its sovereignty and security, and the commission knows its commitments to Iraq. We have allowed teams to inspect what they wanted . . . with the exception of a few early inspections and inspectors . . . [there has been] no serious question of access for

four years. The demands of your inspection teams, UNSCOM 143 and 150, have raised some important questions. . . . The question asked in Iraq after UNSCOM 150 was "why [at] this time?" These sites, ministries and the Special Republican Guard, were symbols of Iraq's sovereignty and important to national security.

. . . Iraq cannot, and should not, under any circumstances, be treated as an occupied state, nor will we accept that the commission considers itself as the occupying force. The same is true of sanctions. More than five years have passed. The question is, when would UNSCOM be satisfied? No answers are forthcoming, only generalities. Now there were allegations that Iraq concealed weapons. These allegations are not only baseless, but also not new. In the past numerous teams have inspected with this claim of concealment. How many have found anything to prove these allegations? . . .

Iraqi sovereignty is not to be discussed. You [Ekéus] work for the United Nations. There are two governments, the U.S. and U.K., which officially or formally say they would like to change the government of Iraq. . . . Iraq cannot take lightly the fact that UNSCOM receives information mainly from these two governments, and then you send teams to the Special Republican Guard sites and find nothing. This is not an easy thing for Iraq.

What had been the urgency of sending the teams in March and June? We in Iraq have serious concerns and suspicions. You [Ekéus] sent your team, UNSCOM 150, anticipating a crisis. This really concerns us. We had created a sound working relationship . . . we had our differences, but we tried to find solutions to them. But this time you met with the council and told them we might be irritated, that there would be trouble and to be ready for it. . . . I am complaining about the timing of the inspections. It might not concern you, but we in Iraq see it differently.

Are you coming here to give us a warning? Tell the U.S. and U.K. we are ready. There were attempts by the two delegations [U.S. and U.K.] to insert the phrase "material breach" in the council statement. We are not worried.

If you and I succeed, we can turn events into future joint work in a civilized and professional manner to achieve the resolution of outstanding problems. If we fail, and the U.S. and U.K. resort to a threat or to exercise the use of force, then we will not make concessions. If your proposals do not accommodate the principle of national sovereignty and national security and the reasonably early [lifting of sanctions], then we will not agree to them, even if the Americans threatened force. . . . Let me tell you, the state of Iraq is one of the most experienced in the region, maybe the world, in terms of war. . . . Iraq knows that a couple of missiles will not win a war. We know their effectiveness, and also their limitations.

Tariq Aziz's opaque references to "suspicions" and "timing" would become clear soon, but Ekéus could not wait. He was aware that if he returned to New York empty-handed he would be unleashing the military forces of the United States and the United Kingdom. He also knew that Iraq would not be intimidated by the use of force. The U.S. and U.K. might have intended for Ekéus to be a messenger but Ekéus was his own man and knew that he had a choice: be tough and lose the inspection process altogether, or seek a compromise and keep the inspection regime in place and functioning, even if flawed.

On June 21, Ekéus and Tariq Aziz signed a new a plan that addressed four areas of concern, among them concealment. Also signed was a secret Agreement for the Modalities of Sensitive Site Inspections, which imposed limitations on inspections of sites that the Iraqis regarded as sensitive in terms of their national security, dignity, and sovereignty. These included various ministries, Republican Guard and Special Republican Guard facilities, the Mukhabarat, the Istachbarat, the Amn al-Amm, and the SSO. Ekéus knew that these "modalities" would be controversial and sought to reach an agreement with the Iraqis that this agreement be kept confidential. However, on his return to New York, Ekéus discovered that Tariq Aziz had already briefed the Russians and French on the deal, and Ekéus had to face off against an irritated and skeptical America and Great Britain. But there would be no war, and the inspections would continue.

Within a month we were back in Iraq, this time with

UNSCOM 155. We had a specific location for this team to inspect: a military barracks located on the southern edge of Saddam International Airport. A combination of U-2 imagery and communications intercepts collected during the course of UNSCOM 150 indicated that this site was involved in the movement of vehicles in response to our inspection team. We needed to investigate this site as a result, and felt that this would be a good first test of Ekéus's new "modalities."

After a smooth start, we hit a wall with the Iraqis, who were again denying access. We were absolutely convinced that this proved that Ekéus's experiment in compromise had died at birth. Some days later, on July 21, Ekéus, having intervened diplomatically, asked us to try again. We approached the site as instructed and met Lieutenant General Amer Rashid at one of the checkpoints where we had earlier been denied passage. He then led us through Saddam International Airport, until we came to the gates of the place we wanted to inspect. Amer Rashid gracefully showed us in. The site turned out to be a combined unit of the Radwaniyah Presidential Security Unit, consisting of the 2nd Company, 1st Battalion, Special Republican Guard, and the Radwaniyah Presidential Security Unit of the Special Security Organization. The Iraqis denied that any vehicle had moved from this site in June, despite our photographic evidence to the contrary. Both sites appeared to have been sanitized, and vehicles were missing from the inventory of the 2nd Company (U-2 imagery taken that same day revealed that two hours before the team had arrived at the checkpoint, vehicles from the 2nd Company had assembled in the courtyard and exited in the opposite direction from which we were coming).

No logbooks existed, no records of any significance. There was, however, a large vehicle garage that housed dozens of sedans and sports cars belonging to the president. Several of the sedans were of the same type observed back in June. These cars were dusty, and a closer look at the trunks showed finger marks where they had been recently opened. The trunks had been sealed, and the seals broken. An analysis of the condition of the seals and finger marks indicated that the trunks had been emptied within the past forty-eight hours. Frustrated, we ended the inspection on Ekéus's orders, and as we feared, it would later be presented as a successful application of the new modalities.

But as we were preparing to leave, I was still looking around for documents that could somehow explain what had transpired here between June and our inspection. The Iraqis were not helpful, but I uncovered a file listing administrative orders from the 1st Battalion to the 2nd Company. Two things struck me about these orders: first, they were signed by the same official who had served on the three-man team that had aided Major Izz al-Din in hiding ballistic missile components at his villa. The second and at that moment timelier document, was an administrative order announcing the transfer of the 3rd Battalion, Special Republican Guard, to the direct subordination of the Special Republican Guard command for "liquidation." This order also listed a new security directive from the director of the Special Security Organization forbidding contact between officers and soldiers of the Special Republican Guard and any foreigners.

My mind was taken back to a recent discussion I had had with an Iraqi minder, a highly educated and personable engineer colonel —clearly under orders from Iraqi intelligence to befriend me. He and I would sometimes engage in conversations, usually about the domestic situation in Iraq. On this occasion, he turned to me and asked forgiveness for a question he wanted to pose. "Fire away," I said.

"Mr. Ritter," he began, "you are a man of honor and logic, and we in Iraq trust you. We know that you believe that your investigations are just, but we also know that you are going down a dead-end street with no answers."

This kind of lecture was unusual from him, but he went on.

"I say this, Mr. Ritter, because we are confused as to why you are allowing yourself to be used by the CIA and Mossad for their purposes." I asked what he meant by that. "Well, perhaps you are unaware of how you are being used, but we have exposed a plot against our president, a plot planned by the CIA and the Mossad. We have interrogated several of the plotters, who have confessed completely. They claim that they were to time the plot to coincide with your inspection in June, that you were supposed to create a crisis that would provide justification to the United States to launch cruise missiles against presidential security using UNSCOM as an excuse. In the resulting confusion the plotters would attack. Unfortunately for them, their plot was known for some time, and they never had a chance. The question is, why did you allow yourself to be used?"

I had no idea what the colonel was talking about, and said so, adding that it sounded a little too contrived to me. But the document I had found about the 3rd Battalion of the Special Republican Guard being liquidated set me to thinking—all the more so when it soon became public knowledge that the Iraqis had indeed foiled a coup attempt against Saddam Hussein in June 1996, and that the plotters included officers from within the Special Republican Guard. The plot had been mounted by the Amman-based Iraqi National Accord. The INA, a creation of the British MI6, had been working with the CIA since at least 1994, as I've mentioned.

As I read these documents and recalled my conversation with the Iraqi colonel, I began to think about Moe Dobbs. There was no proof of Dobbs's involvement but there was a strong set of coincidences. UNSCOM 150 and the attempted coup had both taken place in June. That inspection was directed almost exclusively at Special Republican Guard sites; the coup plotters were from some of the same units we were trying to inspect. Finally, Dobbs and his Special Activities Staff operators were the CIA's covert operations experts, one of whose specialties was organizing coups. As the person in charge of planning the UNSCOM inspections in which Dobbs participated, I have no doubt of the legitimacy of its disarmament objectives. However, looking back at the transcript of Tariq Aziz's statements to Ekéus about the suspicious timing of these inspections, I began to understand the Iraqi point of view.

By the end of July 1996, Ekéus was having a difficult time. The full story of the UNSCOM 155 debacle had emerged, and the Swedish diplomat was under increasing attack over the wisdom of his "sensitive site modalities." The United States in particular was feeling very vulnerable. Ekéus had spurned its decision to make a strong case for the inclusion of "material breach" language. Worse, the hopes that the Clinton administration had planned on getting a new regime in Baghdad had been crushed by the penetration of the

INA coup plotters by Mukhabarat, and the quick arrest and punishment of those involved. The U.S. policy of removing Saddam was falling apart.

The White House called a meeting of the National Security Council in August to review American policy toward UNSCOM. Three conditions were becoming increasingly apparent: Iraq was behaving more aggressively; UNSCOM appeared to be on a path of greater accommodation with Iraq; and finally, as a result, there was a risk that confrontational inspections would strengthen the Iraqi hand. This was something that made U.S. policymakers think twice when considering what support to provide UNSCOM.

Many believed that Ekéus had tricked the U.S. into thinking UNSCOM was going to be tough on Iraq, which had led Washington to turn up the heat to force Iraqi cooperation. But when UNSCOM had let Iraq off the hook, the U.S. had been left looking unduly harsh. The U.S., some policymakers felt, should go no further than it had in support of UNSCOM and allow the economic sanctions to take their toll. Further American efforts on behalf of UNSCOM were unwarranted, since recent experience showed it to be diverging from U.S. policy.

Others argued that Iraq's noncooperation and maintenance of prohibited weapons were clear to all. America had made a full commitment to UNSCOM, and UNSCOM remained a credible operation. If the U.S. were to shrink from that commitment, subsequent failures would be blamed on flagging American support. On the other hand, full support would allow it to judge the results of UNSCOM's work without fear of criticism.

In the end, the White House decided to continue backing UNSCOM broadly, including the aggressive concealment-based inspections. However, Washington wanted assurances from Ekéus that he would not accept any further erosion in UNSCOM's mandate without Security Council approval. Ekéus refused to back down, citing his modalities compromise as an important achievement that had enabled the inspectors to continue their work.

Ekéus saw a fatal flaw in the Clinton Iraqi policy. Like the Bush administration policy, it had no endgame. The Clinton team was willing to confront Iraq, but to what purpose? Washington espoused a policy of indefinite economic sanctions until Saddam Hussein was removed from power. Ekéus knew that this policy was an inherent contradiction of the provisions of Security Council Resolution 687, which had no such linkage. That was why he had defended his compromise so energetically. He believed that it alone had kept the inspection process alive, and therefore all options for some conclusion of the Iraqi problem were still on the table.

# 11

# The Lean, Mean
# Politics of Sanctions

DR. NORBERT REINECKE was a German missile expert, the quintessential rocket scientist. With his goatee and round wire-frame glasses, he seemed a stereotype of the precise Teutonic character. Indeed, he was a hard-driving perfectionist, a disarmament specialist who would tolerate no duplicity. He held the Iraqis to task, exposing their every inconsistency, and they hated him for it, taking to slander in their defense. They accused him of forging the documents he deftly wielded in his quest to uncover truth. No one could accuse Norbert of being soft on Iraq.

In October 1994, Norbert and I were working together trying to bare the secrets of the Iraqi ballistic missile program. We sought to reconstruct the projects in detail, sifting every particle of information, locked in verbal and mental combat with our Iraqi counterparts. The work was as bitter as it was exhausting, our attitudes shaped by ceaseless contact with lies wrapped in deceit. We worked late into the night, often returning to our hotel well past midnight.

By 1994, Baghdad had been under economic sanctions for over four years, and there was a telling effect on the daily life and economy. On my first trip, in December 1991, Norbert and I would tour Baghdad in our off-duty hours. We saw a city that had absorbed the brunt of a major war but had survived. Goods were plentiful in the markets, restaurants flourished, and the city was very much alive night and day. I was surprised how prosperous Baghdad seemed, but

it was already only skin-deep. Baghdad—all Iraq for that matter—
was eating itself from within. Fattened by the plunder of Kuwait,
Iraq was sustaining its lifestyle artificially. Now, this self-
consumption had become evident. Streets that once had bristled
with activity at night were dark and silent. The spoils of Kuwait had
long been depleted, and Baghdad lived now by its wits. Families
bartered their heirlooms for food and medicine. Segments of society
profited from the misery. A black market thrived. The graft and corruption of Saddam Hussein's regime knew no bounds, and the criminal element that had ingratiated itself with the *Issaba* over the years
was reaping the benefits.

Every night as Norbert and I drove home, we passed a square
near our hotel where an impoverished woman no more than thirty
was always camped on the grass with four sleeping children beside
her, their ages ranging from a few months to about five years old. We
had become hardened to such sights, so common in Baghdad now,
but as parents of small children ourselves, we invariably noticed the
plight of this family as we went by.

One night, we saw that the smallest child was gone. When we
got inside the hotel, Norbert was livid. He had already been in a foul
mood, having been called a provocateur by the Iraqis in that
evening's meetings. "This damn government is killing its own people," he growled. He turned to me and asked how much Iraqi money
I had with me. We inspectors purchased local currency, the dinar,
through official U.N. channels, but at black market rates, and in
1994 we were getting several hundred dinar to the dollar. I had just
cashed $20, which bought enough dinar to last me for at least a
week. I handed him a wad of bills. He walked over to some other inspectors in the lobby, holding them up for their dinar. Then he ran
up to his room and was back in a minute with food and mineral
water that he had stashed in his suitcase. Together we walked out to
the square. The woman was in a very bad way, the children no better. Her youngest, about a year old, was emaciated and breathing
weakly. We had collected about $60 worth of dinar, a small fortune
for most Iraqis. We handed it to her along with the food; she wept
and grabbed our hands in appreciation.

The next night, the one-year-old, too, was missing from her

side. There were only two children now. We walked over to her, and she became visibly upset, shaking her head and hands and saying in Arabic, "no, no." She pointed across the square. Two men in black leather jackets were watching us. Mukhabarat. We understood and left quickly. We never saw the family again.

The human toll imposed by economic sanctions was real. Real suffering, real hunger, and real death were taking place all around us. By early 1996 this tragic reality had reached gigantic proportions. Iraq's economic isolation had drained all available resources in support of the dinar. The only recourse available to Saddam was to accept Security Council Resolution 986, which authorized Iraq to sell $2 billion in oil every six months to finance the purchase of food, medicine, and other humanitarian goods as well as pay off war reparations and fund the work of UNSCOM.

Saddam and his government abhorred Resolution 986. "Iraq is not ready to be blackmailed," Tariq Aziz told Rolf Ekéus in June 1996. But Iraq finally accepted the resolution. Neither did the U.S. cherish 986. True, it addressed humanitarian concerns, but it eased the bite of economic sanctions. In agreeing to it, however, Saddam lost some of the leverage he had had in transforming the suffering of the Iraqi people into an imperative for the total lifting of the oil embargo. Saddam sought to use this sympathy in a campaign to show that the sanctions were unjust, causing pain and hardship to his people.

As a result of 986, the United Nations began taking on staff to oversee the distribution of food and medicine. These were committed professionals, veterans of the massive humanitarian relief efforts in Africa and the former Yugoslavia. They saw their work as bringing a sense of hope amid despair. About the same time, UNSCOM began resuming its intrusive inspection activity, and the grouping together of dedicated humanitarians with hard-nosed inspectors was not a match made in heaven. Soon the Baghdad Monitoring and Verification Center and the U.N. Headquarters, sharing the same space in the Canal Hotel, broke into two distinct camps, the UNSCOM "Cowboys" and the humanitarian relief worker "Bunny Huggers."

Neither fully appreciated the other's mission. The inspectors confronted the Iraqi government at its worst, as perpetrators of deceit and terror; inspections were often conducted while looking down the barrel of an automatic weapon. The humanitarian workers saw Iraq at its most vulnerable, hospitals full of sick and dying children. Exposure to hunger, poverty, and sorrow was the relief workers' daily lot. The inspectors got little joy from their work. They grew inured to the grind of confrontation, and it was hard to view the Iraqis in a sympathetic light. The humanitarian workers were able to get immediate feedback in their activity, experiencing firsthand the impact of their labors on the people. The inspectors regarded the relief workers much as a combat veteran regarded his rear-area administrators. The humanitarians saw the inspectors as heartless soldiers, and wondered if sanctions would ever be lifted as long as these thick-skinned bullies were in charge of determining Iraqi compliance.

But the economic sanctions were designed to be painful; they were intended to compel Saddam to disarm. Saddam was the problem. He was not an expression of his people's voice. In June 1990, he told Western reporters that "I am in every glass of milk an Iraqi child drinks." In his mind, everything good in Iraq was because of him. He was insulated from the ravages of the sanctions, coddled by the wealth siphoned off by his family over decades of corruption. His Mukhabarat worked day and night to devise schemes to circumvent the grip of the sanctions primarily to procure hundreds of millions of dollars' worth of illicit material for the regime and its beneficiaries.

These real humanitarian needs were used to full advantage by Saddam for propaganda purposes. His goal was simple—neither sanctions nor disarmament. The Iraqi situation illustrates the moral perversity of economic sanctions applied against a dictatorial regime. In the end, only the innocent suffer, because, in the end, Saddam would not disarm.

Baghdad, June 8, 1997. I was in Iraq as the chief inspector of UNSCOM 194, part of a new wave of inspections. It was to be based on a paper I had prepared a month earlier to muster support from the U.S. and the U.K. for a more aggressive UNSCOM posture regarding Iraqi concealment activities. The team was in good spirits, although our relationship with the humanitarian workers was not going well. Many of them were openly criticizing our work. Relations with the Iraqis were no better. We had been carrying out inspection activity since the beginning of June, and had just finished a grueling day inspecting the Special Security Institute, the elite training academy of the SSO, and the Al-Bakr Military Institute, a senior-level school for Iraqi generals. As we left the Al-Bakr Institute, Hossam Amin approached me. "The minister of oil would like to meet with you tonight at 8:30. We will pick you up at the BMVC [Baghdad Monitoring and Verification Center] at 8:00." It was more summons than invitation, meant for the whole team, but I accepted.

At the appointed hour, we were ushered into the ministry through the dimly lit marble hallways. Minister of Oil Amer Rashid was waiting for us, along with Hossam Amin and two other Iraqis. As usual, the Iraqi hospitality was impeccable, and we exchanged broad smiles, firm handshakes, and warm pleasantries.

"Thank you for coming tonight, Mr. Ritter," said the minister. "I have been asked by Mr. Tariq Aziz to ask about some aspects of your mission over the last couple of days." He was very relaxed, but had taken on an air of seriousness. "The important issue here is the story of concealment. We think that it will lead to endless inspections of our security units and establishments. It is not logical or acceptable. We would like to hear it from you, as there is surprise and disbelief with all this."

I sat looking straight at Amer Rashid, trying to hide the turmoil going through my mind. I, of course, had no guidance concerning this matter. My concealment paper was an internal working document, based on sensitive intelligence sources that UNSCOM's executive chairman may not have been willing to back up publicly. My stomach churning, I shuffled in my seat, and waited for the minister to finish his opening remarks. He went on, reading from notes, but it was when he lowered them and looked straight at me that he got to the point.

"We are very concerned about exposing our security organization to experts outside of Iraq," he said. "We believe that it is also possible that some of your experts are from foreign intelligence organizations. We believe these inspections to be totally irrelevant and

[in]sensitive to our security. So where are we going? It's an endless game. What are the political objectives behind it?"

I didn't know what Amer Rashid wanted, but he certainly had me where he wanted me—thrown. I was a chief inspector; we had the authority to act on our own. This power was granted to deny the Iraqis an avenue for second-guessing chief inspectors, and going over their heads to the executive chairman. The executive chairman was the one who had formulated this policy. He made it clear that the chief inspector was his representative, and on technical issues pertaining to a given inspection, spoke with his authority. So I had been trapped by our own policy, one well known by the Iraqis.

If I backed down, I would lose face in Amer Rashid's eyes. In the high-stakes game of inspection bluff and bluster, such a chink in a chief inspector's armor would be fatal to his mission. A weak performance on my part would give the Iraqis plenty of political ammunition with which to counterattack in the Security Council. Amer Rashid was, in my opinion, banking on a failure on my part to firmly commit the commission to a specific course of action.

Buying time to collect my thoughts, I reached down into my green canvas bag for a copy of my concealment paper, showing the cover page to Amer Rashid. "This is the basis for our investigations," I began, holding the paper so that the Iraqis could clearly read the title—"The Iraqi Concealment Mechanism." I looked Amer Rashid squarely in the eyes. "What came out in August 1995 [after the Hussein Kamal defection] was that much had not been declared by Iraq before then. In the various fields of expertise—chemical, biological, and ballistic missile—the experts were not satisfied with the full, final, and complete declarations submitted by Iraq. I sat down with these experts. And we have an idea of what remains. For instance, in the chemical area, we have information—"

Amer Rashid raised his hand, cutting me off. "Please don't use the McCarthy approach of the 1950s. Tell me you have this information or not. I could say I have two or more documents also. . . . I know your links to intelligence and I could go through them, say I have a document that proves this, that you are an American spy. Either you have information, or you do not. Which is it?"

So, it was put up or shut up. I flipped through the pages of the concealment mechanism paper. "We feel that Iraq has had chemical weapons capability delivered which has not been declared to the commission. After the Gulf War, Iraq received indigenous chemical capability under the guise of pesticide production. This is really a chemical weapons production facility."

"Did we hide it, or did we make it?" he asked. He and the others were scribbling notes.

I continued. "We believe that you have hidden it. We also believe that VX is a major problem. We have information that there was some VX produced in salt form for long-term storage, and that this VX can be used for ballistic missile warheads or aerial bombs."

"And all are hidden till now?"

I nodded. "Yes. The rest of the paper is how I think you hid it." I sailed on now; in for a dime, in for a dollar. "On biological warfare, the information we have is that Iraq has a mobile biological production facility. You have fermenters and processing equipment, and also a drying and grinding facility."

Amer Rashid interrupted once more. "So we are hiding a mobile facility?"

"Yes. We also believe that Iraq has held back some anthrax in dry form, possibly in ballistic missile heads. And this leads us to the issue of missiles. We assess, based upon our information, that Iraq has up to two launchers, and five to seven missiles on operational status, and up to twenty-five missiles retained in storage, for example either as engines or as disassembled missiles. We have access to information which we believe to be very sensitive and reliable, and so we believe what I say here to be true."

Amer Rashid was surprisingly calm. "I tell you briefly now," he said. "Your whole idea is based on two things—hidden material and hidden capabilities. The hidden capabilities are fully covered by your inspections and monitoring teams. On hidden material, we agree there is a discrepancy on a few missiles. On chemicals we are converging. On biological, we are working hard as well." He looked at me directly. "What is important is [Resolution] 687. It is the Iraqi dismantling of its weapons, and making sure that Iraq does not reactivate it. All other issues are irrelevant." He put his pen down, signaling an end to the meeting. I had passed the test. If I had not answered Amer Rashid the way I had, I believe that he would have terminated all cooperation with my inspection team.

That night we inspected the headquarters of the Special Republican Guard, following up with unannounced visits to three other SRG sites the next day. On our last day of inspections, we were stopped by the Iraqis from entering two additional SRG sites, and the team was withdrawn. This prompted the Security Council to condemn the Iraqi actions and impose additional sanctions if UNSCOM did not report complete Iraqi cooperation by October 1997. Sanctions were begetting sanctions. UNSCOM had put action behind its words, but we had embarked on the path of confrontation in which we were hostages to the will of a Security Council that seemed less and less willing to enforce its own resolutions.

New York, September 1, 1997. I was to introduce UNSCOM's new executive chairman, Richard Butler, to the "Israeli connection." Butler had only just taken over from Ekéus in July. We were met in the lobby of the elegant hotel by two men, ushered into an elevator, then down a hall and into a suite. There we were greeted by the Israeli ambassador to the U.N., a colonel of Israeli intelligence, and the director of military intelligence, Major General Ayalon.

The purpose of the meeting was to get Butler to embrace the UNSCOM-Israeli special relationship that had been in place since October 1994. After an exchange of handshakes, we got down to business. General Ayalon started off. "We appreciate what UNSCOM does in Iraq, eliminating and reducing the threat we have witnessed in the past decades. It is our intention to keep Iraq out of the game of proliferation taking place in the Middle East. Weapons, ballisitic missiles, unconventional capabilities, and nuclear—everyone wants to acquire these, regardless of what Iraq does. This is threatening not only to Israel but the entire Gulf. It is in our interest to cooperate with UNSCOM. . . . We are at your service in the future."

Butler seemed pleased by this warm welcome. It quickly became clear that he wanted to give the impression that he was the rough-and-tumble rugby player he once had been. "I continue to be stunned by Iraq's anti-UNSCOM industry—it's almost as big as its weapons of mass destruction effort. These people are absolutely determined to defeat the council and UNSCOM and to keep their weapons. They have created this anti-UNSCOM industry, and it is quite large. We face a determined opponent who wants to prevent us from carrying out our mandate. . . . We have to continue to do our work. Our task is big and vital. We need help, because we cannot do it alone. Our appreciation of Israel is great . . . any success we have is indivisible from the help our friends provide us."

Butler and Ayalon both agreed that Saddam Hussein was difficult to fathom. "What's the answer?" Butler asked.

Ayalon shrugged his shoulders. "There is no rational answer. He thinks in another way, his main values [all relate to] power. If we look at him through Western eyes, with Western values, he is impossible to comprehend. He exists. He survives. He has mechanisms in place to control the internal situation. . . . You can never be sure what he will do. When he has the capacity to use weapons of mass destruction, he will. Iraq is the main threat to Israel. Saddam wants to acquire the capabilties to become a regional superpower, to deter us, to dominate the supply of oil in the Persian Gulf. . . . We are determined to prevent him from acquiring these weapons. We did it in the 1980s. We prefer to do this without using force. . . . We are trying hard to find what he conceals."

Butler nodded. "I am convinced of it. We have a rough time ahead politically."

Ayalon again nodded his agreement. "It is quite clear. The Iraqis use tactics of cooperation, but when UNSCOM comes to a sensitive issue such as concealment, Iraq stops you. We need the help of the United States in some fields. . . . I think the CIA should play a more significant role. I know full well the [intelligence] capabilities of the United States and Israel. I can deploy mine, but they need to deploy theirs. This job cannot be done by inspectors alone. We need to find Iraqi hiding activity—there are such activities. We should improve our ability to detect them."

"Two things are clear," Butler interjected. "The United States sees that this is an important task . . . and says that it is supportive. However, there is a case to clarify, how deep their love is . . . we need to make the case to the United States that their pledge of coop-eration must be real and concrete. The Special Commission under Rolf Ekéus did very well. . . . The other reason for our success is the help given to us, together with the fact that we can rely on Iraq to make mistakes. If they do, we can find things. There is a chance. We have to keep doing our job."

Butler understood the stakes. Decades of working toward non-proliferation and disarmament as attainable goals had resulted in a moral consensus regarding the horrible nature of weapons of mass destruction, the need to control them, and the importance of effec-tive verification. The struggle between UNSCOM and Iraq was a watershed event in the history of international arms control. All that Butler, his predecessor, and their fellow arms controllers had strug-gled to achieve was threatened by Iraqi intransigence.

The pity was that neither the Security Council nor the United States seemed to share these conclusions. The Security Council was bent on a return to the status quo ante of pre-war Iraq, where all could benefit from the oil-rich coffers of Saddam Hussein. Russia was owed $8 billion by Iraq. France's largest oil company, Elf Aqui-tane, fell into dire economic straits following the embargo. China, a major supplier of ballistic missile technology to Iraq prior to the Gulf War, was fundamentally opposed to the work of the commis-sion and was double-dealing behind the scenes with the Iraqis. All had permanent seats on the Security Council, and with it veto power. The U.S. seemed satisfied with the containment policy of keeping the economic sanctions in place indefinitely. This put it at odds with the majority of the Security Council and was further exac-erbated by Madeleine Albright's March 1997 declaration that even if Iraq disarmed, economic sanctions would not be lifted as long as Saddam remained in power. This violated the provisions of the Se-curity Council resolution governing the sanctions regime and un-dermined the very framework of UNSCOM's existence.

# 12

# What's in the Briefcase: The Anatomy of an Inspection

UNITED STATES IRAQ POLICY was inching away from a solid foundation in the Security Council mandate. Washington's antipathy toward Saddam Hussein, while understandable, was unsupportable in terms of the implementation of UNSCOM's disarmament mission. The inability of the United States to separate the two made effective support very difficult as the Clinton administration's national security team became overwhelmed by the contradictory requirements of its Iraq policy. One example of the Clinton administration's shallow understanding of the obstacles to disarming Iraq and the lifting of the sanctions was how it handled the issue of inspecting the so-called Presidential sites.

Early in April 1997, I was briefing the National Security Council in the White House Situation Room. Peter Tarnoff, a deputy secretary of state, asked what UNSCOM's next step might be.

We had just finished a very controversial inspection, UNSCOM 182, designed to detect and flush out a covert Iraqi ballistic missile force. The United States had promised to provide intelligence and technical support for this inspection, most of which it either failed to produce or flubbed—such as U-2 aircraft overflying the wrong targets at the wrong times.

Rolf Ekéus, the consummate diplomat, had not cited U.S. bungling as a reason for the negative results of the inspection. Instead, he had talked about an Iraqi "strategic adjustment" in how they had hid their weapons. UNSCOM 182 had in fact foreseen this "strategic adjustment," which was why it had planned to swoop down on several highly sensitive locations related to the SSO and presidential offices at the tail end of the inspection, if necessary. Ekéus, however, had canceled the presidential sites inspection on the grounds that in the course of the operation we had not turned up anything that could justify such action. At the White House, I had just finished briefing a senior group of policymakers on UNSCOM 182, and had made only a passing reference to the failure of U.S. intelligence to adequately support the mission when Tarnoff raised his question about what we would do next.

The Iraqis had further tightened the circle of control over these weapons, I replied, and getting to them meant that UNSCOM would have to start inspecting residences and properties associated with the president of Iraq. There was a general nodding of the heads around the table. Presidential sites were now very much on the agenda.

In September 27, 1997, I was back in Iraq, leading UNSCOM 207. We had just finished inspecting the headquarters of the 2nd Battalion, Special Republican Guard. This was a facility where we had been denied access in June, and we now were reassessing Iraqi willingness to cooperate. The inspection went smoothly, and on completion we moved out to our next objective, a barracks complex housing three companies of the 2nd Battalion—one of which was known to have played a role in transporting biological agent three years earlier.

We knew the area was sensitive, but under the Ekéus modalities compromise such sites were inspectable within well-specified limitations. In keeping with our mandate, we were going in.

Before we could get very far, however, our minder, Hossam Amin, felt it necessary to consult with Tariq Aziz, who wasted little time in declaring the area "sensitive-sensitive," meaning a presidential site, which placed it in a separate category. I called Butler by secure satellite telephone, informing him that we had been stopped. The new UNSCOM chief instructed me to give it one more try, but if the matter was not resolved to my satisfaction, I was to withdraw the team from the site. The Iraqis would not budge, Hossam Amin's hands had been tied by Tariq Aziz. I had no choice but to pull back.

Two days later, at Jabal Makhul, the mountainside site with marble carvings of Saddam in ancient battledress and splendor, we were again stopped in our tracks on the sensitive-site excuse. When I invoked modalities, the matter was kicked upstairs and I was informed this time by Oil Minister Amer Rashid that there had been a misunderstanding. The site was not sensitive but "residential presidential" and thus another off-limits presidential site. Within the span of two days UNSCOM had been introduced to two new categories of sites—"sensitive-sensitive" and "residential-presidential." A crisis certainly seemed to be brewing, and it did not take long for it to explode.

Butler had pretty much made up his mind that my inspection had run its course. The inspection concept of operations had called for the team to undertake three inspections on October 1, starting with a facility suspected as housing the archives of the SSO and Special Republican Guard. The team was then to shift to the SRG headquarters before closing the day's events with an inspection of several buildings centered on a central landmark near the Republican Palace, the Al Hayat building. These sites were known to have accommodated administrative and communications elements of the SSO. Butler was particularly concerned about this stage of the inspection, which was designed to bring the issue of access to a head, and by the night of September 30, he had only authorized the inspection of the first target, judged to be the more benign of the three.

He believed that the two clear cases of denied access—the 2nd Battalion, the SRG (UNSCOM 207), and the Jabal Makhul palace—were sufficient course for action. He planned on taking these cases to the Security Council for their consultation and direction.

This decision did not take me by surprise. I had sensed an understandable squeamishness in Butler over confrontation at this early stage of his tenure as executive chairman. Nevertheless, I had recommended that the Al Hayatt targets be retained, given their association with the SSO—the enforcement arm of the concealment

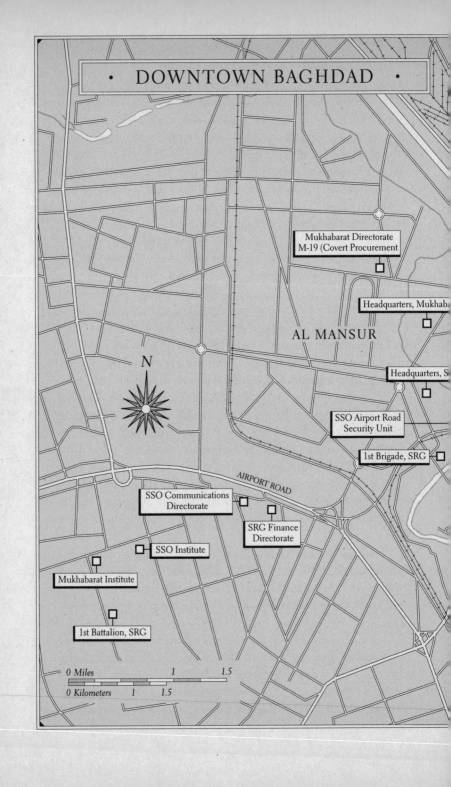

# · DOWNTOWN BAGHDAD ·

Mukhabarat Directorate
M-19 (Covert Procurement

Headquarters, Mukhab

AL MANSUR

Headquarters, S

SSO Airport Road
Security Unit

1st Brigade, SRG

AIRPORT ROAD

SSO Communications
Directorate

SRG Finance
Directorate

SSO Institute

Mukhabarat Institute

1st Battalion, SRG

N

0 Miles          1          1.5
0 Kilometers    1     1.5

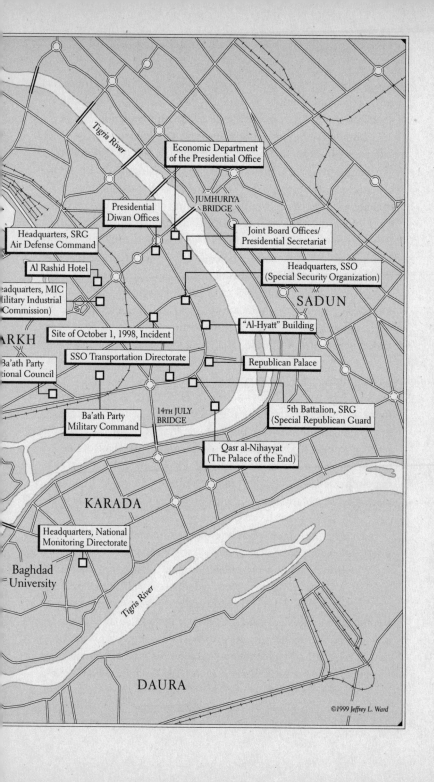

Tigris River

Economic Department
of the Presidential Office

JUMHURIYA
BRIDGE

Presidential
Diwan Offices

Joint Board Offices/
Presidential Secretariat

Headquarters, SRG
Air Defense Command

Headquarters, SSO
(Special Security Organization)

Al Rashid Hotel

SADUN

eadquarters, MIC
ilitary Industrial
Commission)

"Al-Hyatt" Building

ARKH

Site of October 1, 1998, Incident

SSO Transportation Directorate

Republican Palace

Ba'ath Party
tional Council

5th Battalion, SRG
(Special Republican Guard)

Ba'ath Party
Military Command

14TH JULY
BRIDGE

Qasr al-Nihayyat
(The Palace of the End)

KARADA

Headquarters, National
Monitoring Directorate

Baghdad
University

Tigris River

DAURA

©1999 Jeffrey L. Ward

mechanism—and my desire to send a clear signal to the Iraqis that no organizational entity, no matter how sacrosanct, was above inspection. Butler, however, overrode my recommendations.

Butler gave me his decision during a satellite telephone conversation and I informed Hossam Amin that UNSCOM 207 was over. We would withdraw to Bahrain on October 2. Hossam Amin and the other Iraqis were overjoyed. They did not like these concealment inspections and were nervous the entire time our teams were in country. Despite the two cases of access denial, the Iraqis believed that they had emerged with a relatively clean bill of health and that the commission would have no choice but to issue a positive report to the Security Council. This was not just wishful thinking. Iraq's two principal allies in the Security Council, Russia and France, were in close and continuous contact with Tariq Aziz throughout this period. Iraq was certain that a political compromise could be reached concerning access to presidential sites, one that would neutralize their denials of access to the UNSCOM 207 mission.

Normally, in closing down an inspection, I would debrief the team on the day's activities and then release them to prepare for the next day's departure from Iraq. But I was not finished just yet. I felt that Butler was missing the big picture, and it was my duty to point this out to him. I resolved to do something about it, to try one last time to convince him of the merits for reviving the inspections. During discussions with Charles Duelfer earlier in the week, I had been alerted to the potential importance of a recent laboratory discovery.

Dr. Dianne Seaman was a no-nonsense chief inspector of considerable experience, whose stern, taciturn demeanor masked a warm personality and a remarkable human being. She had an insightful, probing mind, and her credentials in biology (she taught microbiology at the University of Florida) made her one of the most formidable members of UNSCOM. Her knowledge and demeanor also caused her to be singled out by Iraq as a perennial troublemaker. The latest troublemaking centered around events that had transpired a few days earlier, when on September 25 Dianne and her team of biologists conducted a no-notice inspection of the Iraqi National Food and Drug Examination Laboratory.

Dianne had decided that for this particular inspection she would alter her normal inspection procedures. Instead of meeting with the director for a cup of tea to explain the purpose of her visit, she surprised Dr. Hilal al-Tikriti, head of the Food and Drug laboratory, leaving him standing in the main entrance as she swept by and proceeded straight up the staircase to the second floor. Approaching the second-floor landing, Dianne spotted two men carrying heavy briefcases and trying to sneak out the back exit of the building.

The two men, who turned out to be members of the SSO, bolted, at first holding a door shut to block her, then running down a corridor. This created an almost comical scene as the diminutive biologist chased after them, forcing them into a laboratory room. Aided by members of her team, who had by this time caught up with her, she was able to take physical control of the two briefcases.

The two Iraqis seemed unduly nervous, but Dianne kept her cool. The first thing she did was check the contents of the briefcases. They contained documents, biological test kits, and unidentified biological samples in test tubes. Dianne, who has a fair grasp of Arabic, examined the documents, somewhat startled to see that many of them bore the letterhead of the Office of the Presidency, Special Security Organization. Furthermore, some of them originated from Staff 7 of the SSO, the Biological Activities Section. Previously alerted by UNSCOM to the potential importance of such documents, Dianne handed the briefcases to one of her inspectors and ordered him to leave immediately for the Baghdad Monitoring and Verification Center, UNSCOM headquarters in Iraq. As her inspector left the room through one doorway, a group of a dozen or so agitated Iraqi minders burst through another.

"Where are the documents, Dr. Seaman?" the senior minder demanded. But it was too late. By then they were in an UNSCOM car speeding back to the BMVC.

Dianne's subsequent analysis of the documents disclosed the existence of a testing program supervised by al-Tikriti's lab that involved a highly toxic biological agent, *Clostridium perfringens*. This substance causes gas gangrene and ultimately a particularly horrible death. It had been weaponized by Iraq in the late 1980s as part of its biological weapons program.

In her examination of the documents, Dianne found nothing that might explain the purpose of the *Clostridium perfringens* material and the related training that had taken place in al-Tikriti's lab. Al-Tikriti refused to answer any of her questions about the SSO's role in the matter. This did little to alleviate her suspicions and she asked me, as UNSCOM's SSO specialist, if I had any ideas on how to proceed.

I was convinced that she had an issue that demanded attention. The commission had been trying assiduously to find a link between the SSO and prohibited weapons that could be brought before the Security Council (almost all our information on the subject prior to her discovery was based on highly sensitive intelligence that could not be presented to the entire council given the relationship that certain members, notably France and Russia, had with Iraq). UNSCOM had good reason to believe that sensitive information had, in the past, found its way from both French and Russian sources into the hands of Iraq. We now had such a link. But Butler's decision to end the current inspections threatened to let this opportunity slip away. On September 30, I had asked Dianne to request a meeting at the Iraqi National Monitoring Directorate with al-Tikriti and other key Iraqi figures to discuss the SSO involvement. In addition, I had asked Dianne to send to UNSCOM headquarters in New York, via secure fax, selected translations of the SSO briefcase documents. When I returned to the BMVC from the last inspection site, I tracked Dianne down in her office and asked if the meeting was on. She said yes, it would go at 8:00 P.M.

For the first time in days, I felt optimistic. Something had to be done to regain the initiative against Iraq, and I believed I had the solution. I turned to Chris Cobb-Smith, my deputy chief inspector and operations officer, formulating a contingency plan in my head as I spoke. Standing six-four, 225 pounds of solid muscle, Chris was a retired major in the Royal Artillery Commando Battery, which made him a former Marine like me. He had started working for the commission in early 1996, shortly after leaving active duty, and by September 1997 had served on seven inspections, six with me. We worked well as teammates and had become good friends. Chris, with his gregarious nature and infectious, booming laugh, was also one of the best operations men I'd ever met. However complicated my inspection concepts might be, I could rely on Chris: every team member would be briefed to the last detail and every piece of equipment would be at the right place at the right time. Chris was aware of my propensity for rapid planning, and could bend any way to accommodate my fluid style.

"Look," I began, "we have a unique opportunity to inspect SSO headquarters. We have a signed NIS [Notification of Inspection Site—an official UNSCOM authorization document]. We may never get the chairman to sign one again. It's now or never. I'm going to give it a shot. I need you to keep the boys occupied, ready to either move out again on two hours' notice or fly home tomorrow. Either way, it needs to be kept low key."

Chris broke a big smile. "Great. No problems, mate. You do what you have to do. I'll have the team cleaning and packing, and we will get together every hour for situation updates." Chris knew the site in question. We had spent many hours in Bahrain prior to this inspection poring over maps and U-2 photographs, memorizing every building, every turn in the road. We already had a plan. We only lacked the order to execute it. I hoped to get that before the day was out.

I left Chris in our team room and proceeded to make my way across the building to Dianne Seaman in the Biological Monitoring Team. We were in agreement over my proposed course of action. Dianne would go to the meeting for discussions with the Iraqis about the contents of the briefcases. I would accompany her as an expert on the SSO. We would play good cop, bad cop. Dianne would patiently try to engage the Iraqis on the subject and when stonewalled (as we expected her to be), I would take over and demand immediate cooperation. If Iraq refused to cooperate, I would launch a night inspection of the SSO in search of Dianne's answers. Surprise was the key. As to Butler's concerns about being too provocative, my hope was that he could be persuaded by the compelling evidence Dianne had uncovered.

My conversation with the chairman was short and sweet. I made my case and he bought it. "This is the right thing to do," Butler said. "We have every reason to take this course of action." It was now time to put the plan into action.

We drove to the Iraqi National Monitoring Directorate for the 8:00 P.M. appointment. Three cars, eight inspectors. The Iraqi officials, expecting to see Dianne and her colleagues, were surprised when they saw us as well. The Iraqis did not know what to make of this; they had believed my inspection to be over.

We met in the main conference room, the Iraqis on one side of the table, UNSCOM on the other. Dianne explained my presence as an expert on the SSO. The Iraqis, headed by Dr. Billal, the senior minder for biology, kept glancing at me. Both sides had video cameras recording the session. Joining Billal were al-Tikriti and Riyadh Abd al-Rahman Faisal al-Duri, an SSO officer attached to al-Tikriti's lab and one of the men nabbed by Dianne in the briefcase tussle. Several other Iraqis were present as note-takers.

The discussions got off to a bad start. The Iraqis evaded Dianne's repeated questioning about the role of the SSO in al-Tikriti's laboratory. There were no records that defined this relationship, they maintained, either at the laboratory or at the SSO. The briefcase documents, they said, stemmed from an agreement with al-Tikriti to conduct biological testing in support of the presidency and other important Iraqi officials, but there was no written agreement. Dianne stated that she found this inconceivable. Al-Tikriti insisted that his facility was nothing more than a food-testing lab.

Dianne then questioned al-Duri, the SSO officer. He admitted he was in the science section of the SSO but refused to discuss the role of the SSO in this matter. Regarding Staff 7, Al-Tikriti said it was a group that he headed, then he downgraded it to a mere label used between the SSO and his department to refer to the samples and sampling process. After about forty minutes of this verbal sparring, I glanced at Dianne, who nodded for me to spring into action. I broke in on al-Tikriti and looked Billal in the eye. "UNSCOM had two ways of conducting its work here," I said. "It would be easier on everyone present if the Iraqi side would provide full and frank answers to our questions." I paused for effect. "But UNSCOM has other means, inspections, which will be more intrusive and have greater impact on Iraq. This is not a threat, but a statement of fact. The executive chairman had instructed Dr. Seaman and me to get to the bottom of this issue. I now recommend that the Iraqi side take a break for five minutes and consider how to proceed."

Billal responded by saying that the Iraqis were telling the truth and that there was no need for a break. We agreed to a brief recess anyway and when we reconvened, the Iraqis had been joined by Hossam Amin. He stated that the inconsistencies in the Iraqi accounts were simply mistakes or failures of memory. We kept going around in circles. Finally, I told al-Tikriti, "Clearly, you have taken a decision not to provide us with any meaningful response to our questions and concerns." I declared the meeting over, then turned to Hossam Amin. "Under orders from the executive chairman, I am informing you that we will be undertaking an inspection tonight. The team will be assembled, ready for departure from the BMVC, at 2300 hours." I requested that Iraq provide the requisite minder support, and that they be ready to depart the BMVC at the same time.

Hossam Amin sagged. It was all a misunderstanding, he said, sadly it seemed. But when he got up he became quite distraught. "Iraq does not recognize night inspections." He spoke sharply, looking at me. "You, Mr. Ritter, have betrayed me. You told me today that UNSCOM 207 had completed its mission. Now it is clear you had intended all along to create a confrontation." He was red-faced, trembling with anger.

I reminded him that al-Tikriti's unsatisfactory answers to Dianne Seaman's and my questioning had left UNSCOM with no other choice but to do an inspection. The blame rested with the Iraqis, I insisted.

Hossam Amin was incensed. Pointing to the ceiling, he bellowed, "I condemn you in the eyes of God! I condemn you in the name of the Iraqi people! You are a criminal, carrying out criminal acts against Iraq!" As quickly as it rose, however, his anger subsided. He assumed his usual fatalistic posture. "We will be there tonight. You will not succeed in your scheme to provoke the Iraqi people. God will judge you." He turned on his heels and exited, followed silently by the remainder of his colleagues.

Our team was aghast, and the degree of emotion exhibited by Hossam Amin did not bode well. But the act was done; we were committed. We drove out of the NMD parking lot at 9:30. We had ninety minutes to get the inspection team ready to move out. I called Chris on the radio, alerting him to the need to prepare the team for action.

We pulled into the BMVC compound at 9:50. The building and surrounding parking area was bustling with activity. Following my earlier instructions, all inspection equipment had been packed for transport to Bahrain the next morning, but it was now being un-packed—boxes containing radios, batteries, cameras, satellite com-munication terminals, generators, food, and water. Everything we needed for a lengthy inspection in a field environment was being re-assembled and repackaged for immediate use. Under the glow of the overhead lighting, the scene took on an almost Hollywood-like set-ting—the roar of diesel engines, shouts of inspectors, the banging of boxes scraped along the ground. But this was real.

I sprinted upstairs. Chris was huddled over a map with some of the subteam leaders in charge of a single, four-man carload of in-spectors. This was our basic operational unit. He was briefing them on the specific actions of each subteam and individual inspector. He looked up from the map, smiling. "Good to go, boss. The team will assemble at 10:45 for your brief." Everything was in order.

I proceeded to the secure telephone, called Butler and briefed him. He was surprisingly calm, reiterating that this was the right thing to do. Iraq's refusal to discuss the relationship between the SSO and the discovered biological material made his decision to inspect the Special Security Organization headquarters a just one. This was not a provocation on our part, he said. It was disarmament. He was right.

At 10:45 sharp I entered the team room. The inspectors were assembled. There was an air of excitement. I looked around for Di-anne; she and her team were present as well. My presentation was brief and to the point.

"Based on Iraq's refusal to discuss with the commission certain topics of relevance to the commission's mandate," I said, "the execu-tive chairman has instructed that this team, working together with members of the Biological Monitoring Group, conduct a night in-spection of certain facilities in the vicinity of Baghdad. The exact lo-cation will be briefed to you in your vehicles on the way to the site itself."

This was standard talk. I moved on to more special instructions. "The site designated for inspection is perhaps the most sensitive site which the commission has undertaken to inspect ever." This hit hard. All eyes were squarely on me now. I continued. "Emotions are high. Iraq does not want this inspection to take place. Your safety is paramount; there is nothing we are doing that is worth getting anyone injured or killed. As such, it is essential that we proceed slowly and carefully. No sudden actions. There will be armed soldiers around, and they are under orders to shoot to kill any personnel attempting to gain unauthorized entry. We will have minders, and it is their responsibility to facilitate our entry into the site in question. There will be no shouting, no shoving on the part of inspectors. We will remain calm. We will not provoke. If everyone follows these instructions, then we should get through this event with no problems. Any questions?"

There were none. It was 10:50, ten minutes to departure. I turned the briefing over to Chris, who presented the order of march. Chris's vehicle would be in the lead, navigating to the site. My vehicle would follow second, Dianne third, our operations van (a large UNIMOG four-wheel-drive ambulance, painted in U.N. white) fourth, with the remainder of the team following, fourteen vehicles in all.

I went downstairs to join with my vehicle mates. The driver tonight was a French air force officer with several inspections under his belt. I'll call him Patrick Herbert, and I'll change the names of all the men on the team, except Chris's. Patrick's understanding of English was workable, but he sometimes appeared to blank out on what was being said. However, driving the vehicle was a point of pride for him, and since my vehicle was not responsible for navigation tonight, I gave it no further thought.

Also in my vehicle was Bill Turner, a warrant officer in the U.S. Army who spoke Arabic fluently and had extensive knowledge of the Iraqi security and intelligence organizations. Like Patrick, Bill was a veteran of several inspections and an invaluable team member who had proven his worth on more than one occasion. I would normally have had a third inspector with me, who would have been driving and navigating. Mark Sanders, a British Foreign Service officer and my reports officer, had been assigned this evening to ride with Chris. Chris normally had two personnel in his vehicle besides himself— Grant Gibson, an Australian army medic-communicator, and John

170   ENDGAME

Sissons, a British linguist. Given the complexity of the command and control requirements of this inspection, Chris had included Mark as a fourth inspector. This had been Mark's first series of inspections, but in the past two weeks he had shown a level of competence that offset any lack of in-country experience.

At 11:00 P.M. sharp I departed the BMVC compound to meet with the assembled Iraqi minders. The remainder of the team stayed behind, awaiting my signal to move. I wanted to set the tone for tonight's work and try to smooth any rough edges that might exist as a result of my run-in with Hossam Amin. The minders were our guarantee of safety; it would do us well to have them in good spirits tonight. The senior Iraqi present was Colonel Basim, who was dressed in full uniform. I walked forward, offering my hand. We shook, smiling at each other. A good sign. This was the first time I had seen Basim in uniform, and I expressed my surprise. He had always worn a coat and tie.

The pleasantries finished, I got down to business. I noted that this was likely to be a tense inspection, and that it was therefore particularly important that we talk things through and keep lines of communication open between each other. I stated, formally, that UNSCOM was to be given immediate and unrestricted access to a site which would be designated on our arrival. After that, Iraq could say whether it was a sensitive site requiring that special modalities be applied. I emphasized that if the team were stopped en route, the NMD minders would be obliged to facilitate our continued movement until we had arrived at the site.

I pointed out that the realities of the situation were well understood by myself and my team. I accepted that we should give the Iraqis a reasonable time to secure our passage, but, if we were blocked and no progress was made in getting us back on the road, I would have no choice but to report the Iraqi actions to the executive chairman. My goal was to maintain calm. If a problem arose that we could not handle on the ground, we would report to our authorities. We both were just doing our jobs, I reminded him, and we had a long record of working well with one another, even when we disagreed.

Colonel Basim stated that he fully understood and agreed with

my approach. He then got all the minders—there were over forty—
into a huddle and briefed them at length. Once Basim signaled that
he was ready, I called Chris and the remainder of the team forward.
We departed the BMVC at 11:15, heading north down the Canal
Highway.

We drove through Baghdad slowly and deliberately. The Iraqi
minders in their vehicles hovered on the flanks of our convoy. We
wound past the huge headquarters of the Amn al Amm secret political police, through the downtown area, and on toward the Four-
teenth of July Bridge. As we crossed the bridge, the Republican
Palace loomed to our right, bathed in a dull yellow light. The Iraqis
expected us to turn right into the palace and seemed disoriented
when the convoy kept moving, passing the palace gate and continuing into the next major intersection. Here we turned right and drove
past the MIC headquarters compound. The Iraqi minders were re-
lieved that we didn't turn into the palace. In the Iraqi radio jeeps, the
operators were speaking animatedly into their microphones, reporting our progress to their superiors.

Approaching the next major intersection, I knew we were getting close. I ordered the convoy slowed to twenty kilometers per
hour and emergency flashers turned on. There was no sign of a
checkpoint at the junction, although our review of the U-2 imagery
indicated there should be. The roads were empty except for our convoy and one or two passenger cars going in the opposite direction. At
the intersection, the traffic light was green. Noting no particular
concern on the part of the minders, Chris instructed Grant, his
driver, to proceed through the intersection. As he did so, the traffic
signal changed to yellow, prompting Grant to accelerate, following
standard practice that once an inspection convoy had preceded
through a traffic signal, the minders would block traffic until the intersection was cleared, even if the light was against us.

Chris's vehicle crossed the intersection at 11:37. As Grant ac-
celerated through the signal, a young soldier from the Special Republican Guard, who was stationed in a sentry box on the junction
to our left, ran out and signaled the rest of the convoy to stop. Chris's
car kept moving forward, unaware of the situation immediately behind him. Two Iraqi vehicles, one belonging to the NMD, the other

to the traffic police escort provided to our convoys, saw that Chris was moving ahead unescorted. They sped through the intersection after him, nearly running over the now frantic young soldier, who waved his AK-47 and slapped the Iraqi vehicles with his hand, trying to get them to stop. The next vehicle in the procession was mine.

I had been closely following everything around me, and was aware that a dangerous situation now existed. The soldier was standing right in front of our vehicle, looking at the Iraqi vehicles racing past him. His weapon was now at the ready. Patrick, behind the wheel, continued to inch our car forward, toward the soldier. I turned to Patrick. "Let's stop the vehicle right here, Patrick," I said. "Stop now." Patrick continued to stare straight ahead, oblivious to my orders. He kept moving forward. The soldier had turned his full attention to our vehicle. His eyes were wild with fear. He raised his weapon at our vehicle. Still, Patrick kept moving forward, looking for an opportunity to steer around the soldier, to follow behind Chris's vehicle. The soldier started shouting at us, and chambered a round into his weapon. I could see his fingers setting the safety switch to the fire position.

"Patrick, stop the car now!" I ordered. The car kept inching on. The soldier, by this time screaming at us and in a state of sheer panic, lowered himself into a crouch, aimed his weapon at our vehicle, and prepared to open fire. "STOP THE DAMN CAR NOW, YOU DUMB SON OF A BITCH!" I was shouting at the top of my voice, my composure momentarily lost. Patrick finally snapped out of his trance and braked. As we lurched to a full stop, my eyes were fixed on the soldier immediately in front of us. I was waiting for the barrel to start spitting flame.

Out of the corner of my eye I saw a green uniform. It was Colonel Basim, who, seeing what was happening, jumped out of his vehicle and raced toward the soldier, his arms spread wide, yelling at him to calm down. This act undoubtedly saved our lives. The soldier pointed his weapon at Basim, still screaming. I was sure Basim was going to be shot down in front of us. Emerging from my left was a uniformed officer of the SSO, who rushed over to assist the soldier. The SSO officer pulled his automatic pistol from his holster and cocked it, pointing it first at Basim, and then, moving across the front of my vehicle, reorienting it at me, aiming it square at my head.

We stayed frozen that way for a few seconds. The soldier, alternately pointing his weapon at Basim and our vehicle, was yelling at Basim in a panicked voice, with Basim shouting back to calm down. The SSO officer, his pistol at my head, shifted his eyes back and forth to Basim and me. The slightest false move on anyone's part would have resulted in gunfire and, undoubtedly, death.

While this played out in front of me, Chris's vehicle kept moving forward. He was followed by the Iraqi minder vehicle and the traffic police car, speeding to catch up with him. About 300 meters ahead of Chris, I could see soldiers moving around a vehicle checkpoint. Machine guns were being leveled at the vehicles rushing toward them. Rocket-propelled grenade launchers were brought out. In my mind's eye I could see what was going to happen. The Iraqis down the road were going to fire off some warning shots, or worse. This would serve as a trigger to set off our still panicky soldier and his SSO partner. The situation had disaster written all over it. I grabbed the radio handset in my car, and called out over the general frequency. "Chris, these bastards have guns. You need to stop right now." I tried my best to sound calm, but I'm sure there was an edge to my voice.

Fortunately, Chris had realized that he was proceeding alone even before receiving my radio call. He ordered his car to slow down, enabling the Iraqi vehicles chasing him to skid to a stop in front of him, blocking his forward progress. Grant brought his vehicle calmly to a stop, without any screeching of tires. He was fully aware of the two SRG soldiers who had dropped to their knees some 100 meters ahead, aiming their rifles squarely at his vehicle.

Chris had not stopped a moment too soon. Later that night the Iraqis informed me that had Chris proceeded another ten meters, the soldiers at the roadblock would have opened fire. We were saved by the thinnest of margins, a matter of seconds.

The situation reached a kind of equilibrium. I got on the radio again and spoke to the rest of the convoy, telling everyone to stay put, not to move until I gave them instructions to do so. The soldier to my front had lowered his weapon by this time, holding it at the ready. He was still quite agitated. The SSO officer had likewise lowered his pistol, although he had yet to put it back in his holster. Basim, white-faced, was still positioned between the soldier and our vehicle. I slowly opened my door and exited the vehicle. My chief concern at this point was the safety of Chris and his fellow inspectors, who were in a precarious situation a few hundred meters in front.

I approached Basim. He looked at me, his voice shrill with tension. "Mr. Scott, you need to get Mr. Chris back here now. He is in danger." I couldn't have agreed more. After receiving assurances from Basim that the situation had stabilized to the point that Chris could move without getting shot, I ordered Chris over the radio to return to my location. He closed with the main convoy at 11:43, and positioned himself to my immediate rear. I was now the lead vehicle. Only six minutes had passed since Chris's car had driven through the intersection, the longest six minutes of my life.

I walked to Chris's location, trying to put some structure to this situation. "Get the SATCOM [satellite telephone] up. I need to talk to the chairman now. Ensure that everyone stays in their vehicles, and keep movements to a minimum." Chris seemed oblivious to the danger he had been in, a real cool customer. "Right, boss," he responded and went off to the command van where the communicators were situated. Right about now a car backfired near the rear of the convoy. Everyone flinched, thinking the worst, then calm returned once the source of the blast had been identified.

Basim was off with the Iraqi minders, obviously instructing them the way I had with my team. I walked a few steps ahead, trying to put everything together. Other than my outburst at Patrick, I had been quite in control of myself, and was able to think clearly. Now, alone, the reality of what had almost happened hit. For the first time, I became nervous.

Suddenly, a half-dozen white sedans came racing into the intersection. The doors flew open and out came plainclothes SSO officers. They approached Basim, waving their pistols. They were obviously keyed up. Dressed in white shirts and pants, with highly polished black shoes, these were the boys from Tikrit, all thick necks, mustaches, barrel chests, and swagger, filled with unflinching support for their president and hatred for anyone seen as a threat. Well, we sure as hell weren't there to deliver flowers, and their uneasiness was understandable.

After exchanging heated words with Basim, they gestured in my direction, brandishing their pistols and scowling menacingly. Several returned to their vehicles, and drove off at high speed toward the palace grounds. The others strutted across the road, chests puffed out, pistols tucked into their belts, their coal-black eyes burning into me. I stared back. Behind me I could feel the similar stares of my inspectors drilling into the back of my head, as they looked to me for guidance.

Someone, Mark, I think, came up from behind and told me that Oil Minister Amer Rashid was on his way to the scene. Another voice, probably Chris's, informed me that the communicators were having trouble getting a clear satellite link to New York. A slight breeze blew against my face. Baghdad may have been cooling down, but at this intersection, things were just beginning to heat up. There were serious faces and drawn weapons surrounding me. Here I was, in the heart of Baghdad, smack in the middle of a storm of my own creation. No cavalry was going to ride to the rescue. It was up to me to get us out of this.

I lifted the bill of my blue U.N. baseball cap and scratched my head. "Welcome to UNSCOM," I muttered to myself. I looked around once again—a few inspectors standing toe-to-toe with the elite of Iraq's security apparatus. Blue hats against automatic weapons. This wasn't war but it sure as hell wasn't peace. Amer Rashid arrived, and it became clear that we would not be allowed to proceed. The team withdrew.

This evening's outing had yielded an indisputable case of denial of access. In a matter of hours, I would deliver all the facts Butler needed to make that case to the Security Council. Our future would then lie in their hands. They would rule whether this night had been worth the effort or whether we had been engaged in nothing more than the futile pursuit of politically unattainable objectives.

# 13

# Black-Umbrella Days

RICHARD BUTLER, true to his word, delivered a scathing report to the Security Council based on our account of the incident at the Baghdad intersection.

He would not vouch for Iraqi compliance with its disarmament obligations until his inspectors could inspect. And it was clear that what we wanted to inspect was something the Iraqis did not want us to see. The Security Council adopted Resolution 1134 in October 1997, which imposed additional sanctions. Unlike previous resolutions, however, this one passed without a unanimous consensus. Ten members voted yes, but five abstained, including France, Russia, and China. The Iraqis viewed this as a split in the council, and they made an immediate move to exploit it. They announced that they would no longer allow Americans to participate in inspections. Then at the end of October 1997, they expelled all the U.S. inspectors. Butler responded by pulling all UNSCOM inspectors out of Iraq. The IAEA followed suit, and there was suddenly a full-blown crisis.

The realization that Saddam was not bluffing hit Washington hard. No one had anticipated a crisis of this magnitude. The Pentagon scrambled to mobilize a military force to counter Saddam. At the State Department and the White House, Secretary of State Madeleine Albright and National Security Adviser Sandy Berger struggled to reassemble a coalition they thought they had in place.

The poor showing on the vote for Resolution 1134 made the Clinton team uneasy about the foundation of international support for military action.

Desperate for an alternative, the U.S. agreed to a Russian-brokered deal, created by Foreign Minister Yevgeny Primakov. Russia would get Iraq to allow resumption of inspections in exchange for its active engagement in the Security Council on behalf of Iraq. The French government gave its full support. In early November 1997, Primakov called for a meeting of the five permanent members of the Security Council to discuss this approach. Secretary Albright cut short her visit to India to attend, and the deal was sealed. Once again, the Clinton national security team found itself reacting to an initiative put forth by others, in this case a very pro-Iraq Russia.

Primakov, a longtime Arabist and friend of the Iraqi leadership, had a history of questionable dealings with the Iraqis. Senior Iraqi defectors from the Istachbarat claimed that Primakov was often paid by the Iraqis to spread pro-Iraqi propaganda through Russian and other foreign newspapers in the guise of reporting. During an inspection of the covert operations directorate (M-4) of the Mukhabarat, I saw lists of Russian journalists that the document indicated were on the Iraqi payroll. In 1993, while serving as the head of the Russian Foreign Intelligence Service, Primakov was lobbying for Russian acquiescence to the establishment of Iraqi covert procurement fronts in Moscow. This sort of friendly relationship with Iraq led me and others to doubt whether Russia was conducting fair and objective diplomacy.

Part of the Russian plan to support the Iraqis lay in the notion of calling an emergency session of the Special Commission. UNSCOM's semiannual meeting to review progress (or lack thereof) had taken place in October, but the Russians felt that the new situation required reconvening to provide guidance for UNSCOM's future dealings with Iraq. The emergency session was scheduled for November 21. The Russian, French, and Chinese representatives got together in advance to plan strategy for this meeting. Their goal was to get Special Commission approval to close several of the weapons files, including the nuclear, missile, and chemical files. They also sought to reduce U.S. influence by restructuring UNSCOM's staff. However, their strategy backfired. The strength of the technical arguments put forward by the UNSCOM experts in defending their positions in each of the weapons areas, combined with the clear record of Iraqi noncompliance, carried the day. The emergency session ended with a ringing endorsement of the work of the commission, making a case for strengthening—not weakening—the resources available to the inspectors. Primakov, however, had an ace up his sleeve—Madeleine Albright. The two had somehow hit it off and shared a mutual respect. Albright was determined not to be seen as undermining Primakov's diplomacy. Her stance would have direct repercussions for the work of UNSCOM.

UNSCOM had built an impressive inspection machine designed to investigate Iraqi acts of concealment. Butler had authorized the creation of the counterconcealment unit in August 1997, formalizing an activity that had existed unofficially during the tenure of his predecessor. This unit, which I headed, consisted of a small staff in New York to manage the intelligence liaison between UNSCOM and supporting governments. It also directed an operational team deployed to Baghdad with Chris Cobb-Smith as its chief. This was as finely tuned an instrument of on-site inspection as had ever existed in UNSCOM's history, composed of professionals who could carry out an inspection of any location in Iraq within hours of notification from New York. Chris's team also conducted the most sensitive information gathering on behalf of UNSCOM, including the operation of communications intercept equipment. These were stallions, and they needed to be run. The Iraqi refusal to cooperate with UNSCOM, followed by the ejection of the American inspectors, had put a damper on their activities. But when in late November—as part of the Primakov compromise—the Iraqis agreed to the return of the inspectors, both the team and I were champing at the bit.

Our opportunity arose just before Christmas 1997. Butler went to Iraq to discuss a wide range of issues, and in an illuminating exchange with Tariq Aziz, appeared to draw the battle lines over the issue of UNSCOM inspections of presidential sites.

BUTLER: Finally, with respect to presidential and sovereign [i.e., ministries] sites, what am I to say [to the council]? Are they absolutely off-limits in the view of the Iraqis?

AZIZ:  Read the sentence in the presidential statement about respect of security, dignity, and sovereignty of Iraq. . . . That is the interpretation. . . .

BUTLER: Yes, but help me here. I know what that says. I am very well aware what went into it and how closely it was negotiated. I am asking for your help. What do I tell the council? That Iraq's interpretation of this concept of sovereignty and dignity means that in this category of sites there can be no inspections?

AZIZ:  Yes. Tell them that.

While Butler was in Baghdad talking with Tariq Aziz, I was in Bahrain, assembling a team of inspectors who would join up with Chris to carry out a series of inspections relating to Iraqi concealment efforts, including some in the category of presidential sites. We were to wait in Bahrain until Butler finished with Tariq Aziz so that Butler could provide specific guidance concerning our mission. He flew in from Baghdad on December 16. In Bahrain, he held off on signing authorization paperwork until he could get a feel for how the inspection would be supported back in Washington. He spent the afternoon on the phone with National Security Council and State Department officials at the U.S. embassy in the capital city of Manama.

We had scheduled a dinner at the Manama Holiday Inn. It was fish night, a local weekly gastronomic event. There were four of us at the table: Butler, Duelfer, Chris, and I. While we were eating, Duelfer received a call on his cell phone. He stepped away to take the call and in a few moments came back. The White House had given the go-ahead. There was now an air of excitement around the table. The U.S. had, for the past few months, built an impressive array of military force in the region. The White House had grown increasingly frustrated with the pace and intentions of the Russian diplomatic initiatives and was in no mood to be dictated to by the Iraqis. Primakov and the Russians had promised to put pressure on Baghdad to heed its disarmament obligations, but instead they had become mere mouthpieces for Tariq Aziz. The glow of the Primakov-Albright deal had faded away. Tariq Aziz's stance on presidential sites was the last straw. The decision was taken to support UNSCOM's desire to inspect certain facilities inside presidential areas.

After a false start, I was back in Iraq in January 1998, heading UNSCOM 227, which had an ambitious agenda. The inspection machinery was in full swing, and I moved into action on the 12th with over forty inspectors. We inspected seven sites that day and found ourselves hot on the trail of a 1995 Iraqi program of testing biological and chemical agent on humans.

We had received a detailed intelligence report on this human-guinea-pig matter, which included the involvement of the DGS in rounding up prisoners from Abu Ghraib. We had dates, names, and activities to help us uncover a paper trail as proof that such tests had indeed taken place. At Abu Ghraib and DGS headquarters we discovered that all the files corresponding to our dates were missing. It was clear that the Iraqis had become alarmed. That same day, Iraq issued a statement refusing further cooperation with my team on the grounds that it was dominated by American and British inspectors. The truth was that my forty-one inspectors were nationals of seventeen countries. A more plausible explanation was that the Iraqis wanted to halt our work until they could clean up any loose ends from the human-experiment program before we could get our hands on any evidence.

Three days later our team was pulled out. Butler flew to Baghdad hoping to caulk the cracks, only to be scolded and insulted by Tariq Aziz. He returned to New York, reporting the latest breach to the Security Council. The drums of war began to beat along the Potomac.

Washington now had a casus belli. The Clinton national security team initiated a set of talks with members of Congress to elicit their support and launched a concerted public relations offensive to bring the message to the American people. This, however, turned into a major embarrassment for the administration when Albright, Berger, and Defense Secretary William Cohen went to Ohio State

University for a nationally televised public forum to justify action against Iraq. The ill-prepared trio laid out a mishmash of incomprehensible arguments that collapsed under a barrage of withering questions from a savvy audience. Their poor performance all but guaranteed that in such circumstances military force would not yet be unleashed.

Watching the televised debacle along with the rest of the foreign principals was a new player on the block, recently appointed U.N. Secretary General Kofi Annan. Soon motions were being put forward by the French, the Russians, and even the secretary-general's office to seize the moment and send Kofi Annan to Baghdad in a last-ditch effort to forestall hostilities. The U.S., playing hard to get, made it clear to Kofi Annan that as far as it was concerned he was going to Baghdad to demand compliance with the Security Council resolutions. This was reinforced by the dispatch of a special U.S. delegation, led by U.N. Ambassador Bill Richardson, to brief Kofi Annan on Washington's "red lines" — the nonnegotiable points.

Two days later, however, Secretary of State Albright flew to New York in secrecy, went to Kofi Annan's home, and told him to disregard the Richardson briefing. Unbeknownst to Richardson, she assured the secretary general that the U.S. would back any agreement that allowed the inspectors to return to Iraq. This was music to Kofi Annan's ears, and on February 23, the fateful Memorandum of Understanding was signed between the secretary general and Tariq Aziz. It established new procedures for the inspection of presidential sites. The deal was a sham, and we at UNSCOM knew it. We had a copy of a highly confidential letter from Tariq Aziz to Kofi Annan, dated the same day as the Memorandum of Understanding, that constituted a secret protocol. It outlined Tariq Aziz's view of an unwritten agreement with Kofi Annan that the inspections of presidential sites would be a one-time event, after which the secretary general would seek to get the economic sanctions lifted.

Kofi Annan hailed the Memorandum of Understanding as a great triumph of diplomacy and returned to New York to receive the adulation of a grateful U.N. staff, much like Caesar returning to Rome after a conquest abroad. At UNSCOM we regarded his return more like a much later historical event and gave serious thought of attending the secretary general's welcome-back party holding black umbrellas as a reminder of Neville Chamberlain's return from Munich in 1938 with his ill-fated statement that he had secured "peace in our time." The cooler heads among us prevailed.

Now the U.S. had the inspectors on the way back to work. But what to do next eluded everyone on the Clinton team. U.S. UNSCOM policy became completely confused as the weaknesses of the Kofi Annan agreement revealed themselves.

Butler, Duelfer, and I were discussing the situation in Butler's 31st floor office at the U.N., and we all agreed that the deal was a betrayal of UNSCOM. Since we had no inkling of Albright's backchannel to the secretary general, we were at a loss to explain the U.S. about-face, particularly because of Bill Richardson's strong warnings to Kofi Annan not to yield the rights of the inspectors. What made it worse was the secret prorocol. We were shaking our heads in bewilderment when the telephone rang. It was Madeleine Albright. Recognizing Butler's need for privacy, we stepped outside, and when he called us back in after he'd hung up, he said, "Madeleine is very nervous. The heat coming down from Trent Lott [the Republican Senate Majority Leader] is upsetting the administration. She wants me to hold a press conference and endorse the Kofi Annan agreement."

By midday Butler was on worldwide television praising the agreement not for its content but for its signatures, which resulted in the memorable soundbite, "It's not the fine print, but the thumb print." Duelfer and I, however, felt that Butler's participation in the domestic politics of a member nation was not in the best interests of UNSCOM.

The Republican criticisms, however, continued to sting, and the Clinton team could not allow itself to be seen as weak on this issue. They called for a test of Iraqi compliance.

Some weeks earlier Tariq Aziz had gone on record saying that if UNSCOM tried to inspect its Ministry of Defense, "it would mean war." But now in a stunning reversal it seemed that was where the U.S. was heading, and the Ministry of Defense became the test site of choice.

We had been aiming for an inspection of that ministry for some time, but both Ekéus and Butler had rejected it on the grounds that the arms control justification was too weak. When I asked Charles Duelfer why he though Butler might approve it now, he replied, "The Americans really want this . . . they'll push him."

I put together two options for the conduct of such a test, one "heavy," involving close to 150 inspectors, and one "light," with around forty. In view of the significance of either one, we sought U.S. intelligence support that would allow UNSCOM to send communications intercepts back to Bahrain via satellite for rapid assessment, with turnaround capability to feed anything of importance back to the team in Baghdad.

Support of this kind required senior authorization, and on February 26 Duelfer and I briefed a White House deputies-level committee on the proposed inspection and the need for American backing. The briefing was well received—until the question was raised about who would lead the mission. When Duelfer replied that I was the best one for the job I could see some of the White House people shift uneasily in their chairs. I knew what was up.

A month earlier, I had learned that I was under investigation by the FBI for espionage. The bureau had somehow come up with a theory that I was working for the Israeli government. It was questioning my motivations for pushing ahead so aggressively in carrying out my job. What if I was part of an Israeli plot to force the United States into a conflict with Iraq? I expected the FBI to eventually catch up with the truth, but for now I had become an issue.

The "Ritter issue," I would learn shortly, was being compounded at this very moment in a separate meeting Butler was having with Albright and Berger. The Americans were laying out their plan for military action against Iraq—a seven-day air campaign that had to end on March 15 because of the holiday pouring-in of pilgrims to Mecca for the Haj. Thus the test, and of course the inspections, had to be concluded by the 8th. Albright also made it clear she was not happy about me leading the inspection. "We want this to be about the issues, not about a person," she told Butler.

As the deadline for the inspection fast approached, Butler had to make a decision. While he contemplated, he kept me working as the mission planner. He still hadn't decided until a day before my scheduled departure to Bahrain, when he went on a Sunday to Kofi Annan's residence to inform him of the inspection.

"Who will lead?" the secretary general asked.

"I'm thinking about Ritter," Butler responded.

"Why him? Haven't you anyone else?" A week earlier, while briefing the Security Council on the results of his Baghdad trip, Kofi Annan had derided the UNSCOM cowboys. "It would be very provocative," he added.

Butler said that no final decision had been made yet.

The issue had reached a crescendo. On Monday, March 2, I went to the U.S. mission to the U.N., together with Butler and Duelfer, where we met with Ambassador Richardson. Of all the people on the Clinton administration's national security team, Bill Richardson was the only one I considered to be a stand-up person. Affable, warm, and armed with a politician's ever-ready smile, he had been an able representative for the people of New Mexico. Although he may have been faulted for a lack of foreign policy experience or diplomatic polish, no one could doubt the sincerity and sense of purpose he brought to the table. With his offbeat sense of humor, Richardson made every meeting a memorable one, and this was to be no exception.

I briefed him on the inspection, questioning the feasibility of trying to rush it through. This was when I was let in by Butler on the secret about the military campaign and the need to have the inspection wrapped up by the 8th. The degree of collusion surprised me, but it was good to know that the U.S. appeared serious this time about backing us up. When the question about my leading the team arose, Richardson told Butler that "if Ritter's your man, then that's who we go with."

What I wasn't aware of when he said that was that a week earlier the Ritter issue had been discussed in Richardson's presence at a meeting in Washington. The FBI again was raising questions about my loyalty. Richardson had had enough. He slammed his hand on the table, and demanded that the FBI "put up or shut up." If they had something of substance behind their assertions, Richardson wanted to see it. If not, they were to back off and let Butler pick whoever he felt best qualified to lead. The FBI, of course, had nothing, and that was that. But it wasn't over yet.

I arrived in Bahrain on March 3, and was immediately handed a message that instructed me to call Butler. "Madeleine is not happy about you being chief inspector," he said. "We need to consider options."

Meanwhile, back in New York, the leadership situation was about to be turned into a scene straight out of the Keystone Kops. The options I had prepared for Butler—which ranged from me in a support-role position to outright cancellation of the inspection—had found their way to the U.S. mission. Bill Richardson was briefed by his political counselor on UNSCOM affairs.

"What the hell is Butler up to?" Richardson asked. "I thought he had committed to Ritter staying on."

The counselor replied that Secretary of State Albright had put pressure on Butler. Richardson was incensed. He told the counselor to get Butler on the phone. The counselor moved into the foyer to make the call, but Butler was nowhere to be found. Suddenly, Richardson called out to his counselor, who returned to the ambassador's office. Richardson was on the phone, covering the mouthpiece.

"Did you get Butler yet?" he asked. The counselor shook his head no, and started to explain, when Richardson held up his hand, signaling silence. It was Madeleine Albright on the line. "Listen, Madeleine," Richardson said. "Butler is really irritated at your intervention. He says Ritter's the guy, and that he resents your meddling into his affairs. He may resign."

Albright was flabbergasted. "But I just talked to him," she said, meaning Butler. "He didn't indicate any of this when I was on the line. I don't believe it."

Richardson pressed. "Believe it," he said. "Ritter's on, or Butler's out."

Still stunned, Albright said she would call Butler right away to clarify the matter.

Richardson hung up and looked at the counselor, who was standing by in disbelief. "This is high stakes, my friend," Richardson said with a laugh. "Find Butler before Madeleine does, or we're both screwed."

The race was on. Knowing that State Department Operations would be calling all of its resources in New York to track Butler down, the counselor stuck to the few numbers he knew, especially Butler's pager and cell phone. Finally, after incessant ringing, a voice answered the cell phone. It was one of Butler's sons. Butler was at the *Time* magazine seventy-fifth anniversary party, which Richardson and the president were also attending. He had left his pager and cell phone at home.

The counselor rushed into Richardson's office. "Look," he said, "I need to use your security detail to get Butler. It's our only chance." Richardson agreed, and the counselor called one of the agents serving in Richardson's advance party. "Find Butler," he instructed. By this time Richardson had changed into his tuxedo and was moving toward the elevator to go to a waiting car. He told the counselor, "Come with me."

While they were driving crosstown to the *Time* event, the car phone rang. It was the advance security detail man. He could not find Butler. There were over 2,000 people at the event, he said. Richardson was furious. He grabbed the phone. "Don't give me excuses, find Butler!" He slammed the phone down. The senior security agent picked up the receiver and tried to reassure the advance agent. But when Richardson had slammed down the receiver, he had activated the speaker phone. When the senior agent got on the line, the advance agent, livid with rage, shouted, "Who the hell does that short fat son of a bitch think he is?" Richardson, hearing this, grabbed the phone again. "You're fired!" he shouted, and hung up.

Within a few minutes the advance agent called back. He had Butler. Richardson got on the line. All was forgiven, he told the agent. "Keep Butler away from anyone with a phone. Don't let him talk to anyone until I get there and talk to him myself."

At the event, Richardson and the counselor collared Butler. "You've got to keep Ritter on," Richardson said. "The inspection will fall apart if he doesn't go in. We can pressure Washington to back off. Just tell Madeleine that you're mad about this interference." Butler agreed. To seal the deal, Richardson arranged for an audience between Butler and the president and the first lady. Richardson told Clinton that Butler wanted to keep his best chief inspector on the case for this inspection. Clinton shook Butler's hand. "We are very supportive of you and your organization," Clinton said. "Of course it makes sense to go with your best leadership. Send in your best in-spector." Mrs. Clinton nodded in agreement. Later, when Albright finally managed to get through to Butler, he played his role per-fectly. The secretary retreated. I was back on the job. But despite all the heroics of Bill Richardson and his people, I still had serious con-cerns about this particular mission.

The cozy relationship between Butler and the U.S. in aligning the inspection timelines with those for military action was disturb-ing. So was the pressure to include the Ministry of Defense. If the U.S. wanted to launch military action in support of UNSCOM, the reasons had to be unimpeachable. Iraq had to be held accountable for any refusal to cooperate with the legitimate work of the inspec-tors. But I was concerned that this inspection was not a proper test of accountability. In its Republican-induced panic, the Clinton na-tional security team had adopted an approach that would be coun-terproductive. A limited military strike would only expose the weakness of the U.S., further isolating Washington from world opin-ion. Moreover, UNSCOM being used as a "trigger" for military ac-tion would be seen by the Security Council as nothing more than a provocation, and UNSCOM would lose its claim to objectivity and independence.

We flew into Iraq on March 5, and on the 6th and 7th carried out inspections of various SRG and SSO facilities without incident. The Iraqis were cooperative and praised the behavior of the inspec-tion team. During these first two days, however, I began receiving re-ports from our communications monitoring effort that indicated the SSO was getting instructions from Presidential Secretary Abid Hamid Mahmoud to remove and destroy documents at a site prior to the arrival of the inspection.

This spectacular piece of real-time information confirmed two things: the involvement of the presidential secretary and the SSO in concealment activity, and that the communications monitoring pro-gram could develop information that would have a meaningful im-pact on the inspection.

We ourselves had been caught up in one of these document sweeps. At one point we were delayed at a crossroads while the

Iraqis, pretending to be confused, allowed several vehicles loaded with documents to exit the facility we intended to inspect. Once the vehicles had departed, we were suddenly permitted to move—into the cleaned-out complex.

March 8th was crunch time. We finished inspecting the old Defense Ministry complex in the morning and were moving on to the most controversial site: the new Ministry of Defense. A grand building that formerly housed the Ministry of Oil, this was the site that Tariq Aziz had put UNSCOM on notice not to try to inspect. As anticipated, we immediately ran into difficulties. When on arrival I informed Hossam Amin that I wanted to enter with twenty-eight inspectors, he contacted Tariq Aziz, who cut the number to six. Unacceptable, I replied, and soon we were in a Mexican standoff.

Back in New York, Bill Richardson was sitting with Kofi Annan, waiting for the inspection results to trickle back. I called Butler, who instructed me to make an offer of twenty-two and to be prepared to go to twenty.

In the interim Minister of Oil Amer Rashid appeared on the scene. To avoid a crisis, he said, we could have twelve. Not acceptable, I said, but to avoid a crisis I would settle for as low as twenty.

Amer Rashid looked at me. "Mr. Ritter, we know that right now your government is kissing our feet to make a crisis. We have no intention to do so. We know that there is a threat of war, and we are not afraid. But we do not want a crisis. You are the chief inspector. You are right; the agreement states that it is the chief inspector who determines how many inspectors. Tariq Aziz has said twelve, but on my own authority I am proposing sixteen. Please, help avoid a crisis. On your authority, accept sixteen, and let us begin our work."

I thought about it. I had already dropped the number of inspectors to twenty. Was it worth a war to get four more inspectors inside a building the Iraqis were clearly willing to allow us to inspect? What could I ever say to the families of any U.S. servicemen or women who might lose their lives in a resulting military strike? I am sorry your son or your daughter was killed because I couldn't do my job with four fewer people? I looked at Amer Rashid, and said, "If accepting sixteen inspectors means avoiding a crisis, then it is probably a good deal." And the inspection began. Eleven hours later we were finished. We had found nothing. The inspection was over. I believed that I had performed my duties in a manner befitting an international civil servant. The next day my team returned to Bahrain. I didn't know it then, but it was the last inspection I would ever lead in the field.

# 14

# The End of UNSCOM As We Know It

THE UNITED STATES was hamstrung. In allowing Madeleine Albright to encourage the mission of Kofi Annan to Baghdad in February 1998, the Clinton administration set the stage for the full endorsement of the Memorandum of Understanding, with its self-defeating secret protocol. But this was a bad agreement for all sides. It placed the severest restrictions on the rights of the UNSCOM inspectors since the Agreement for the Modalities of Sensitive Site Inspections of Rolf Ekéus in June 1996. The U.S. was furious at Rolf Ekéus at that time, and yet suddenly it welcomed a similar pact in February 1998. But even worse for the Iraqis, it locked them into agreeing to grant access to inspectors to all sites; there were no more forbidden areas. Kofi Annan's secret agreements with Tariq Aziz notwithstanding, UNSCOM now had procedures in place that would actually facilitate concealment inspections. That would gradually allow UNSCOM to squeeze the retained Iraqi weapons into a few sanctuaries, which would then be subjected to no-notice inspections. Twin inspections of that type in March and April 1998 established absolute precedents concerning access from which it would be impossible for the Iraqis to back down without exposing themselves politically.

UNSCOM now felt compelled to inspect, not for the purpose of setting off a confrontation with Iraq, but rather to bring closure to its disarmament mandate. If Iraq failed to comply, then

UNSCOM could in clear conscience report as much to the Security Council. That was the limit of what UNSCOM could do. The problem would then be political and would invariably invoke the questions that the U.S. did not want to answer: What weapons were left in Iraq? What threat did Iraq represent to regional peace and security? The inability to provide these answers meant that any UNSCOM-based confrontation with Iraq would inevitably lead to a split in the Security Council, isolating the United States and again raising the issue of continued sanctions. Sanctions, however, were the cornerstone of the Clinton team's policy, and thus had to be maintained at any cost, including reining in UNSCOM.

In an April 1998 report to Congress, President Clinton stated that Iraq's acceptance of the provisions of the Kofi Annan Memorandum of Understanding made it imperative that UNSCOM be allowed to carry out its inspections, including those related to the concealment mechanism. At the same time that the U.S. president was making this important policy statement, however, his national security team was in fact implementing a completely different policy—one of holding UNSCOM back.

In trying to generate support for aggressive UNSCOM inspections, the U.S. encountered the lack of consensus in recent years about whether to use force to compel Iraq to comply with the will of the Security Council.

By 1998, many of the countries that had supported Desert Storm no longer viewed Iraq in the same threatening light as they had in 1991. The Iraqi military was a mere shadow of its former self, unable to sustain any meaningful military action beyond internal suppression of the Kurds and Shi'a. Such a weakened Iraq, these countries argued, surely would not invite a bombing campaign by obstructing the work of UNSCOM. Given the undisputed effectiveness of UNSCOM as an ongoing deterrent to Iraq's ability to reconstitute its weapons of mass destruction programs on any meaningful level, others maintained, any military action would result in the termination of UNSCOM while doing nothing to resolve the remaining outstanding disarmament issues.

The U.S. was being criticized for advocating the continuation of sanctions without end, without offering any incentive to Iraq to cooperate. Some nations argued that the ruthless oppression of Iraq represented a double standard when compared with Washington's tolerant treatment of a nuclear-armed Israel.

Worse, actions by the U.S. in the Persian Gulf over the past seven years had almost always been taken in response to UNSCOM-initiated confrontations with Iraq, which meant in effect that UNSCOM held the lever that could launch American military forces into combat.

This was something that the National Security Council wanted to rectify as soon as possible. The power to unleash American military might belonged the U.S. president and that was where they indisputably wanted it to be. They had to slow UNSCOM down to a pace that was diplomatically sustainable by Washington.

These were the difficulties that had to be addressed by the Clinton national security team to construct a policy that would realize the stated U.S. goal of eliminating the security threat posed by Iraq. But in the end, one policy issue rose above all others: the perpetuation of containment through economic sanctions.

This objective required the U.S. to strike a delicate balance. On one side a credible UNSCOM inspection effort had to be maintained to report to the Security Council on Iraqi compliance. On the other, UNSCOM itself had to be kept in tow—not permitted to rock the boat, so to speak, to prevent any split in the council over Iraq. An UNSCOM actively carrying out its mandate to disarm Iraq would force the U.S. and all members of the council to deal with those problems of the extent of the Iraqi arsenal and the threat it poses to peace and security in the region. Those were the very questions about which there was no consensus, yet which would have to be answered satisfactorily if the U.S. hoped to generate any broad support for decisive military action in support of UNSCOM.

U.S. policy toward Iraq in the spring of 1998 was born of frustration, namely, the Clinton national security team's inability to hold together the international coalition of Desert Storm, one of the most successful in history. The Clinton team's insistence on maintaining sanctions regardless of Iraq's compliance, a fundamental flaw in American policy toward Iraq, destroyed the coalition, for which the Clinton team deserves harsh criticism.

America was bound by a confusing strategy based on four precepts:

1. Continued control by the U.N. of the Iraqi checkbook through the application of economic sanctions, while mitigating the suffering of the Iraqi people by a massive relief effort paid for under an oil-for-food agreement.
2. Continued disarmament of Iraq through the work of UNSCOM.
3. Continued containment of Iraq through regional and international isolation.
4. Destabilization or overthrow of the regime of Saddam Hussein.

Unfortunately, the primary precept, economic sanctions, was proving to be ineffective. In addition, it had become more and more difficult to support on moral grounds.

Under the provisions of the oil-for-food agreement, which was significantly expanded in early 1998, Iraq today derives more oil-based income ($5.2 billion) than at any time since 1986—four years *before* the Gulf War. The expanded program actually allows Iraq to pump more oil than it possibly could with its present capability. As a result, the United Nations authorized Iraq to upgrade oil field infrastructure, an action that resulted in Iraqi contracts with foreign companies worth hundreds of millions of dollars.

This surge in economic activity directly contradicts the basic objectives of sanctions. True, the U.N. controls the purse strings, but the dramatic economic benefits of this arrangement—the oil-for-food agreement infused desperately needed dollars into the Iraqi economy, propping up the failing dinar and saving Saddam from disaster—more than compensate for the limited loss of national prestige. It is difficult to see how this circular policy of sanctions and sanctions relief is anything other than self-defeating. It has certainly failed in forcing Iraq into compliance. Indeed, Saddam Hussein has shrewdly turned the issue of sanctions against the U.S., portraying them as unjust and a symbol of American imperialism against an Arab people, a message that resonates throughout the Arab world.

From the very beginning, the U.S. pointed to the work of

UNSCOM as the justification for continuing economic sanctions. Sanctions had to be maintained until Iraq disarmed. But after seven years of the most intrusive inspection program ever undertaken in the history of arms control, some nations ask, "What has been accomplished?"

The view from France in the spring of 1998 was very different from that in America. The French believed that Butler was depicting the arms inspection process as unsuccessful, and thus playing too great a role in prolonging sanctions. There was, however, according to the French, a distinct separation between the disarmament process (i.e., the physical destruction of weapons) and the inspection process. One was technical, the other political. While there were problems on the political side—implementing inspections that offended Iraqi sensitivities—UNSCOM had been generally successful on the technical side. Butler, in the eyes of the French, mixed the two together, creating a misleading impression about Iraq's overall disarmament progress. His close relationship with the U.S. only contributed to the stalemate in the Security Council.

Paris wanted Butler to back away from the concept that it was somehow up to him to decide whether the sanctions would be lifted and to state clearly that he was a disinterested party, whatever the policies of the United States. The French felt that the U.S. was using UNSCOM in a dispute that was basically between Iraq and the U.S. The French favored scaling down U.S. military forces in the region as a means of easing tensions. UNSCOM should not allow its credibility to be put on the line by Washington's political agenda, particularly since UNSCOM was setting the standards for the future of nonproliferation.

The French assessment in many respects was shared by Russia, although Moscow had its own credibility problem because of the clear self-serving interests driving its policy toward Iraq. But French opinion was another matter. While the differences between Paris and Washington extend over a wide range of UNSCOM issues, France shares the same core beliefs as the United States. The French were a major force behind the creation of UNSCOM and consistently supported Iraqi disarmament. Moreover, the French position in the early part of 1998 today seems prescient.

The British, in early 1998, viewed the Iraqis as making headway in the Security Council not only with the French, Russians, and Chinese, but also with the ten middle-ground, nonpermanent members. The British were eager for UNSCOM to regain the initiative. London believed that intrusive inspections that did not turn up actual evidence of prohibited material were counterproductive. Intrusive inspections, which they supported in principle, had to be carried out only when armed with top-grade intelligence. The key was how to develop that intelligence.

In many ways, the British and the French were not very far apart. Both feared the overwhelming U.S. influence on UNSCOM and its potentially disastrous effects in light of the capricious character of U.S. foreign policy objectives in Iraq. The British "special relationship" with the United States precluded overt criticism, which was further constrained by British confusion over what the Americans were actually up to.

Confusion was the name of the game. After Saddam's decision in August 1998 to cease cooperation with UNSCOM, Washington completely misread the new state of affairs. The U.S. clearly occupied the moral high ground in terms of who was to blame for the crisis, but the absence of any vocal support for Iraq was understood by the Clinton national security team as a mandate for an intensive bombing campaign. By early November 1998, the lines were drawn. Having been repeatedly frustrated by Saddam's cycles of "cheat and retreat"—a tactic that had eroded American prestige by exposing it to ridicule as a paper tiger—the Clinton administration had already decided that the next time forces were deployed, it would be for real.

As it turned out, a last-minute diplomatic initiative by Kofi Annan resulted in a temporary halt to the planned bombing campaign in November. Saddam agreed to let the UNSCOM inspectors back in, but no one believed he would comply. Few were more certain than Sandy Berger, who immediately met with Butler to coordinate inspection schedules in the framework of the all-but-inevitable military strike. Butler had the customary test ready to go, one that he knew would be confrontational. It was a reworking of the UNSCOM 255 inspection that had been canceled in August (the one over which I resigned) on the grounds that it was *too* confrontational. Now, however, Butler and Berger knew what they wanted, and the newly numbered UNSCOM 258 delivered in spades. Delays, blockages, evacuated buildings—the classic pattern of Iraqi obstruction—all were provoked and carefully catalogued. I'm not suggesting that Iraq wasn't to blame. It was Baghdad that undertook not to live up to its obligation to fully cooperate with the inspection teams. On the other hand, Butler appeared to have forgotten that he was a servant of the Security Council, not the United States.

The Butler-Berger hand-in-glove relationship during UNSCOM 258 was too cozy. Prior coordination, daily Butler-to-Berger situation updates during the inspection, and a mutual review of Butler's report before its submission to the secretary general infringed on the Security Council's powers. The final insult came on December 16. In the middle of Butler's presentation of his report to the council, and without prior consultation, a four-day bombing campaign, Operation Desert Fox, began.

Like most Americans watching the televised briefing of the chairman of the Joint Chiefs of Staff, General Hugh Shelton, my eyes were glued to the photograph on the screen. He was pointing out the battle damage done to one of the sites struck by cruise missiles.

Here are their barracks [he said] . . . along with the headquarters. . . . You see over here that this headquarters is now rubble. If you go from these barracks, the prestrike to the post-strike, you'll see out of the five barracks, four of the five were destroyed. . . . The barracks area that belongs to the Special Republican Guard, these are the units that, in fact, guard the [weapons of mass destruction] and help transport it. They're the ones that basically help move it. They deny UNSCOM access on occasion. This is part of the apparatus that Saddam uses to maintain control of his [weapons of mass destruction] facilities.

Unlike most Americans, I knew that site almost as well as my own backyard.

It was the headquarters and barracks of the SRG's 8th Battalion. This particular unit had played a key role in the overall concealment plan orchestrated by Iraq since 1991. It had provided command and control, personnel, and transportation resources for the purpose of hiding nuclear weapons production equipment from the United Nations, and played a central role in the dramatic confrontations that took place in June 1991, when inspectors closed in on this material. We had inspected the 8th Battalion facility, collecting data that, when combined with the results of similar inspections, eventually compelled Iraq to admit that the SRG, including the 8th Battalion, had played a significant role in the concealment of material from UNSCOM inspectors in 1991.

In the image displayed to the world by General Shelton the headquarters building was destroyed. But I was certain that it was unoccupied at the time it was bombed, the battalion staff safely ensconced in their operational bunker located several hundred yards away. I looked in wonderment at the devastated barracks, trying to fathom why these structures had been chosen for destruction. Why weren't the armories and ammunition bunkers hit? Why wasn't the vehicle park destroyed? What about the fighting positions along the perimeter, which would be fully manned and therefore susceptible to crippling casualties? None of this. Just an empty headquarters and barracks. How did this strike advance the stated U.S. goal of containing Saddam Hussein? How did it diminish Iraq's ability to attack its neighbors with weapons of mass destruction? If, as Shelton insisted, the reason for the bombing was to destroy this unit's mission of protecting weapons of mass destruction, what had been achieved by destroying an empty building? If the bomb damage assessment teams were interpreting these photographs as examples of mission success, then there was something fundamentally wrong with this entire effort.

It has been said that UNSCOM destroyed more of Iraq's weapons of mass destruction than the entire aerial bombing campaign of Desert Storm. This is true, and it raises the question, therefore, about what remains. The simple truth is that no one really knows. But Iraq has an endgame strategy: get sanctions lifted, and keep its remaining weapons of mass destruction. Against this dedicated pursuit, the United States hurls inchoate campaigns of punishment and degradation, the goal of which is to undermine the rule of

Saddam while destroying Iraq's weapons capabilities, in short, a military version of its policy of open-ended containment.

But where does this lead us? Open-ended containment means the continuation of economic sanctions for which there is no international support. The inherent inhumanity of economic sanctions damages those who impose it. As an American, I resent having my national character stained this way. The containment policy implies renewed military action whenever the United States determines that Iraq has violated its restrictions but this again leads nowhere unless the military action is decisive.

Iraq, having no incentive to cooperate, will provoke, counting on its ability to absorb punishment, until the United States exhausts its political capital in dishing out military punishments. The regime of economic sanctions is on the verge of collapse. Our allies are already distancing themselves from this morally reprehensible policy. In using UNSCOM's disarmament mission to justify its own ill-defined objectives the Clinton administration has discredited UNSCOM. As a result, the U.S. has ceded its moral standing to others, such as the French, who now seek to salvage a situation spinning out of control.

Sooner or later we will be forced to choose: do we turn right, toward escalation of military confrontation, or do we turn left, into the realm of diplomatic engagement? If one makes that right turn, how far down the road of confrontation is one willing to go? Lacking an answer to that question before undertaking such a step virtually guarantees that the result will be a quagmire.

France, Russia, and China have already embarked on diplomatic engagement. If the U.S. is unwilling to take military confrontation to its logical conclusion—the removal of Saddam—when it finally embraces diplomacy, as it must, it will be playing in a game with rules already formulated by others.

The policy of containment has failed. It is time for the United States to discard it and adopt a new policy of engagement. The question is, what kind of engagement will achieve the best results with Iraq: military or diplomatic?

# 15

# Trumping Saddam

ANY REASONABLE ANALYSIS of Saddam's Iraq today would find that while it maintains a big (and impressive) bark, it has little bite. The politics of Saddam's regional ambitions are evident in his every speech as well as those of his subordinates. There can be no doubt that an unrepentant and rejuvenated Iraq would again attempt to throw its weight around using bullying, blackmail, and naked force. But in 1999 Iraq is all bluster with nothing to back it up.

The Iraqi army is in total disarray, capable of little more than manning security pickets along the Iran-Iraq border, in northern Iraq (Kurdistan), and in southern Iraq. I have visited numerous Iraqi military barracks and have seen soldiers in tattered uniforms and bare feet. Military training is without substance, barely sufficient to convert recruits into simple soldiers, let alone provide skills in the intricacies of modern combined-arms combat—the integration of infantry, armor, artillery, and air power in a single military action.

Reduced to five corps from seven before the Gulf War, the army today relies on an armored force whose centerpiece is the T-55 tank, a relic of the 1950s. The bulk of the armored personnel carriers are likewise vintage 1950s. The few T-62 tanks and BMP armored fighting vehicles are only one generation newer, and countless generations behind world-leading U.S. battlefield technology. I have seen Iraqi transport vehicles on concrete blocks without wheels, hoods up and engines stripped for spare parts. All of these antiquated vehicles are short on spare parts, and have undergone jerry-built rehabilitation campaigns just to enable their engines to run. This is an army that poses a threat to no one.

I have seen the Republican Guard, too. Better equipped than the regular army, it remains a viable fighting force, as was proven in its 1996 suppression of the Kurds at Irbil. However, the same logistical shortfalls that haunt the regular army also plague the Republican Guard, and it is currently unable to do much more than conduct operations on the same scale as it carried out against Irbil—enough to put down internal unrest, but not enough to match the armed forces of any of its neighbors.

The Republican Guard has been divided into two corps, a northern and a southern. This reorganization reflects the reality that it cannot operate too far from its supply center. Although its T-72 tank is a powerful machine, the Republican Guard suffers from the same lack of training as the regular army, and combined-arms operations are but a dim memory. Even at its *best*, the Republican Guard was decimated in a matter of hours once it engaged the U.S. Army in 1991. Any international threat from today's Republican Guard is imaginary.

The air force has aircraft, but in the current shortage of spare parts most training consists of simply taking off, circling the airfield, and landing. Training like this does nothing to impart combat skills, as any fighter pilot would confirm. Its best fighters are the MiG-29 Fulcrums and the Mirage F-1; nevertheless, these pilots at the top of their skills were pulverized in 1991. Saddam's air force in action could be shot out of the sky by any of the modern air forces of its neighbors.

The one area where Iraq could represent a threat is in employing weapons of mass destruction, but it is highly unlikely that Saddam would authorize the use of such controversial weapons until he has completely rebuilt his conventional arsenal. Iraq simply lacks the stocks of chemical and biological agent needed to have any militarily significant effect. Tens of thousands of munitions would be required, and at best Iraq has but a few hundred. The political losses that would be accrued by using weapons that it has declared it no longer possesses would far outweigh any short-lived battlefield benefits. In any event, the U.S. trains to fight in this environment on a regular basis, and if anything American forces are better prepared for combat than during the Gulf War.

Although Saddam today cannot be regarded as a military danger, he will eventually pose a threat to his neighbors. Throughout the Middle East Saddam is regarded with almost universal disgust, scorned and repudiated for his repressive brutality. But he is also the president of Iraq. He lives in a tough neighborhood, where realpolitik is the order of the day. Lost in all the rhetoric of today, at least in Washington, is the fact that before the Gulf War, the United States had undertaken an active program of economic and political engagement with Saddam. Some of the current problems between the U.S. and Iraq have origins in problems that confronted Iraq in early 1990, before the Kuwait invasion, when the U.S. lined up against Iraq as Iraq looked desperately for economic help.

Since August 1990, Washington has vilified Saddam as the Middle Eastern equivalent of Adolf Hitler. His monstrous behavior makes such a comparison easy, but it is mistaken. Saddam Hussein is a uniquely Iraqi leader, a product of regional forces. While he has molded modern-day Iraq in his own image, he himself has been molded by the realities of modern-day Iraq. The bloody, ignoble soap opera of his personal life bears heavily on the nature of his regime. Nevertheless certain forces shaped Saddam and Iraq that to some extent would shape any Iraqi ruler—pan-Arabism, tribalism, Islamic fundamentalism, anti-Zionism, regional megalomania. While doing business with Saddam is certainly not an attractive idea, when contrasted with the unspeakable horrors of war, or the mindless and morally corrupt policy of indefinite economic sanctions, it does represent a lesser evil.

The current U.S. policy of trying to overthrow Saddam is misguided. The underlying problems will continue to exist. Saddam did not create the animosity between Iraq and Iran, nor did Saddam fabricate the Iraq-Kuwait border issue. He is not the source of the Israeli-Arab conflict. His extreme positions and irresponsible actions have exacerbated these problems, but they would have arisen without him, and his disappearance would solve none of them. Similarly, his removal would not change the nature of Iraq. It would have to be followed by a "de-Saddamization" of two generations of Iraqis and their institutions. It could succeed, but it would not be easy, quick, or cheap. Nor would it be acceptable to the majority of the Arab world, who would view such an undertaking as a clear example of Western imperialism.

Practically speaking, there is virtually no chance that opposition groups could overthrow Saddam. Past attempts by the CIA and the British MI6 to orchestrate a coup from within all met with disaster. Rumors of CIA efforts to foment a revolt by Iraqi army generals in southern Iraq during Operation Desert Fox were also accompanied by reports of officers from these units being summarily executed by Saddam's security services. Anyone contemplating engineering a coup from within ought first to consider that every officer in the Iraqi military today is a product of post-1968 Ba'athist Iraq. These officers have been trained along lines approved by Saddam; they and their families have been thoroughly investigated by his security services. These are Saddam's officers, and any independence they may have once had has long since atrophied. In short, there is no effective way to organize such a coup. Saddam is imbued in the very fabric of Iraqi society; he is, to quote his boast, in every glass of milk, whether the taste is sour or sweet. Getting rid of this man is much more than a one-bullet job.

What are the chances that anti-Saddam opposition abroad might succeed? I have met repeatedly with Achmed Chalabi, the head of the Iraqi National Congress. He is an imposing, highly educated man with an admirable passion for a free Iraq. I know from firsthand experience that Chalabi and the INC have a network of well-placed informants in Iraq. Some of the information they provided proved to be of considerable value to UNSCOM's work but the feasiblity of a successful incursion by Chalabi is another matter.

The INC believes that if adequately funded it can recruit and train a force of about 3,000 men. Special units, including a 200-man commando force, would also be raised for ambushes, raids, and other guerrilla-style actions. Under the INC plan, this force, to be known as the Iraq Liberation Army, would be inserted into safe zones in southern and southwestern Iraq—zones protected as no-fly/no-drive (air and armor exclusion zones) by the U.S. Air Force. A provisional government would be established, and an extensive information campaign initiated to promote defections from the local population and military units. Manpower from these defections would be trained and equipped to swell the ranks of the ILA, leading to a massive revolt to be sustained until Saddam's fall from power. The INC would make use of existing opposition forces in the north of Iraq (the Kurds) and in the south (the Shi'a rebels) to strengthen INC forces and positions.

This is a plan that even under Chalabi's able leadership is doomed from the start. The experience of March 1995 in northern Iraq shows the limitations of any INC-Kurdish alliance. Despite all of the efforts expended by the U.S. in recent months to forge an agreement between the rival PUK of Jalal Talabani and the KDP of Massoud Barzani, the animosity between the two groups is so strong that prospects for long-term cooperation are very slim. Chalabi himself does not command wide support outside the Shi'a membership of the INC.

Most of the repeated calls by respected members of the U.S. Senate for the overthrow of Saddam support the INC plan. However, the current political situation in the Persian Gulf would not allow the United States to sustain a no-fly/no-drive exclusion zone, and any insertion of INC forces into Iraq would result in a desert version of the Bay of Pigs, this time with thousands, not hundreds, dead. Many INC sympathizers have disseminated the idea that once Saddam is deprived of his tanks and artillery, his helicopters and aircraft, he would be powerless against an opposing force because Iraqi soldiers would defect in droves. I have seen videotapes of 'Ali Hassan al-Majid, the "fighter staff general" on whom Saddam places so much trust, pistol-whipping beaten Shi'a rebels. I have seen tapes of the SRG pouring into a Shi'a-held village and, with all of the viciousness of the Nazi SS, crush the opposition. The SRG would be reduced to so many corpses in a fight with the U.S. Marines or the U.S. Army, but they are well trained to destroy the very type of rebellion that the supporters of the INC would like to see. INC fighters on the ground in Iraq would need a lot more help—direct, massive intervention by the United States military, including ground troops that would inevitably see combat.

If the United States were to become involved in a military campaign against Iraq, what form should it take? The most important objectives, I believe, should be the swift, decisive defeat and removal from power of Saddam Hussein, the Ba'ath party, and the al-Bu Nasir clan, all of which have dominated Iraq for so long and have pursued policies that seek Iraqi hegemony in the Gulf through intimidation—including the possession and use of weapons of mass destruction.

A key element to this scenario would be the indictment of Saddam Hussein and the leadership of Iraq as war criminals by an international criminal court. Although such a court is at best still years off, the concept is sound and would provide legitimacy to the process of removing Saddam Hussein. In February 1998 Senator Arlen Specter introduced a Senate resolution that called for: 1) the creation of a U.N. commission to establish an international record of the criminal culpability of Saddam Hussein and other Iraqi officials; 2) an international criminal tribunal to indict, prosecute, and imprison Saddam and other Iraqis responsible for crimes against humanity, genocide, and other violations of international law; and 3) a long-term plan for the removal and capture of Saddam Hussein so that he can be brought to trial.

Any military campaign to remove Saddam Hussein must have such a legal foundation, and it is encouraging that the U.S. Senate has at least considered the proposal. However, the Specter resolution was not part of a concerted military plan to overthrow Saddam, but rather an alternative to such action. Such an indictment without arrest powers is a noble but ultimately futile gesture. And it will take more than a United Nations policeman to deliver the warrant; the warrant will have to be delivered from the barrel of an M-1 tank, because Saddam will never surrender voluntarily.

President Clinton's endorsement of the campaign to indict Saddam also provides no method for execution. "The best way to end that threat once and for all," Clinton said, "is with a new Iraqi government—a government ready to live in peace with its neighbors, a government that respects the rights of its people." True enough, but how will that happen?

Senator Richard Lugar, the influential co-chair of the Foreign

Relations Committee, expressed the frustration of many in the Senate when he said, "Relying on containment, even accompanied by concerted bombings, is doomed to failure. Such a policy treats the symptoms rather than the disease. It presupposes the continued reign of Saddam Hussein despite his fundamental goal of harming the United States and our interests. There can be no compromise in such a situation. Saddam Hussein has never stopped being at war with us, even if we have stopped being at war with him."

In the end, the hard reality always surfaces: to remove Saddam, we must employ the military forces of the United States. No one can doubt that the United States has the military might to overthrow Saddam Hussein. What is required is the proper mix of assets to remove him quickly, with the minimum loss of American lives.

But before we can overthrow Saddam Hussein we must be certain that the United States government has the authority to undertake such an action, both domestically and internationally. The United States is the world's leader; if it leads decisively, the world will follow. The United States must make a convincing case that in the future Saddam will represent a serious menace to his neighbors. When Iraq rebuilds its economy and its military, and seeks to reestablish itself as a regional superpower—probably equipped with WMD capability—it will present a real threat. The time to solve this problem is now, when the cost in terms of lives and resources will be far less than it would be in the future. However, it is very difficult to mobilize support for war based upon a potential threat. It is easier to hope that containment through a combination of economic sanctions and limited military action will suffice. But the framework of containment is collapsing, and Iraq is on the verge of breaking out. And when it does—perhaps three to five years down the road—the world will face a serious confrontation. So if the only way to prevent Saddam from igniting conflict is to overthrow him through military action, that is what we must do.

Any military action, however, while representing the clearest solution to the Saddam problem, is fraught with obstacles. It would require the full support of Congress, indeed total commitment: total war, total victory, total restructuring of a defeated Iraq. Only in this way can we ensure that the Saddam phenomenon is gone forever.

This campaign will succeed, but only if the American people are behind it.

In his opening statement at my Senate hearing, Senator Carl Levin of Michigan, the ranking Democrat on the Armed Services Committee, said, "If I introduced a resolution this afternoon to authorize the president to use all necessary and appropriate force to compel Iraqi compliance with U.N. resolutions, how many senators would be willing to support it? I have real questions as to whether or not a majority would, indeed, support a resolution." I believe that those questions remain.

Americans are by and large a society driven by moralistic-legalistic norms. We don't approve of military action in support of ill-defined foreign policy objectives. We need to feel a sense of outrage before agreeing to the mobilization and dispatch of American servicemen and women overseas to fight and die for a cause. The cause must be about right against wrong, about the forces of good conquering the forces of evil. When we didn't feel this way about the war in Vietnam, we withdrew. When the television screens showed dead U.S. soldiers in the streets of Mogadishu and no one could explain satisfactorily why we were there, we withdrew.

So the first step in any military confrontation intended to remove Saddam from power and transform Iraq into an international law–abiding nation is to convince the American people that this is a morally just fight. Saddam has provided the world with a massive body of damning evidence from which to assemble such a case, some of which I've discussed in this book. There is certainly moral justification to take action to overthrow Saddam.

At the end of the Gulf War U.S. Army planners developed a contingency plan to move on Baghdad, surround the city, and facilitate the occupation of Baghdad by insurgent forces, supported by American Special Forces. The U.S. military incursion was to have removed Saddam Hussein and the Ba'ath party from power, install a friendly government, and stabilize the situation in Iraq. Following the decisive victory in the Gulf War, military planners believed that this mission could be accomplished with a minimum of forces—two divisions and an armored cavalry regiment supported by combat service support units (transport, engineering, and logistics capabilities beyond those inherent in a division's normal complement) and the Special Forces elements.

This plan, known as the Road to Baghdad or the Arnold Plan (after its author, Brigadier General Steve Arnold, the operations officer of the Third Army during the Gulf War), was shelved almost as soon as it was written. Nevertheless, the Arnold Plan was based on the U.S. Army's experience in ground combat against Iraq. The Iraqi army was incapable of opposing the United States military. In the intervening years, the U.S. military has become more effective while Iraqi forces have declined considerably, as I've mentioned.

An expanded version of the Arnold Plan would almost certainly work today. If the U.S. deployed ground troops in Iraq for the purpose of overthrowing Saddam, I believe that the number of soldiers required would be about 250,000. Such a large number would guarantee victory as well as reduce casualties. During the Gulf War Iraqi soldiers surrendered as often as they fought. In my opinion, Americans would spend more time processing prisoners than fighting the forces of Saddam.

As with any serious undertaking, the devil is in the details, and when assembling any military option, the specifics of acceptable force ratios are best left to the experts. A quick victory with as few casualties as possible depends on the use of overwhelming force. There will be many Iraqi casualties, but every month that we hold back and do nothing, several thousand innocent children die in Iraq. Prior to Desert Storm the annual mortality figure for children under the age of five in Iraq was a little over 7,000. Today it is over 50,000. That increase of 43,000 can be directly attributed to the effects of sanctions on Iraq. I bet there would be fewer Iraqi casualties in an all-out attack than the number of Iraqi children who die each year from malnutrition or untreated disease.

The United States must be prepared, if necessary, to go it alone. But going alone means just that. There is a real possibility that the United States, in embarking on major military action against Iraq, might not attract any allies to its cause. Gaining the support of Kuwait, Saudi Arabia, Jordan, and Turkey for the military defeat and occupation of Iraq will be impossible unless they are convinced of the seriousness of the United States to carry this mission to completion on its own. Such a demonstration of national will would redefine America as a leader around whom an international coalition could be formed.

The actual military campaign would be relatively short-lived. Once military forces are established in theater, the battle for Iraq should be over in less than a month. As soon as the reality of Saddam's impending defeat is established, the glue of fear and oppression that holds Saddam's Iraq will begin to weaken. There is a distinct possibility that Saddam would be assassinated by those closest to him in the belief that by doing the job themselves they may save themselves. The target, however, is not the man but the regime. They all must go.

And so the endgame. Military occupation. Military government. Nation building. All difficult problems but not insurmountable ones. The role of the organized opposition would become crucial now. The U.S. would set about the task of working with, say, Chalabi's INC from the perspective of rebuilding Iraq and establishing basic democratic forms of government, the faster the better. The thought of American troops putting down civil unrest in Tikrit is not a pleasant one. There should be a residual military presence in Iraq after Saddam has been overthrown and a transition government set up. The new government would establish its own police force and its own military. The assistance of the GCC states, Jordan, and Egypt would be vital in this effort. Nation building should be an Arab endeavor as much as possible. The job of the United States in the post-military phase of Saddam's defeat should be facilitating Iraq's economic recovery.

But in reality such a large-scale military confrontation between Iraq and the United States has been rendered highly unlikely by Operation Desert Fox. The December 1998 bombing campaign accomplished the inconceivable: it renewed the world's sympathy for the plight of the Iraqi people and isolated the United States, revealing that the U.S. has no plan for how to solve the problem in Iraq. The legal-moralistic argument for decisive military conflict that existed before Desert Fox was clear:

- Iraq violated international law by invading Kuwait;
- International law served as the basis of Desert Storm and a cease-fire agreement;

- Iraq's noncompliance with disarmament provisions invalidated the cease-fire;
- Saddam Hussein was the prime mover behind Iraqi noncompliance;
- Military action should seek to solve the problem of Iraqi noncompliance;
- Therefore, the focal point of military action should be Saddam Hussein.

But not today. UNSCOM is dead; the shards of the inspection regime lie on the floor of the Security Council, where a new regime is being constructed that whitewashes Iraq's failures to disarm with vague language about a future monitoring system. In the U.S., mobilizing domestic support for a war now seems impossible; not many Americans would be willing to lay down their lives for a discredited United Nations organization, which is what the once proud UNSCOM has become. The case for war against Iraq on the grounds of its refusal to comply with the provisions of Security Council Resolution 687 (1991) is no longer sustainable. What was once an international cause to rid Iraq of weapons of mass destruction has turned into a squabble between the U.S. and Iraq, beyond the framework originally put together by the Security Council in its resolutions. As long as the struggle was about UNSCOM and disarmament, the United States could hope to gather international support in overthrowing Saddam Hussein. However, given UNSCOM's demise, a military campaign would have no legal justification.

Let's take a closer look at the diplomatic engagement option.
The appointment of a special envoy for Iraqi affairs would go a long way to help in gathering support domestically for a new diplomatic opening to Iraq. The Clinton team would have a hard time doing a convincing about-face after its support for military action and sanctions. The new policy would require new leadership on this issue.
Since the end of Operation Desert Fox, the United States has found itself on the defensive in dealing with Iraq. All initiative rests with Iraq or those countries that are sympathetic to Iraq, especially France and Russia. Unless the U.S. undertakes some form of dra-

matic new policy, it will be left playing a secondary role to Paris, Moscow, and Beijing at a critical time when the balance of power in the Persian Gulf is being reshaped. This would be terrible since these countries appear to have a high tolerance for Iraq's residual weapons of mass destruction capability, which can be reconstituted almost at will. The hollow post-UNSCOM monitoring schemes suggested thus far would place little restraint on Iraq.

The new American initiative that I am proposing has a successful historical precedent, President Nixon's trip to China in 1972—a surprise, bilateral move that broke the deadlock between the U.S. and China. The United States, through its special envoy, would engage in direct diplomacy with Saddam Hussein's Iraq. Carried out in good faith, this would be an exercise in credible diplomacy seeking a peaceful accord that takes into account the needs and concerns of both nations. It would also be a bitter pill for the United States to swallow after years of demonization of Saddam Hussein and Iraq. Regardless of the distastefulness and uncertainty of entering into an agreement based on trusting Saddam Hussein and Iraq to abide by its terms, the reality is that the Security Council is well on the way to brokering such an agreement.

Given the difficult nature of such a diplomatic initiative, both in terms of selling it domestically and abroad (especially to the Iraqis), the special envoy would have to be a person of special character. My ideal candidate for this position would be Bill Richardson, the tough-talking secretary of energy and former ambassador to the United Nations. Alone among the Clinton administration's national security team involved with Iraq, in my opinion, Richardson behaved with honor and rectitude. This would be an especially important trait in seeking to reestablish American bona fides with the Iraqi government, and gaining the support of Iraq's Middle East neighbors.

Another ideal candidate would be Richard Holbrooke, the no-nonsense negotiator of the Dayton Peace Accord, who rescued Bosnia—and the United States and Europe—from the morass in the former Yugoslavia. He is one of the few diplomats with the combination of skill, intelligence, and determination in dealing with brutal dictators that would be required in hammering out a solution with the likes of Saddam Hussein. Yet another such diplomat would be George Mitchell, who helped to broker the Northern Ireland–IRA peace agreement. Making peace with Iraq would represent hurdles of at least the same magnitude as those Holbrooke faced over Bosnia and Mitchell over Belfast.

As with any negotiation, there would have to be room for wiggle and at the same time a bottom line—the core values that cannot be ceded. In my judgment they would include:

1. *Iraqi recognition of Kuwait and the Iraq-Kuwait border as presently drawn.* This is essential to any peace and regional stability accord, and would represent a major concession on the part of Iraq. The issue of the so-called nineteenth province, unless resolved, would seed future conflict. The United Nations has established clearly defined frontiers between Iraq and Kuwait, and they cannot be negotiated away. Once this basic principle is agreed, other outstanding issues can be addressed, such as slant-drilling and Iraqi facilities on Bubiyan island. Such negotiations would be treated as separate issues, to be resolved between Kuwait and Iraq based on the understanding that Iraq no longer has claims on these territories.

2. A *pledge by Iraq not to possess any weapons of mass destruction and to permit monitoring.* This would be formulated in a new Security Council resolution that would supplant Resolutions 687 and 715, but would include export-import controls. There is no way to return to the UNSCOM-type searches for retained Iraqi capabilities. The new agreement would assume that Iraq would dispose of any remaining capabilities and not institute new ones. Agreeing to accept Iraq's declaration that it has destroyed its weapons of mass destruction capabilities and agreeing not to impose any supervision would constitute recognition of the possibility that the Iraqi claim of not having any weapons of mass destruction might be accurate. If Iraq's past claims are not accurate, this offers a face-saving way for Iraq to move the issue forward without becoming mired in past issues. Insistence on a United Nations monitoring regime recognizes the importance of accepted norms of international arms control. Although there is ample evidence that Iraq lied about its past WMD programs, it is virtually impossible to envisage reconstituting an UNSCOM-like investigatory body. If the U.S.

insists on such a capability, it will stand alone. The days of the detective inspections are over. An Iraqi declaration that it no longer has WMD would have to be taken at face value—but a credible monitoring system would also have to be installed before such a declaration can be accepted. This is not as difficult as it might appear. Iraq cannot rebuild a significant WMD capability without the requisite industrial infrastructure, and such an undertaking cannot be concealed from adequate monitoring.

3. *Acceptance of the autonomy of Kurdistan within the state of Iraq.* The Kurdish problem has haunted Baghdad for decades. Providing an independent state for the Kurds is not realistic (Turkey, Iran, and Syria would all balk at this because of their own Kurdish minorities.) The concept of an autonomous Kurdish homeland within a greater Iraq could serve to defuse tensions that have been at the root of so much strife over the years.

4. *An end to the state of war between Iraq and Israel.* While it is probably impossible to get the Iraq of Saddam Hussein to enter into a framework of peace with Israel along the lines of the Camp David accords, ending the state of war between the two countries could go a long way to make Israel more accepting of an American rapprochement with Iraq, and would tone down the harsh rhetoric coming out of Baghdad that has heightened tensions in the past. Getting Israel and Iraq to stop viewing one another as an imminent threat would go far in stabilizing the entire region. Such an agreement is no more implausible than a peace accord between the Israelis and the Palestinians—and probably no easier to achieve.

5. *A cease-fire between Iraq and the Iraqi opposition groups.* This would be monitored by a United Nations or a regional observer force. Recognizing the sovereignty of Iraq would open a door to discussions between Iraq and the opposition aimed at a nonviolent resolution to current differences.

These core values would serve as the minimum requirements that the United States would have to obtain from Iraq to make rapprochement possible. In return, the U.S. would have to put some serious collateral on the table. This might include:

1. *On Iraqi signing of the pledge not to possess weapons of mass destruction, the United States would support the immediate lifting of all economic sanctions.* Iraq would still be required to fund reparations and would have to agree to United Nations weapons monitoring, including the monitoring of exports and imports to ensure that no weapons of mass destruction material was procured.

2. *The creation of an Iraqi Marshall Plan to rebuild the infrastructure of Iraq.* The plan would be developed on a regional basis, with the full involvement of the GCC states, Europe, and perhaps Japan, which relies on the resources of the Persian Gulf. Money would come from major International Monetary Fund loans, favorable loan guarantees from the United States and Europe for oil field revitalization, lump-sum grants from the United States, the GCC, Europe, and Japan to jump-start the Iraqi economic engine, perhaps an OPEC agreement to stabilize oil prices and to set higher quotas for Iraqi oil production, which would be offset by a voluntary lowering of the oil quotas of other OPEC nations. This would allow Iraq to generate much needed income in a stable manner.

3. *Military-to-military contacts to assist in the modernization and training of the Iraqi military.* Such contacts were actually proposed by April Glaspie during her tenure as ambassador to Iraq. Such contacts would not only benefit Iraq, but also serve as a moderating influence, promoting peace and stability in the region.

4. *Allowing Iraq to resume peaceful nuclear activity under the stringent monitoring of IAEA safeguard inspectors.* The Iraqi nuclear bomb manufacturing infrastructure has been eliminated, and any resumption would be readily detected. Iraq wants a nuclear energy program and has a large scientific community trained for and dedicated to this task. In a controlled and carefully monitored setting, such a concession would represent a low-risk vote of confidence in Iraq's good intentions.

The Iraqi government has set forth its own requirements for a diplomatic solution. Its conditions stipulate that there must be a linkage between any Iraqi solution and the Israeli-Palestinian problem, namely that conditions imposed on Iraq must be imposed on Israel. This, of course, is a deal-breaker, but one could reasonably expect that Iraq, eager to take advantage of an unexpected opportunity to engage in high-level diplomacy with the United States directly, and standing to benefit economically from doing so, would back away from this demand, which is little more than a propaganda ploy for public consumption.

Further, Baghdad insists that in addition to lifting the economic embargo, Iraq be found in compliance with its disarmament obligations. It also wants linkage between its disarmament status and a regional disarmament plan, which includes Israel. Iraq wants compensation for harm done to its economy, and assurances that any settlement of claims on Iraq be in accordance with international law and not imposed. Iraq wants the costs of any United Nations presence in Iraq to be borne not only by itself but by all parties involved. Iraq demands an end to the no-fly zones, and the recognition of its sovereignty over all territory encompassed within its borders.

These are genuine obstacles to a comprehensive peace with Iraq, but the record of past peace initiatives contains many successful agreements reached from starting positions that were further apart than those cited here. This is not mission impossible; mission unpleasant, yes. But this may be the only way that the United States can shape its own destiny.

The United States today is losing ground in its fight with Iraq. The failure of U.S. policy is evident. The U.S. is the most powerful country in the world, and if there is to be a settlement with Iraq, it must play a leading role in developing a solution.

In the end, a military solution may prove to be the only certain way to solve the Saddam problem. At present, however, a military solution is impossible. There is neither domestic nor foreign consensus. A bold diplomatic initiative, no matter how distasteful, is the only way the U.S. can express leadership in the Persian Gulf and the Middle East.

In engaging Iraq diplomatically, the United States would not only be replacing its defeated policy, but also rebuilding a foundation of principle in U.S.-Iraqi relations based on coexistence under international law. If Saddam Hussein's Iraq were to violate such an agreement, then all bets are off. At that point the U.S. would have reestablished the moral and legal grounds for a major military confrontation with Iraq.

On the night of March 8, 1998, my last inspection, I was in the office of the deputy chief of staff of the Iraqi armed forces. Amer Rashid was sitting across from me. I had approached him earlier, after the inspectors had begun their work. On my own initiative, I had asked him to identify those places in the facility that were considered to be the most sensitive to Iraqi dignity, sovereignty, and national security. He enumerated them as the offices of the minister of defense, the Defense Council, the chief of staff, and the deputy chief of staff as well as the situation rooms of the planning and operations directorates.

I proposed that he and I walk through these places. This would allow me, I said, to determine their size and layout and decide whether any detailed inspection would be required. He was somewhat wary but he agreed, and we toured the rooms. When I finished, I turned to him. "Could I now, if I thought I had to, order my inspectors to inspect these rooms using the full capabilities of the team?" I asked. "Yes, of course," he replied, "but that would be seen as an affront to Iraq."

I had just been inside the minister of defense's office, had opened his desk drawers and skimmed through his papers. I had seen the map boards in the situation rooms, which listed the precise locations of every military unit in Iraq. None of this, however, related to my mandate. "I will place these rooms off-limits to inspectors," I informed Amer Rashid, and passed the word down to the inspectors.

Amer Rashid had brought dinner into the deputy chief of staff's office. Chris Cobb-Smith and I dined with Amer Rashid and some of the most senior military men in Iraq. My decision to respect those three concerns—dignity, sovereignty, and national security—had put Amer Rashid and the others at ease regarding my intentions. As the evening wore on we began to discuss the situation in Iraq, especially Amer Rashid's work as the minister of oil. Surrounded by generals from the Defense Ministry and in the midst of one of the most controversial inspections ever, I watched Amer Rashid transform.

His eyes brightened as he discussed the potential of Iraq to produce oil, and the problems associated with maintaining current output. He spoke of important research and discoveries concerning oil explorations that had been carried out before the Gulf War, and of the vast potential these proven oil reserves held for Iraq. He spoke about the promise of the future. This was a man who had been one of the architects of Iraq's weapons of mass destruction programs, and yet became quite another person when talking about the reconstruction of his country—not military reconstruction but rebuilding the basic fabric of Iraqi society. In his eyes that night, I saw an ardent desire, a wish for all this conflict between us to end so that Iraq could get on with the overwhelming task of rebuilding and moving forward.

I am often asked if there is any chance of a peaceful settlement with Iraq. Invariably, knowing what I know about Saddam Hussein's regime, my inclination is to respond negatively. But whenever I think back to that night in the Ministry of Defense, I have to pause and reflect. Perhaps. Perhaps there is such a chance. For the sake of the American servicemen and women who would be called on to fight Saddam if the military solution were invoked and for the sake of the innocent Iraqi people who would ultimately pay the heaviest price, I hope that there is a chance for a peaceful solution to the crisis in Iraq. But we have to take decisive steps and assume some degree of risk to make it happen.

# Afterword

IN THE SEVEN-AND-A-HALF YEARS that I participated in the inspection process, I was vilified by the Iraqi government as an agent provocateur, a spy for the CIA, and a troublemaker sent into Iraq for the sole purpose of creating crisis. During these trips, my fellow inspectors and I flew into a military airfield outside Baghdad where we were ushered through Iraqi immigration and customs with little fanfare, our entry guaranteed by the United Nations Security Council. Iraq had no choice but to let us enter, but oftentimes the tension and hostility were palpable. It was for good reason, therefore, that I believed my aborted inspection mission to Iraq in August 1998 would be my last visit to that country. So it was with no small amount of surprise, and more than a little trepidation, that I found myself at the end of July 2000 approaching the Iraqi border, this time via an overland route from Amman, Jordan, not as a weapons inspector, but rather at the head of an independent film crew shooting a documentary movie on the current status of Iraq's disarmament saga.

It was nearly midnight as our two-car convoy pulled up to the border. As we neared the checkpoint, our driver veered onto an empty lane designated for VIP traffic. Our vehicle was flagged down by an armed border guard, accompanied by a phalanx of plainclothes security types I was long familiar with. My on-board interlocutor rolled down his window and spoke to the guards. Several looked into the back of the vehicle, where I sat, and smiled. "Welcome back, Mr. Scott," they said, waving us through and on into Baghdad, where I was about to resume, in a different fashion, my search for the elusive truth regarding Iraq's program to develop weapons of mass destruction that had begun nearly a decade ago.

Several days later, I found myself seated in a room on the second floor of one of the several major buildings comprising the Republican Palace compound in downtown Baghdad. Seated across from me was the Deputy Prime Minister of Iraq, Tariq Aziz, a man who only months before had led the process of personal denigrating and damning me and my work in Iraq. We now spoke civilly about the weapon-inspection process, with the film crew capturing the moment. Tariq Aziz was dressed in a sharp, gray suit. An Iraqi flag and portrait of Saddam Hussein were in the background as in any meeting with an Iraqi official of ministerial rank. We sat side by side in matching plush armchairs. The table between us held a crystal ashtray that serviced the trademark Cohiba cigar Tariq Aziz smoked during such tête-à-têtes.

"Well, Mr. Ritter," he said, "the question of inspectors is part of the whole story. There are U.N. resolutions, mainly Resolution 687, and we had to implement it. And we did. We accepted this resolution formally, and we implemented this resolution for seven-and-a-half years. And I can say also that we still abide by this resolution." Throughout our discussion, the Deputy Prime Minister remained reserved, professional, always in control—every bit the cool diplomat who had confounded the Security Council and successive American administrations for the past decade. "We are ready to be a party to a comprehensive solution to the problems of the region, in the area of weapons of mass destruction, in the area of maintaining peace and security in the whole region." Pausing for effect, Tariq Aziz tapped the cigar in the ashtray. "So what else do they want?" he asked, "they" being the United States. "We are ready to do that. But to pick on Iraq, to focus on Iraq, that is a political attitude made by the United States of America with the support of Great Britain. Other members of the Security Council do not share that attitude with the United States. And that shows that this has become an American political policy towards Iraq. It's not the United Nations' policy. It's not a Security Council policy."

Tariq Aziz was repeating the mantra of the Iraqi government, playing the innocent in the face of incontrovertible evidence that established that Iraq in fact had not fully complied with Security Council resolutions concerning its disarmament obligation. And yet now, more than ten years after the Iraqi invasion of Kuwait that had set this whole chain of events into motion, Tariq Aziz's words rang with a new credibility. As the lead investigator for UNSCOM, I knew firsthand the lengths to which Iraq would go to keep the inspectors, and the international community, at bay. And yet I also knew that, during the course of our difficult work, we inspectors had uncovered the lion's share of Iraq's illegal arsenal. What was left, if anything, represented nothing more than documents and scraps of material, seed-stock, perhaps, for any reconstitution effort that might take place in the future, but by and of themselves, not a viable weapons program.

My analysis was shared by no less an authority than Rolf Ekéus, the distinguished Swedish diplomat and UNSCOM's first executive chairman, who had reminded me during a meeting after my 1998 return from Iraq that "by February 1996, we had really managed to get our hands or arms around all the issues: nuclear, chemical, biological, and missiles." The silver-haired Swede, resplendent in his open-collared shirt, silk cravat, and tailored tweed coat, had an air of reflective sincerity as he mused about the past. "So . . ." he murmured in his heavily accented English, "we were very far down the road there."

Apparently, however, not far enough. In the larger scheme of American policy objectives toward Iraq, the results of our inspections seemed to mean little. It had become frustratingly clear to me that, after seven-plus years, the United States cared less about the actual progress of disarming Iraq than about using the inspection process to justify the continuation of economic sanctions against Iraq. In this way, the United States would be able to pursue its policy of the "containment" of Iraq until it could put into effect its ultimate policy objective—the removal of Saddam Hussein from power. Successive administrations in Washington had articulated policy positions that stressed that economic sanctions would be maintained against Iraq regardless of its disarmament status until Saddam Hussein was gone.

It seemed to matter little in Washington, D.C., that such a

stance contradicted the objectives of the Security Council resolutions, propelling the United States down the path of pursuing
contradictory policies that, on the one hand, held Iraq strictly accountable to Security Council resolutions, but on the other dis-
carded these resolutions as irrelevant because of a larger American
objective. Several CIA-sponsored coups, all of which failed, reinforced the reality, and weakness, of America's Saddam-centric position not only to Iraq, but also many nations around the world.
Adding to the crisis in international confidence about America's Iraq
policy was the "Iraqi Liberation Act," passed by Congress in November 1998. This law proposed the removal of Saddam Hussein from
power even as the United States claimed to Iraq and the world that
all Saddam and Iraq needed to do to get sanctions lifted was to comply with the will of the Security Council. The result of such inconsistent policy posturing was that the United States lost credibility in
many capitals around the world as a nation interested in international cooperation.

The only hope the United States appears to have of rebuilding
a coalition to confront Iraq militarily seems to be first to rebuild the
foundation of legitimacy enjoyed when Security Council Resolution
687 was passed, nearly a decade ago. But President George W. Bush
and his national security specialists have inherited a nightmare situation in Iraq. During the eight years of the Clinton Presidency, the
United States undertook actions that sullied the original mandate set
forth in Resolution 687, repeatedly manipulating the work of UN-
SCOM weapons inspectors in order to better fit American policy objectives. The demise of UNSCOM made it very difficult for the
Security Council to reach any sort of consensus on how to move forward on the issue of Iraq's disarmament.

The collapse of UNSCOM's credibility came during the tenure
of Richard Butler, the outspoken and personable Australian diplomat who succeeded Rolf Ekéus as UNSCOM's chief in the summer
of 1997. As though he were somehow unsure of himself from the
very start, between September 1997 and August 1998, Richard Butler permitted the United States to intervene in UNSCOM's affairs in
a way his predecessor never did, enabling Washington to stop or
postpone scheduled inspections no fewer than seven times because

the timing was "inconvenient" to the domestic political climate in America. I bore frustrated witness to these actions, as each intervention involved inspections under my direct control.

Worse still, Butler broke faith with his mandate and obligations to the United Nations by allowing the United States to use UNSCOM as a vehicle for the conduct of unilateral intelligence operations targeted not at Iraqi weapons capabilities, but rather the security of Saddam Hussein. This was especially true of Butler's actions in mid-1998, in which he closed down a sensitive communications-intercept operation I had led since its inception in February 1996. This operation had been designed to penetrate the circle of Iraq's innermost leadership to learn about the suspected retention by Iraq of prohibited weapons, and indeed it had succeeded to a large degree. However, while the goal of the effort had been to further the disarmament mandate of UNSCOM, the "take" was considered a gold mine to those elements in the United States that saw the effort as allowing them for the first time to get a clear look into the inner workings of Iraq's government and, more importantly, the previously unknown world of Saddam Hussein's security apparatus. For many in the national security circles of the United States, this intelligence was too valuable to be entrusted to a United Nations operation. Despite my repeated and emphatic warnings, Butler acceded to American pressure to close down my team and turn the ultrasensitive job of eavesdropping on Saddam over to the intelligence services of the United States.

The end of UNSCOM came in December 1998, when Butler coordinated closely with then–National Security Advisor Sandy Berger to discuss the timing of an intrusive series of inspections— Mission 258—designed to be deliberately confrontational and which, at the bidding of the United States, did away with the modalities for sensitive site inspection agreed to in 1996 by Ekéus. The National Security Advisor was, at the time, preparing for military strikes against Iraq and was looking to Butler to provide the justification for such action, in this case inspections that would provoke the Iraqi government into acts of "noncooperation." Such collusion was not only fundamentally inconsistent with Butler's position as a United Nations official, but it demonstrated to many in the Security Council and elsewhere (including Iraq) that the UNSCOM inspection process had become little more than a tool of American foreign policy. The resulting military campaign—Operation Desert Fox— was not only unsanctioned by the Security Council, but, because it relied almost exclusively on information derived from weapons inspections to target Saddam Hussein and his security apparatus, represented the death knell of the inspections process. The entire debacle reinforced the long-standing Iraqi allegation that the inspections were little more than a tool of American espionage. Since that time, no inspectors have been allowed back into Iraq, preventing any verification of Iraq's disarmament obligation and thereby extending economic sanctions indefinitely.

This result is exactly what many in Washington wanted. Their goal is to contain Iraq until a way can be found to remove Saddam Hussein from power. However, the heavy-handed methodology used to achieve this end, namely the blunt instrument of economic sanctions, has resulted in a backlash of international opinion, especially because of the horrific cost that these sanctions have extracted from the 22 million innocent Iraqi people. Denis Halliday, the former United Nations Humanitarian Coordinator in Iraq, has spoken out in defense of the Iraqi people. Halliday resigned from his post in August 1998, shortly after I left my work with UNSCOM. Perhaps because humanitarian work didn't have the same panache and media appeal as did weapons inspections, Halliday's departure from his post received relatively little notice when compared to the media storm brought about by my own resignation. A soft-spoken and highly articulate man, the Irish-born, lifelong United Nations professional brings a focused passion to the issue of Iraq's humanitarian crisis. Since his resignation, Halliday and I have had the opportunity to meet and discuss Iraq several times. Together we present an interesting combination of personalities and backgrounds, the mild-mannered Irish Quaker joined by a more brusque, combative former American Marine officer. But the dissimilarities vanish once Halliday begins speaking about Iraq. His sharp recitation of fact and analysis has the impact of a military briefing.

"Iraq in 1990 had a mortality rate equal to Southern Europe

[fewer than 15 deaths per 1,000 live births]. Today it's 131 deaths over 1,000 live births." Drawing on firsthand experience, Halliday continues, "There is massive malnutrition throughout the country, for both children and adults, and political consequences which we're all going to have to live with in the years ahead . . . you do not punish people, you do not punish innocent children and adults of a country because of the crimes committed by their leadership."

Economic sanctions continue to be the centerpiece of the U.S. efforts to contain the regime of Saddam Hussein, and the U.S. resists loosening these sanctions. As long as weapons inspections justified the continuation of economic sanctions (i.e., by illustrating Iraqi noncompliance), the U.S. favored them. But when the inspection process threatened the larger objective of containment either by finding Iraq to be in compliance (i.e., disarmed), or by forcing confrontation to the point where the Security Council began seriously to debate what its ultimate objectives were regarding Iraq, and whether something less than 100 percent disarmament would be acceptable, then the inspection process—disarmament followed by the lifting of sanctions and the monitoring of Iraq's industrial infrastructure to prevent reconstitution of its proscribed programs—itself suddenly became expendable. The United States has been clear that its policy is to contain Saddam through sanctions until the means can be found to remove him from power. The inspection process, which offers the promise of the lifting of sanctions with Saddam still in charge, represents the opposite direction in policy. The Clinton administration sought the demise of inspections, and now the Bush administration denigrates the value of inspections. Weapons inspections are a poison pill to the policy of containment.

However, in forgoing the inspection process, the United States surrendered its justification for the ongoing humanitarian tragedy inside Iraq. Overseas the United States fell under increasing pressure to do something to break the impasse.

This wave of humanitarian concern forced the United States to craft a diplomatic solution that attempted to shift the burden of the suffering of the Iraqi people onto the shoulders of Saddam Hussein. The result was a new Security Council resolution, 1284, passed in December 1999. Resolution 1284 replaced UNSCOM with a new inspection body, the United Nations Monitoring, Verification, and Inspection Commission (UNMOVIC). However, the resolution was purposefully vague in defining Iraq's disarmament obligation, leaving the United States the ability to "raise the bar" at will, should it ever be confronted with the specter of Iraqi cooperation. In addition, Resolution 1284 backed away from the concept of the lifting of sanctions should Iraq cooperate with a more loosely defined "suspension" of sanctions. Both clauses proved to be unacceptable to Iraq, a point driven home to me by Tariq Aziz during our meeting: "1284 is not a solution. We cannot deal with it, because it brings us back into a vicious circle which will not lead to any positive result."

As a stopgap measure, Resolution 1284 bought the United States a year-long extension of economic sanctions covered by the thin veil of diplomacy. However, the veil soon wore through. By the summer of 2000, the support for comprehensive economic sanctions began to collapse under the combined weight of international revulsion at the humanitarian disaster unfolding in Iraq and simple corporate greed on the part of companies and countries who longed to gain access to the Iraqi coffers. By the time George W. Bush was sworn in as the forty-third president of the United States, the American policy of containing Iraq through continued economic sanctions had failed. Saddam was gaining nearly $3 billion in revenue from oil smuggling operations outside the U.N. oil-for-food operations, and the Iraqi economy had stabilized to the point that Saddam was no longer at risk from a total collapse of his nation. Saddam was succeeding in strengthening his position inside Iraq, and because of his diplomatic successes in exploiting the humanitarian suffering of the Iraqi people, gaining political support around the world. Rather than keeping Saddam in his "box," America's policy of economic sanctions–based containment was isolating the United States from the rest of the world.

Today the Bush administration rejects the one issue that has served as the bulwark for a hard line against Iraq over the past decade—sending inspectors to evaluate Iraq's program to develop weapons of mass destruction. Secretary of Defense Donald Rumsfeld and Vice-President Dick Cheney denigrate inspections as "ineffective" and "a waste of time." Some in Washington have gone so far as to say that even if Iraq allowed inspectors back, and the inspectors found compliance with U.N. disarmament resolutions, the policy of "regime change" would still be in effect. The Bush administration seeks regime removal because of the threat posed by weapons of mass destruction in the hands of Saddam, but then admits that, in the end, it is not concerned about weapons of mass destruction, but about Saddam Hussein himself.

The administration says that it cannot permit Saddam to have weapons of mass destruction. However, experts closely tied to American policy offer another rationale for overthrowing Saddam. Charles Duelfer, the former deputy executive chairman for UN-SCOM, retired State Department official, and currently a guest scholar at the Center for Strategic and International Studies, put it to me this way during a telephone conversation: "I think it would be a mistake to focus on the issue of weapons of mass destruction. To do so ignores the larger issue of whether or not we want this dictator [Saddam Hussein] to have control over a nation capable of producing 6 million barrels of oil per day. We simply cannot allow Iraq to have that kind of power and influence. If you focus on the weapons issue, then the first thing you know, Iraq will be given a clean bill of health, sanctions will be lifted, and then Iraq will, at the first excuse, kick the inspectors out. We will be left having no leverage over Iraq or how Saddam chooses to spend his money." This was a stunning statement from a man who was the number-two official responsible not only for overseeing weapons inspections in Iraq, but also preserving the credibility of the premise of the whole exercise in Iraq, which promised the lifting of sanctions in exchange for Iraq's disarmament.

Duelfer's comments reminded me of my meeting in Baghdad with Amer Rashid, the minister of oil. A gruff, well-spoken man who met me dressed in the military uniform of an officer of his grade, Lt. Gen. Amer Rashid was a man well known to me and others who pursued Iraq's weapons of mass destruction. One of the principal architects of the Iraqi weapons programs, and the chief interlocutor between Iraq and UNSCOM during the years of inspection and crisis, Amer Rashid was not a man who shied away from the center spotlight, a role he had slipped into as minister of oil. "We will definitely accommodate," General Amer told me, "the legitimate interest of the United States of America in this area . . . they want to have a secure supply of oil strategically? Okay. Fair enough. But this has to be done on equal grounds between independent countries and not when dictating." But such an approach is not what America has in mind when dealing with the issue of Iraq's oil-based wealth.

One of the key concerns that many American experts have regarding a renewed focus on weapons inspections and disarmament is that Iraq might actually cooperate, and the world would be confronted with the reality of a disarmed Iraq. "The attitude of Iraq regarding inspections?" Amer al-Sa'adi, who, like Amer Rashid, was a former head of Iraq's weapons programs and currently serves as the scientific advisor to Saddam Hussein, asked rhetorically when I interviewed him. "That can only take place after sanctions are lifted. I would certainly advise that. Because we have nothing to hide. We have accepted Resolution 687 and its consequences, and we abide by that. So monitoring inspections in that area are expected from us, under the resolution."

Absent weapons inspections, however, the lifting of sanctions will be no easy task. In the summer of 2002, the United States and Great Britain orchestrated the passing of a new Security Council resolution that dramatically restructured the decades-long program of economic sanctions imposed against Iraq. These so-called "smart sanctions" eliminated restrictions on the importation into Iraq of humanitarian items such as food and medicine, and also consumer goods (including some nominal "dual-purpose" items that could have potential military applications), while keeping in place a program of "military" sanctions. Another key component of this new resolution is the continuation of the practice of depositing all income generated by Iraq through the sale of oil into a U.N.-controlled escrow account, effectively withholding control of the Iraqi economy from Saddam.

Meanwhile, the world continues to turn, and so, too, does the sad tale of Iraq. One of the more curious, and for the United States, frustrating, aspects of the ongoing Iraqi saga is the massive scale of the illicit trade taking place between Iraq and its neighbors, mainly Jordan and Turkey (amounting to several hundreds of millions of dollars per year). The United States, for reasons that reek of regional politics, has been, to date, powerless to stop this trade. The economies of Turkey and Jordan, critical allies in the ongoing struggle with Baghdad, have been damaged by the decades-long economic embargo. Iraqi oil fuels the respective economic engines of these two nations, and the United States, unable to provide alternative economic relief, simply looks the other way at the long line of Iraqi trucks that pour across the borders with Turkey and Jordan. This gaping hole in the blanket of sanctions against Iraq provides close to a billion dollars in funds to the regime of Saddam Hussein per year, free of United Nations controls. This source of revenue all but guarantees the long-term viability of the current Iraqi government, something that frustrates the Bush administration to no end. However, rather than seek a diplomatic resolution to this matter through the resumption of weapons inspections, the Bush White House insists on regime removal.

This will not be as simple as some proponents of removing Saddam would like the American public to believe. While the Bush administration struggles to define how exactly it plans to achieve regime removal, Iraq continues to persevere, a reality best illustrated by a statement made to me by Tariq Aziz in his second-floor office in the Presidential Palace. "What can we do?" he said. "We have to survive. And the Iraqi nation is a great survivor. We have survived for six or seven thousand years. We have survived aggressions. We have survived occupations. We have survived blockades. Many of our cities lived under blockades from the Persians, the Mongols, and others . . . and they survived." Tariq Aziz looked at me for emphasis as he finished his thought.

"This nation is going to survive."

This quote eerily echoes the words of the same Tariq Aziz, spoken to Secretary of State James Baker in January 1991, on the eve of the Gulf War: "We'll be here long after you're gone."

The absence of weapons inspections in Iraq has fueled speculation over what has transpired inside Iraq since we inspectors left that country in 1998. This in turn has led to wide-ranging speculation about what, if anything, Iraq retains in the way of weapons of mass destruction. The paucity of evidence regarding any Iraqi retention of weapons of mass destruction is highlighted in the details of the classified presentations made by the Bush administration to NATO in the spring of 2002, in an effort to drum up European support for military action against Iraq. In this report, which I have read, the United States told NATO that Iraq continues to possess three tons of unspecified biological agent, without providing any supporting evidence. It also claims Iraq continues to possess enough growth media (the nutrients needed to grow a biological agent) to produce 21,000 liters of anthrax. But even if Iraq had retained this growth media (and there is no information suggesting it has), the media has long since expired and therefore would be useless. The U.S. paper cites unaccounted-for, unfilled munitions (bombs and artillery shells) as evidence of a continued Iraqi chemical-weapons program, but fails to explain that any nerve agent produced by Iraq prior to 1990 would have degraded to the point of being useless today, making the point of Iraq's retention of such weapons moot. The U.S. paper speaks of launchers (five) and long-range missiles (thirty) as if they were a present threat, without mentioning that the launchers are dismantled and stored in a desert scrap yard where they are readily monitored, and the missiles are sheer conjecture based upon no substantiated fact. Although the U.S. paper acknowledges that Iraq's nuclear program had been largely dismantled, it speaks of so-called dirty bombs as if they existed, even though Iraq had declared its research into such weapons to U.N. inspectors, and no evidence exists that the Iraqis ever took such programs beyond research and development.

The U.S. presentation to NATO only reinforces the fact that the case for war being made by the Bush administration is a sham. The uncertainty about Iraq's proscribed programs could be dispelled if U.N. weapons inspectors were returned to Iraq. Such a move is opposed by Secretary Rumsfeld and Vice-President Cheney. Yet such inspections, properly led and mandated, could readily detect any effort by Iraq to retain and reconstitute programs for weapons of mass destruction.

Inspections offer the best solution for resolving the overall issue of Iraq. If the Bush administration continues to oppose the return of U.N. weapons inspectors to Iraq, then it will be clear that Washington's only objective is the removal of Saddam Hussein. But if Iraq doesn't possess prohibited weapons, what threat to U.S. national security interests does Saddam pose? And if Saddam doesn't directly threaten U.S. national security interests, then on what basis can America go to war? There is a real concern among many observers that the Bush administration, by investing such a tremendous amount of political capital behind the policy of regime removal, has actually boxed itself into a rhetorical corner, where speculation has far outstripped the facts. The danger here is that politically driven ideology has hijacked the national security decision-making machinery of the United States, creating the possibility that the United States may go to war not because there is a real threat to the national security, but rather because war represents the best means of saving political face for those in the White House who have been such heavy proponents of regime removal in Iraq. War under any circumstances is never good; a war with Iraq for this reason would be a travesty, a total failure of American democracy.

President Bush seems willing to go to war with Iraq, even if the United States must act unilaterally. This would be a mistake. To succeed against Iraq, the United States must act within the framework of broad international consensus, which can only be derived through the unified action of the United Nations Security Council. This means that more effort should be expended on the return of weapons inspectors to Iraq as opposed to seeking a replay of Operation Desert Storm in 1991. Throughout this debate, one should keep in mind that this is a problem of Iraq's own making. Saddam Hussein has a history of irresponsible behavior, including twice invading his neighbors (Iran in 1980, Kuwait in 1990), using chemical weapons against Iran and his own Kurdish population, threatening Israel with chemical weapons (not to mention launching thirty-nine SCUD missiles against Israel during Operation Desert Storm in 1991), and developing nuclear- and biological-weapons capabilities in direct violation of Iraq's international agreements not to do so. Once the international community rightfully outlawed weapons of mass destruction in Iraq, following the 1991 Gulf War, Iraq failed to fully declare the totality of its weapons programs and played a frustrating seven-year game of cat and mouse with U.N. weapons inspectors. Clearly Iraq is not without blame. It should also be noted that if

Iraq continues to possess weapons of mass destruction, or is actively seeking to reacquire such capability, more than ten years after the international community outlawed these weapons, then Saddam Hussein is a pariah leader, a rogue menace who must be dealt with decisively and harshly. This is the essence of the case for the resumption of weapons inspections in Iraq. If Saddam Hussein resumes his hide-and-seek tactics, then the United States—and the world— would be right in assuming that he has hostile intentions, and the case for war would be apparent.

However, one cannot lose sight of the fact that the United States itself is culpable in the demise of the inspection process. Presidents George Bush and Bill Clinton supported the containment of Iraq through continued economic sanctions and endorsed a policy of regime removal. Both of them and President George W. Bush authorized the CIA to carry out covert action in Iraq to overthrow Saddam. As I've mentioned, the CIA used the U.N. weapons inspections to spy on the security of Saddam Hussein. Iraq must be held accountable for its obligation under Security Council resolutions to disarm and must allow the unconditional return of U.N. weapons inspections to verify compliance. But it is only fair that Iraq be given some assurance that the United States will not again misuse the unique access afforded the inspectors to spy on Saddam or otherwise engage in activities inconsistent with their disarmament tasks. This is especially important given the heated level of rhetoric in the White House concerning regime removal.

The biggest impediment to the rapid overthrow of Saddam Hussein is his security apparatus. Historically, the most effective penetration of Saddam's security apparatus was achieved by U.N. weapons inspectors. Saddam Hussein would be foolish to allow weapons inspectors to return, thus enabling the United States to more effectively target his regime, without assurances that inspections would never again be so abused. The Canadian Government is considering offering its services as such an "honest broker" to the U.N. Secretary General, if Iraq agrees to the unconditional return of inspectors. But until such time as the Bush administration places disarmament ahead of regime removal, even diplomatic initiatives like this one are doomed to fail.

The prospect of unilateral American action against Iraq represents an illusory path to victory. The victorious coalition against Saddam in 1991 had as the foundation of its legality a Security Council resolution. Likewise, the coalition that has been assembled to confront terror today has similar legitimacy from the U.N. Security Council action. Anyone thinking that the U.S. can go it alone against Iraq should only consider this: could the successes against the terrorists in Afghanistan today have been achieved without the support of Russia, Pakistan, Uzbekistan, and other nations? The answer is surely no. And yet these three nations, along with a score or more additional nations (including such U.S. allies as France, Turkey, and Germany), have stated clearly that they feel there is not a sufficient case for war with Iraq.

Any unilateral U.S. military action against Iraq would face the real prospect of fierce resistance from the Iraqi people and army (not because they support Saddam, but because they oppose an American invasion), and with it the probability of heavy casualties, especially if Saddam delivers on his promise to fortify every Iraqi village, town, and city. But a unilateral invasion would probably cause the fragile coalition assembled to confront international terror since September 11, 2001, to rapidly collapse. Given that the forces of Osama bin Laden and the al Qaeda terror network, although still intact, have been dealt a harsh blow in Afghanistan and elsewhere, such a collapse would be a regrettable snatching of defeat from the jaws of victory by the United States. The unfortunate reality is that if the United States proceeds with its invasion of Iraq, we may succeed in overthrowing Saddam Hussein while losing the war on terror. Our unilateral military action will push many moderate and intellectual Arabs and Muslims into the bin Laden camp by giving credence to the concept that the United States has in fact declared war on Islam and the Arab world. Hosni Mubarak, the President of Egypt, has warned that an American invasion of Iraq could unleash forces of radicalism that no moderate Arab government could contain. If America invades Iraq, we run the real prospect of condemning ourselves to twenty years of terror, in which suicide bombers become a daily reality in the U.S. as they have in Israel. That is a life to be wished on no one.

# APPENDIX:
# Iraq's Arsenal
# of Weapons of
# Mass Destruction

CHEMICAL WEAPONS (CW). The Iraqis maintain, at a minimum, the capability to produce, weaponize, store, and employ chemical weapons. Additionally, Iraq has not accounted for hundreds of tons of precursor chemicals used in manufacturing the VX nerve agent, as well as precursor chemicals used in manufacturing GA, GF, and GB nerve agent. All four agents were produced by Iraq in binary form.

The Iraqis have not accounted for at least two complete production lines associated with CW agent production known to have been delivered to Iraq prior to the Gulf War. In addition, information available to UNSCOM indicates that precursor and possible agent production are taking place inside Iraq.

A CW production facility, under the guise of a pesticide production plant, was shipped into Iraq in 1994–1995, according to UNSCOM information. The Iraqi intelligence service used an Iraqi front consortium, the Baghdad-based Al-Eman Establishment for Trade Investment, involving the company's offices in Amman and a subsidiary firm in Poland (Dalia). The shipment of helicopter spare parts is believed to have been undertaken to hide this transaction. Of twenty-three such shipments made in 1994–1995, some may have transported toxic precursor chemicals.

Of two mobile CW munitions filling stations acquired before the war, one is not yet fully accounted for. Further, the declared destruction of a CW filling plant at Muthanna State Establishment is suspect, and in any case, filling limited numbers of munitions with CW agents is relatively simple.

The entire range of agents available to Iraq prior to the Gulf War may have been retained. The focus of concern is GB/GF and VX nerve agents, which are highly lethal and persistent, and as binary weapons, conducive to safe, long-term storage. (VX salt becomes VX agent when mixed with sodium carbonate. Iraq had designed, and probably manufactured, true binary munitions for VX which would have the precursors mix in-flight.)

From Italy (SNIA-BPD) and Spain (ITESA), Iraq procured thousands of empty munitions casings not immediately declared to UNSCOM, and which were being used by the Iraqis as the core of their binary weaponry. While much of these weapons were destroyed in the 1991 unilateral destruction, it is very likely that several thousand of these empty casings are being stored by the SSO.

High-quality intelligence also indicates that Iraq has loaded VX agent into dozens of aerial bombs of the R-400 type, seven warheads for Al-Hussein missiles, and hundreds of 122 mm rocket warheads and 155 mm artillery shells. All of these weapons are under the control of special Chemical Corps weapons-handling units that have been subordinated to the SSO.

The R-400 bombs and the Al-Hussein warheads are for strategic use, and would be issued to special-designation air force units and the surface-to-surface missile force only on orders of the president of Iraq. The 122 mm rocket warheads would be issued to Republican Guard artillery units equipped with BM-21 multiple-rocket launchers, and the 155 mm shells would be issued to Republican Guard field artillery units equipped with advanced GN-45 systems. These weapons would be used as a last-ditch measure in the defense of Baghdad from an attacking force.

Information indicates that Iraq retained 500 155 mm artillery shells filled with mustard agent. These shells are for use by Special Republican Guard artillery units to provide final protective fires in defense of the president from any mob or military coup. Other weapons include spray tanks, which could be fitted onto fighter aircraft or helicopters. The filled munitions could be stored underground, but most likely are mounted in vehicles garaged at SSO-controlled facilities around Iraq. Spray tanks could be deployed at the airfields in question, or at intermediate storage locations, again all of which would be under the control of the SSO.

The equipment for the two chemical agent production lines that remain unaccounted for could be transported in fifteen to twenty trucks. This type of mobility plays to the strength of the SSO-run concealment mechanism, and makes targeting—by weapons inspectors as well as by the U.S. military—extremely difficult. These plants can be installed in a matter of weeks, and are capable of producing chemical agent in less than two months. In addition, because they are built out of corrosion-resistant material, they can be stored either underground or underwater.

The Polish pesticide production plant may have been carried in at least two dozen vehicles. The filling plant could be carried in one to four standard metallic shipping (ISO) containers. Information indicates only small-scale ongoing production. To produce ten tons of agent, the Iraqis would need 200 to 300 tons of precursors. This is equal to 1,000 to 1,500 barrels of precursor. Precursor chemicals need to be stored in temperatures of less than 40 degrees centigrade. If stored in trucks, the precursors would need to be kept in special warehouses possessing temperature control or other relatively cool locations, such as caves. SSO garages, which are located in highly protected presidential areas, are off-limits to no-notice inspections as of 1998. Moved at night, such vehicles are all but impossible to locate. This would frustrate military targeting planners in establishing sites for selective, pinpoint air strikes. Lacking this, the military would need to strike in an indiscriminate fashion, something it has been loath to do.

Producing CW agent requires that certain levels of personnel, technical, and documentation administration be maintained, as well as centralized coordination and direction of such production. Supporting documentation required for a covert CW program consists of production procedures ("cookbooks"), facility configuration designs for the dismantled facilities and their material, as well as designs for converting existing civilian chemical production facilities (fertilizer plants, pesticide plants, petrochemical refining plants). Such records could be concealed in a half-dozen or so metal footlockers, easily transported in one light truck, or the trunks of a few Mercedes sedans.

BIOLOGICAL WEAPONS (BW). The Iraqis have at least the capability to produce, weaponize, store, and employ biological weapons. This activity appears to revolve around the maintenance of the capability to produce agent using civilian biological laboratories, as well as making use of retained equipment that is outside UNSCOM's control and protected by the SSO. According to sensitive information, Iraq has probably retained several Al-Hussein warheads filled with a dry BW agent, probably anthrax. Additionally, Iraq undertook a program, run by the office of the president and involving a special MIC office, Unit 2001, either to produce new agent, or test agent that was retained from pre–Gulf War stocks. In 1995 Unit 2001 conducted tests on live human subjects taken from the Abu Ghraib prison, using BW and binary CW agent. Around fifty prisoners were chosen for these experiments, which took place at a remote testing ground in western Iraq. The purpose of these experiments was to test the toxicity of available agent to ensure that the biological arsenal remained viable. As a result, all the prisoners died.

Biological agent for military use is relatively simple to produce. There is reason to believe that the Iraqis possess a mobile BW agent production facility, consisting of three to five semi-trailers, containing fermentors and processing equipment. The equipment for use in these mobile facilities probably came from the Italian OLSA company and the Swiss firm Chemap. There are also numerous biological weapons projects known to have existed in Iraq before the Gulf War and never declared to UNSCOM. In addition, Iraq has the capability to produce its own mobile BW agent drying and grinding facility, able to be mounted inside a single semi-trailer. Together with the mobile agent production facility, this would give Iraq a significant and difficult-to-detect BW agent production capability.

The biggest problem in assessing Iraq's remaining biological weapons capability lies in its refusal to discuss this matter fully with UNSCOM, significantly hindering any understanding of Iraq's past and present capabilities. Real concern exists that Iraq desires to retain a large-scale biological agent production capability. After the Hussein Kamal defection revealed the existence of such a capability, at the Al Hakam facility, it was destroyed by UNSCOM. The dual-use nature of biology, however, where innocent-sounding civilian projects can be readily converted into BW production, means that one must also look at the overall context of any biological project to properly assess its purpose. UNSCOM had several examples of this, the most prominent being the discovery of minutes of meetings held between Iraqi biologists and Russian government officials in Moscow in June 1995. The Iraqis were from the Chemical Engineering Design Center, part of the MIC family of research centers formed after the Gulf War. The purpose of the CEDC visit to Moscow was to gather information concerning production and research assistance in biotechnology that could be provided by Russia, as well as the possibility of Russia supplying Iraq with a complete factory for the production of single-cell protein, ostensibly for use as an animal feed factory. Production of single-cell protein, however, was the same cover story used by the Iraqis to explain the Al Hakam BW production facility.

One of the main areas of concern about the Iraqi-Russian deal was that four of the Iraqis present at the discussions were senior officials with the Al Hakam BW facility, including the head of reasearch and development, and another person who was a senior participant in the Iraqi botulinum toxin production program. All four had worked with Dr. Taha at the Technical Research Center BW plant in Salman Pak, and three of the four had been with Taha at the Muthanna State Establishment. These BW experts were in Russia to buy a facility that would have dwarfed the Al Hakam facilities—a plant with a 50,000-liter capacity, twenty times the Al Hakam figure. In July 1995 the MIC accepted the Russian offer to provide this and gave instructions to move the project forward. The Russian firm involved was Biopreparat, a longtime Soviet BW conglomerate. A senior Russian scientist claiming knowledge of the transaction, Ken Alibek, has indicated that the plant was specially configured for BW applications. The current status of this project is unknown. Moscow has not been forthcoming on this matter.

All of Iraq's retained BW material could be carried in fewer than ten thirty-five-ton trucks, and three to five semi-trailers. They could be stored mounted in their vehicles, inside a warehouse, or buried underground. The supporting documents for this program could be easily kept in a single sedan-sized vehicle.

**BALLISTIC MISSILES.** Iraq retains a limited operational capability for using long-range (i.e., over 150 kilometers) ballistic missiles. Reliable information as recent as 1996 reveals that the SSO supervises a special Al-Hussein brigade, managed by the commander of the surface-to-surface missile force. This brigade is kept in a cadre status, and consists of a commanding officer, his deputy, and two battalion commanders (the 1st, or ready battalion, consisting of a launcher in full operational status, and the 2nd, or standby battalion, consisting of a dissassembled launcher. Information dating back to 1995 indicates as many as four launchers of Iraqi design that use Russian parts imported into Iraq in violation of sanctions. The SSO also directs the activities of Unit 2001, a special MIC entity responsible for the storage, maintenance, and transportation of Iraq's retained CW and BW munitions, including the warheads for the Al-Hussein missile brigade.

Iraq has been conducting top-secret training in support of an operational long-range ballistic missile force. Training conducted in December 1992 involved the actual dispatch of a launcher with missile to a launch site in western Iraq. Analysis of this data indicates that the Iraqis may have been preparing to strike Israel in response to a potential heavy bombing campaign. Such a campaign was feared as a response to a planned Iraqi challenge to the United States on the southern no-fly zone. Iraq would have denied UNSCOM the right to fly its transport aircraft from Bahrain to Baghdad. In any case, the missile went back into hiding.

In 1995 the Iraqi surface-to-surface missile force directed that the Al-Hussein brigade conduct an exercise known as Samoukh 48. This exercise was designed to ascertain the brigade's launch proficiency. Iraq had just finished manufacture of two to four mobile launchers, which were kept under the control of the SSO. For this exercise, the SSO released at least one of these launchers along with at least one operational Al-Hussein missile. In January 1996 the SSO carried out detailed inspections of all involved forces to collect any documentation referring to the Samoukh 48 exercise.

The launchers and missiles for the Al-Hussein brigade are kept under direct presidential control. They are stored inside the same presidential security triangle (Baghdad-Tikrit-Diyala) that the president operates in. The seven operational missiles are most likely the seven Iraqi-produced missiles referred to in a document accounting for missiles at the end of the Gulf War. They were listed as operational. Iraq later declared that these missiles were misidentified as operational and were destroyed during the 1991 unilateral destruction of missiles. However, when UNSCOM excavated this site to account for destroyed missiles, there was no trace of any Iraqi missiles, only those of Soviet manufacture. When confronted, Tariq Aziz informed UNSCOM that these Iraqi missiles were part of the excavated debris melted down into ingots. More likely, these seven missiles are extant and at least five are ready for launch at any one time. Information states that Unit 2001 maintains a mix of warheads filled with VX and dry anthrax for use on these missiles.

Iraq has an active ballistic missile research and development and manufacturing capability that was extensively bombed during Operation Desert Fox. This capability is run by the Karama State Establishment at two primary manufacturing facilities (the main plant, in Wazariyah in downtown Baghdad, and a secondary facility, the Ibn al-Haytham Missile Research and Development Center on the northwestern border of Baghdad) and the Al-Rafah Missile Test Facility, west of Baghdad in Amoriyah. It is currently involved in the production and testing of the Al-Samoud missile, a Scud clone with a stated range of less than 150 kilometers. This entire project is dedicated to developing specific technologies applicable to short- and long-range missiles, such as guidance and control, liquid propulsion engines, and warheads. As with the Scud-B, the Al-Samoud can have its range extended simply by increasing the amount of fuel used. Defectors have reported that Saddam has issued instructions that the Karama State Establishment be prepared to produce a long-range missile (650 kilometers) within six months of receiving such an order.

Iraq is currently working on improving manufacturing capabilities for guidance and control systems (it recently tried to purchase an entire guidance and control production plant from Romania, where it procured specific technology, tools, and components required to assemble complete guidance control sets for the Al-Samoud missile). Iraq has procured high-precision computer-controlled machine tools for use in its missile production plants. The high-priority Al-Samoud project is closely watched by Saddam, who personally approved the budget for the covert procurement activities undertaken in Romania (such as CW warheads for FROG-7 rockets).

At present, it is believed that Iraq is unable to produce from scratch ballistic missiles of a prohibited range. It can, however, reconfigure its current manufacturing base and, within six months, produce long-range missiles based on the Al-Samoud. It can also produce up to twenty-five Al-Hussein missiles assembled from components, engines, and guidance and control sets from the pre–Gulf War programs. Key manufactured components from the old Al-Hussein projects remain unaccounted for, especially Project 1728, the Iraqi liquid-fuel-engine production unit, and much of the infrastructure required to produce a ballistic missile of a prohibited nature remains in place. The main production threat is its ability to assemble retained components into an operational missile. The matériel required to do this, amounting to up to twenty-five Scud engines and guidance and control sets, could fit into six to ten thirty-five-ton trucks.

Iraq may possess CW warheads for the FROG-7 artillery rocket. Retained proscribed missiles are needed to deliver BW, CW, and nuclear payloads. Iraq has at least two mobile missile launchers and seven missiles on operational readiness. Warheads, fuel, oxidizer, and support equipment for such a force are also being retained. While the components of the twenty-five retained missiles are kept in a manner conducive to long-term storage, the operational force must be ready for use within thirty-six hours. This requires a more mobile and active storage profile. Missiles stored the long term can be kept in trucks (up to three missiles per truck), in a warehouse, or underground (in the form trenches as opposed to complete burial). Vehicles associated with this storage would include two to eighteen thirty-five-ton trucks for the missiles, and one to ten additional thirty-five-ton trucks for the support equipment. Fuel and oxidizer would be stored in standard Soviet containers designed for that purpose, of which there should be between twenty-five and 100. These containers can be stored buried or in a warehouse, and if mounted on vehicles would require fifteen to twenty thirty-five-ton trucks.

An operational force would require secure fixed locations, as well as mobility capability. The missiles in operational standby status could be transported on three to four thirty-five-ton trucks. Operational warheads and guidance and control equipment could be transported on three to four additional thirty-five-ton trucks. There should be two to four fuel trucks, and two or four more oxidizer vehicles. There are also two mobile missile launchers. The maintenance of an operational force of ballistic missiles requires that certain levels of personnel, technical, and documentation administration be maintained, as well as centralized coordination and direction of such production. The supporting documents for this program could be easily stored in a single truck, transported in the back of a sedan, or carried by several trusted personnel.

**NUCLEAR ENRICHMENT AND WEAPONIZATION.** The Iraqis maintain, at a minimum, the capability to conduct active research and development in the field of gaseous centrifuge enrichment and the weaponization of a nuclear device.

Iraq has retained a considerable nuclear weapon manufacturing production base. This consists of numerous declared and undeclared dual-use machine tools which have been dispersed among a wide variety of enterprises and plants. In addition, there are several vital undeclared instruments capable of carrying out machining operations essential for nuclear weapons manufacture. Finally, despite the official termination of the nuclear weapons program, the vast majority of its intellectual infrastructure remains in place. Much of this work is being done quite openly, under monitoring. Covert manufacturing takes place, on a small scale, at several secret machine tool centers in and around Baghdad. Concerning uranium enrichment, Iraq has retained critical centrifuge-enrichment capability in operation possibly since mid-1994. Undeclared feedstocks are also thought to be retained in support of this effort. The centrifuge program would operate out of a fixed site. It is likely that the feedstock is stored at this site.

Iraq has retained components relating to the most recent weapons design, which have not been turned over to the IAEA. These components may be complete enough for assembly into several weapons, lacking only the highly enriched uranium core. They can be moved in a small convoy of three to five vehicles.

With the exception of the secret machine tool centers, storage requirements for the retained infrastructure are negligible. The secret centers could operate from a fixed location about the size of one to two warehouses. A retained weapon is likely to be more mobile, moving from one hide site to the next every several days or weeks. A special fleet of dedicated vehicles would be required for this. Retained components are either installed in a secret workshop, or stored in a secure warehouse, either on trucks or in a manner that could be rapidly loaded on vehicles should the situation require. Documents supporting a retained nuclear program would fill a small room, and could be carried in ten to fifteen footlockers.

# Note on Sources

THIS BOOK is a critique of U.S. policy toward Iraq, especially the absence of any discernible vision—or endgame. As the architect and principal implementer of the controversial UNSCOM policy of countering the Iraqi concealment mechanism—the systematic methodology employed by Saddam and his lieutenants to safeguard and hide their weapons of mass destruction—I spent a great deal of time studying Iraq and Iraqi policies. This book is based mainly on these personal experiences, which serve as the source of most of the narrative. I have drawn upon my memory, supplemented by my personal notes and documentary material accumulated during my seven years' work as an inspector.

I have made extensive use of certain books to help shape my analysis and provide a factual basis beyond the scope and span of my own direct knowledge and experience. I am deeply indebted to Professor Amatzia Baram for his unmatched scholarship on modern Iraq and the interplay among tribes, politics, the military, and religion. While I developed my own feel for this situation during my years as an inspector, it was Professor Baram who helped give my observations a grounded framework through hours of conversations. I have drawn upon those conversations in writing this book, as well as Professor Baram's considerable writings on the matter. I made extensive use of his *Building Toward Crisis: Saddam Husayn's Strategy for Survival* (The Washington Institute for Near East Policy, Policy Paper No. 47: 1988), which is a wonderful piece of scholarship and analysis. All of Professor Baram's writings are informative, but one other which I drew heavily upon in shaping my ideas for this book was "Neo-Tribalism in Iraq: Saddam Husayn's Tribal Policies, 1991–1995" in *International Journal of Middle East Studies* (Volume 29, February 1997).

Untangling the complicated web that is Saddam's tribal and family history and relations required considerable analysis on my part of a disparate body of data. Two books which I found particularly useful in helping me in this endeavor were Adel Darwish and Gregory Alexander's *Unholy Babylon: The Secret History of Saddam's War* (New York: St. Martin's Press, 1991) and Mohamed Heikal's *Illusions of Triumph: An Arab View of the Gulf War* (London: HarperCollins, 1992). Both of these books were written by distinguished Arab journalists and offer a viewpoint often missing from Western writings on the same subject. Kenneth Timmerman's *The Death Lobby: How the West Armed Iraq* (New York: Houghton Mifflin, 1991) provides useful information from someone who had unique access to Iraq's weapons industry prior to the work of UNSCOM. I have also made use of insights in Latif Yahia and Karl Wendl's *I Was Saddam's Son* (New York: Arcade Publishing, 1997), which despite certain self-serving passages has proven to be a remarkably accurate portrayal of life inside Iraq's inner circle. Recent interviews given by Uday Hussein's former personal secretary, Abbas Janabi, to both the *Guardian* and *Al-Hayat* newspapers were also useful in assembling more information on how Saddam operates behind the scenes.

The Iran-Iraq War was a pivotal period in the shaping of Saddam's Iraq, and I made extensive use of the outstanding study on that war written by Anthony H. Cordesman and Abraham R. Wagner, *The Lessons of Modern War, Volume II: The Iran-Iraq War* (Boulder: Westview Press, 1990).

Deciphering the intricacies of the foreign policy of the United States is a complicated task. I was greatly aided by several works, most notably Robert D. Kaplan's *The Arabists: The Romance of an American Elite* (New York: The Free Press, 1995). James Baker's memoir, *The Politics of Diplomacy: Revolution, War and Peace, 1989–1992* (New York: G. P. Putnam's Sons, 1995), and George Bush and Brent Scowcroft's *A World Transformed* (New York: Alfred A. Knopf, 1998) both provided insights into the complicated world of U.S.-Iraq relations from a firsthand perspective. For the Gulf War and the state of the Iraqi armed forces, I have relied upon what I believe to be the best volume on the war, Bernard Trainor and Michael Gordon's *The Generals' War: The Inside Story of the Conflict in the Gulf* (Boston: Little, Brown, 1995).

There is, however, no one source of complete information about Saddam's Iraq. Although I am indebted to the references listed above in providing me with insights and factual information, in the end I have relied upon my own extensive database gained from years of inspecting the inner sanctum of Saddam's Iraq, together with the invaluable information gleaned from debriefing Iraqi defectors of all types. My travels throughout the Middle East and Europe put me in contact with analysts who provided their own unique perspectives on Iraq. What I have written here is not only a critique of the foreign policy of the United States toward Iraq, but also a unique piece of scholarship of modern Iraq that cannot be found elsewhere.

Despite all the sources I have drawn on, any errors that the book might contain are mine alone.

# Index

321. 00
150. 00
———
471. 00